The Select Documents on India-China Relations

Politics of Resources, Identity and Authority

Volume 1

A Comprehensive Introduction by
K.R. Gupta

ATLANTIC
PUBLISHERS & DISTRIBUTORS (P) LTD

Published by
ATLANTIC
PUBLISHERS & DISTRIBUTORS (P) LTD

7/22, Ansari Road, Darya Ganj, New Delhi-110002
Phones : +91-11-40775252, 23273880, 23275880, 23280451
Fax : +91-11-23285873
Web : www.atlanticbooks.com
E-mail : orders@atlanticbooks.com

Branch Office
5, Nallathambi Street, Wallajah Road, Chennai-600002
Phones : +91-44-64611085, 32413319
E-mail : chennai@atlanticbooks.com

Printed in India at Nice Printing Press, A-33/3A, Site-IV, Industrial Area, Sahibabad, Ghaziabad, U.P.

Preface

Not much has changed in the rhetoric of India-China relations since Mao Zedong, founding father of the People's Republic of China who ruled China as the Chairman of the Communist Party of China from its establishment in 1949 until his death in 1976, speaking in 1951 in honour of the first anniversary of Indian constitution, declared that 'excellent friendship' had existed between the two countries 'for thousands of years'. Yet few of the lofty proclamations made by Chinese and Indian leaders over the years truly reflect the reality of relations between the two giants of the Asia. It is surprising that two neighbouring states with such a rich and sometimes fractious history, including a border conflict in 1962, should have what appears to be a largely reactive relationship. But neither has developed a grand strategy about the other. An unshakeable and largely unprofitable preoccupation with the past on the Indian side and an equally intense preoccupation with domestic consolidation on the Chinese side, have left the relationship under-tended. It might best be one of geostrategic competition qualified by growing commercial cooperation.

China is a more fraught subject in Indian national debates than India is for China, which does not appear to feel threatened in any serious way by India, while India at times displays tremendous insecurity in the face of Chinese economic success and military expansion. To outsiders, India and China show some striking similarities. Both are ancient civilisations reincarnated as modern republics in the mid-twentieth century and are now rising powers. Both have nuclear weapons, burgeoning economies, expanding military budgets and large reservoirs of manpower, and seem to be vying for influence in the Indian Ocean, the Persian Gulf, Africa, Central and East Asia. Yet little attention is paid to the relationship between them. Most attention has been focused on China's relations with the United States, Japan and East Asia or India's relations with Pakistan, South Asia and the United States. Whereas China-United States ties are often cast as one-to-one contest for global preeminence, moreover, the India-China relationship is more often seen in terms of the countries' interactions with extraneous actors such as the United States, Pakistan and other South Asian nations. It is also defined by contrasting polities and models of development, with the parties silently competing not just for capital, resources and markets, but also for legitimacy in the arena of great and emerging global powers.

The book *The Select Documents on India-China Relations: Politics of Resources, Identity and Authority* draws on evidence from interactions between India and China over the years to make an empirical case for the existence and impact of asymmetrical perceptions of threat and friendship between the two countries. The major issues of India-China relations, including the boundary problem, the nuclear issue, the Tibet issue, water diplomacy, regional competition and cooperation, and India-China relations in the global context, have been examined in the Introduction of the book. The book highlights the asymmetry of the threat perceptions between India and China and has explained the interactions of India-China relations. The India-China relations are constrained by the asymmetry between their threat perceptions. Due to the asymmetry in perceptions of threat, India has tried to reduce the sense of insecurity by adopting some countermeasures, such as developing nuclear weapons, allying with other countries, and undermining China's influence. However, India is also very cautious and avoids angering China. On the other hand, China is in favour of the status quo, and feels no urgent need to sort out the boundary disputes. China has ignored the asymmetry and does not want to share India's expectations and concerns. Thus, the asymmetry has made it difficult for India and China to forge shared knowledge and to set a common agenda around which their expectations could converge.

All the documents related to India-China relations have been arranged in chronological order beginning from 1954 to establish the direction of relation between the two countries. Three documents of National Intelligence Estimates of the United States have also been added to show how the world is concerned regarding India-China conflicts.

The book will be useful to the students and researchers of Political Science and International Relations. It will also be useful to all those who are interested and want to explore India-China relations.

K.R. Gupta

सत्यमेव जयते

Contents

Volume 1

Volume 2

INTRODUCTION

An Introduction to India-China Relations

India and China, the two giants of Asia with oldest and living civilization of the world, have a lot in common, and in fact they have had the longest uninterrupted history as a nation. Sindhu and Ganges gave birth to Indian civilization, which influenced South and Southeast Asia. Similarly, Huang He (Yellow River) and Chang Jiang (Yangtze River) gave birth to the Chinese civilization, which influenced Northeast and Southeast Asia. Both India and China have a considerable influence on world economy due to their bigger geographical area and population. They have got independence in the same century (India on 15th August 1947 and China on 1st October 1949), but the manner in which freedom was won speaks volumes about their policies. India won freedom after a prolonged non-violent struggle, on the other hand Chinese independence was a result of a never seen before military backed aggression. An analysis of India-China bilateral relation also determines the policies adopted by the respective countries in terms of dealing with international order. Traditionally China has used a confrontationist approach, for example, its actions in the South China Sea, its conflicts with South Korea and Taiwan, its role in the Vietnam-Cambodia-Laos conflict, etc. On the other hand, India has never been pro-active in declaring war with any of its neighbours. Even in the case of China, India (Pt. Jawahar Lal Nehru to be specific) tried its best to assuage Chinese apprehensions. As a nation that was struggling to grapple with the task of nation building, India saw in China an ally thanks to its socialist ideologies. Pt. Nehru also believed in socialist policies, much to the angst of his political contemporaries. China's breaking of the Panchsheel policies was a setback from which India unfortunately never recovered.

Existing in close proximity for thousands of years, the ancient civilizations of India and China had surprisingly little political interaction for most of that time. However, the twentieth century saw tensions between the two increased over disputed borders and geopolitical competition for power, influence, resources, and markets. As ancient civilizations, India and China coexisted in peace and harmony for millennia, but as post-colonial modern nation-states, except for a very short period of bonhomie in the early 1950s, relations between the two Asian giants have been marked by conflict, containment, mutual suspicion, distrust, and rivalry. Just as the Indian sub-continental plate has a tendency to constantly rub and push against the Eurasian tectonic plate, causing friction and volatility in the entire Himalayan mountain range, India's bilateral relationship with China also remains volatile and ridden with friction and tension.

During the 1950s the relations between India and China were cordial, based on the peaceful coexistence, but the Tibet issue, followed by a border dispute poisoned the climate of India-China entente cordiale. Pt. Nehru's policy of no-dispute and no-negotiation policies finally led to a war in 1962. From then on, India-China relations entered an era of cold war which lasted nearly for 20 years. However, during the era of Rajiv Gandhi (1988), the tension between the two countries was minimized and initiatives were taken for improvement in the relations. Since the end of cold war, the relations between the two countries has steadily improved, and also strengthened in various fields of mutual interest. The regular visits between the heads of state and officials have strengthened the relations and various issues including the border issue have been in the discussion for resolution by mutual cooperation.

Over the past six decades relation between India and China has undergone dramatic changes—ranging from the 1950s with a deep hostility in the 1960s and 1970s to a rapprochement in the 1980s and a readjustment since the demise of Soviet Union. The post-cold war era has offered enormous opportunities to India and China to move in the direction of a productive relationship. Both the neighbours have realized the imperative need for cooperation in diverse areas, especially in the trade and economic domains, in the long-term interest of peace and stability in Asia as well as for faster economic development and prosperity at home. The fast-changing economic and strategic milieu punctuated by uncertainty brought about by globalization in macro-cosmic terms, has created challenges as well as opportunities for both the neighbouring countries to free themselves of 'historical baggage' in terms of bilateral relations.

India-China Relations: Historical and Cultural Legacies

The reliable literature records of India-China interface could be traced from Han Dynasty (206 BC—220 AD). The first information is provided by Sima Qian (135 BC—86 BC), father of Chinese historiography, in his masterpiece Shiji (Records of the Grand Historian). He has narrated that people in the Shu (another name of Sichuan, Southwestern Chinese province) were wearing clothes that were brought from Shendu (Sindhu from India). Later Ban Gu (32 AD—92 AD), Chinese historian, politician, and poet best known for his part in compiling the Book of Han, the second of China's 24 dynastic histories, writes about Kashmir (Jibin State) in his book Qian Hanshu and talks about state of affairs there, its weather and products like pearls, corals, lapis lazuli, etc.

From the above-mentioned facts, it could be established that by 4th to 5th century AD there was already a sea route between India and China; and India supplied the trade items that were in demand in China and available only in India. According to literary sources, imported items transported from India to China included coral, pearls, glass and fragrances. On the other hand, silk appears to be the major item transported from China to India. Trade relations further developed during Tang Dynasty (618 AD—907 AD), Song Dynasty (960 AD—1279 AD), and Yuan Dynasty (1279 AD—1368 AD). By this time maritime activities were intense and it has been found in various sources that in Guangzhou (Canton) there were ships of Indian, Persians, and Sri Lankan merchants. Meanwhile, Indian astronomy, colander, medicine, music and dance, sugar manufacturing technology, etc., made their way to China. Chinese silk products remained popular among the trading items. Historical literature and archeological discoveries have established that there was a continuous flow of cross-cultural currents between India and China. The two elements of the exchange between India and China could be categorized as material exchange and spiritual cultural exchange. This two-faceted exchange was carried through the following four routes of communication:

(a) The Central Asian Route (or Silk Route),

(b) Assam-Burma and Yunnan Route (or Southern Silk Route),

(c) Tibet-Nepal Route, and

(d) The Sea Route (or Maritime Silk Route)

The Central Asian Route was the main overland route though this was not the earliest one to be discovered. This route was especially vital for the traders and missionaries from China to India and vice-versa. The route started from Chang'an passed through Dunhuang and Kashgar. From Dunhuang, it bifurcated into Northern and Southern route. The Northern route passed through the oasis between the Northern edge of Taklamaken Desert and the Tianshan mountain ranges. The Southern route ran through the Southern edge of the desert and Kunlun Mountain. These two smaller routes further merged at Kashgar in Xinjiang autonomous region. The route further splits into two from Kashgar—the Northern route passed through Kokand and Samarkand (now in Kirghizstan) and Southern route which ran through modern Bectria and merged with the Northern branch at Merv in Margiana (present Turkmenistan). From Bactria, the route ran through Kapisi and Kabul to Peshawar and Taxila. From Taxila it was connected to Mathura and Ujjain. Another route from Kashgar ran through Gilgit in Kashmir. Assam-Burma and Yunnan route originated in Chengdu, Sichuan province of China and entered Dali, Baoshan and Tengchong of Yunnan province. From Yunnan it passed through the Northern part of Burma and entered Assam in the Northeast of India.

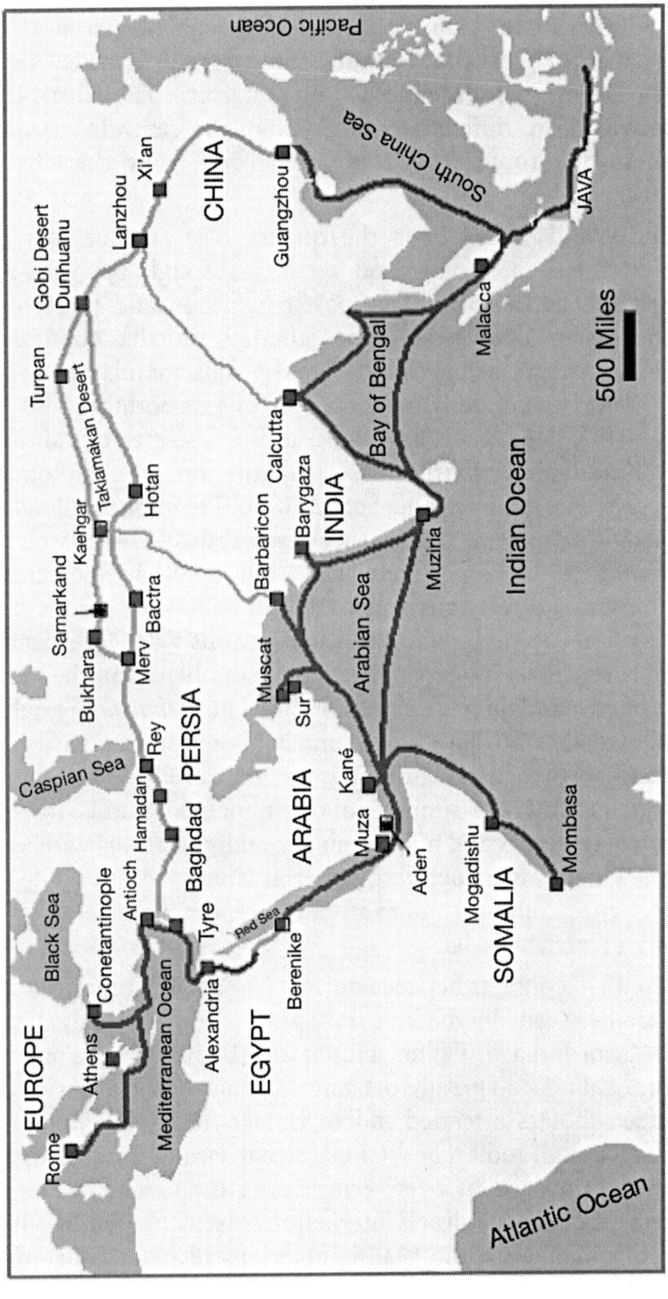
Pacific Ocean
South China Sea
JAVA
Malacca
500 Miles
Guangzhou
CHINA
Xi'an
Lanzhou
Gobi Desert
Dunhuanu
Turpan
Taklamakan Desert
Calcutta
Bay of Bengal
Indian Ocean
Hotan
Kaehgar
Samarkand
Barbaricon
Barygaza
INDIA
Muziria
Bactra
Bukhara
Merv
Muscat
Sur
Arabian Sea
PERSIA
Rey
Caspian Sea
Hamadan
Baghdad
ARABIA
Kané
Muza
Aden
Mogadishu
Mombasa
SOMALIA
Antioch
Conetantinople
Black Sea
Tyre
Red Sea
Berenike
Alexandria
Mediterranean Ocean
EGYPT
Athens
EUROPE
Rome
Atlantic Ocean

The Southern silk route further ran through Bengal and then finally merged with the Central Asian route. It is believed this was earliest route for the India-China interface. The Tibet-Nepal route was more difficult to access than the central Asian and Southern Silk route. This route came into being the late 7th century.

India and China have the quality of resilience that has enabled them to survive and prosper through the ages and against the odds. During the past three thousand years, each of the Asian countries—some situated on the continental landmass, others being islands off the Asia mainland—has at some stage been directly influenced by one or both of these two great civilizations. Both have long and rich strategic traditions. Both Kautilya's *Arthashastra*—a treatise on war, diplomacy, statecraft, and empire; and Sunzi's (Sun Tzu's) *Sunzi Bingfa*—the art of war, were written over two thousand years ago in India and China, respectively. The traditional Chinese concept of international relations was based on concentric circles from the imperial capital outward through variously dependent states to the barbarians. It bears remarkable resemblance to the Indian concept of mandala or circles as outlined in *Arthashastra*, which postulated that a king's neighbour is his natural enemy, while the king beyond his neighbour is his natural ally. The Chinese dynasties followed a similar policy of encircling and attacking nearby neighbours and maintaining friendly relations with more distant kingdoms. Much like imperial China, tribute, homage, subservience, but not annexation, were the rightful fruits of victory in ancient India.

Political contacts between ancient India and China were few and far between. In the cultural sphere, it was mostly a one-way—from India to China. Hindu and Buddhist religious and cultural influence spread to China through Central Asia, and Chinese scholars attended Indian Universities at Nalanda and Taxila. Though Indian and Chinese civilizations reacted to one another during the first few centuries of the Christian era, the process of religious-cultural interaction ceased after tenth century BC, coinciding with the Islamic invasions in India. Since then, the two neighbours lived as if they were oblivious to each other's existence for over a thousand years, until the advent of the 19th century, when both came under the influence of European powers. Before the age of European colonization, India accounted for about 25 percent of the world's manufactured goods and China for about 33 percent. China under the Song and Qing dynasties was the world's superpower. Under the Guptas and Mughals, India's economic, military, and cultural prowess was an object of envy. Then in a complete reversal of fortune, both the mighty Asian civilizations declined, decayed, and disintegrated and were finally conquered by European powers.

India-China Relations: Pre-Independence

India and China share plenty of common concerns and stances on a variety of important issues concerning world peace and development right from pre-independence era. A look at Indian and Chinese independence struggles shows that the anti-imperialistic efflorescence of the Indian and Chinese people manifested in a major way as a challenge to the colonial order for the first time during the First War of Independence (1857-59) in India and the Taiping Uprising (1850-64) in China. The reaction of Indian and Chinese people against their common enemy (Britishers) was the same. For the first-time Indian soldiers were stationed in China and switched over to the Taipings (Taiping Rebellion, radical political and religious upheaval that was probably the most important event in China in the 19th century. It lasted for some 14 years, 1850-64, ravaged 17 provinces, took an estimated 20 million lives) and fought shoulder to shoulder against imperialists and Qing government. It was due to the synergy between the cultures of India and China that the nationalists and revolutionaries of India and China developed deep mutual contact that turned into friendship amidst their anti-imperialist struggle. India and China became the natural allies and used various ways to remove the intruder. They supported Bal Gangadhar Tilak (first leader of the Indian Independence Movement), who carried out activities like Shivaji's commemorative meetings as far as Tokyo to make the Indian voice of anti-imperialism reach outside India. Besides, the nationalists like Ananda Mohan Bose (co-founder of Indian

National Association—one of the earliest Indian political organizations, and a senior leader of the Indian National Congress), Rash Behari Bose (a revolutionary leader against the British Raj in India, one of the key organizers of the Ghadar Mutiny and later, the Indian National Army), Manabendra Nath Roy (an Indian revolutionary, radical activist and political theorist), Abdul Hafiz Mohamed Barakatullah (an Indian revolutionary with sympathy for the Pan-Islamic movement), Lala Lajpat Rai (also known as Punjab Kesari), and many others outstanding pioneers of Indian freedom movement maintained good contracts and friendship with Sun Yat-sen (a Chinese physician, writer, philosopher, calligrapher and revolutionary, the first president and founding father of the Republic of China) who whole heartedly supported the Indian cause and rendered all possible help to them.

With the rise of Mahatma Gandhi in Indian politics, the entire Indian freedom movement turned into a mass movement, which had caught the attention of Chinese rulers. Mahatma Gandhi took spiritual world order or spiritual management of society and worked to bring in order through civilized means such as *Satyagraha* and *Ahimsa*. He made nonviolence his principle creed and never compromised with it. He also opposed Japanese attack against China during the 2nd World War in an open letter to Japanese people saying how he "intensely disliked it", criticizing the move by saying "Japan has descended to imperial ambition". Chinese people had upheld him as a symbol of Eastern civilization who manifested himself to represent this civilization in various shapes and forms. The Chinese media had also paid utmost attention and widely covered the Indian freedom struggle in various newspapers and journals.

A new chapter was written in the history of India-China relations during the war of Resistance and Second World War. So long as China suffered at the hands of Japanese, the reverberation affected India too. India dispatched a medical mission to China in 1938 to help them in their War of Resistance. Jawahar Lal Nehru made bonds of friendship even stronger when he visited China in 1939. The period from 1905 to 1947 was the period when both the people of India and China rendered support and sympathy to each other in their common struggle for independence from Britishers. It was the demand of time that India and China should necessarily come nearer to each other for the vast and tremendous potentials of economic cooperation in the New World after the war.

India-China Relations: Post-Independence

The gradual Westward expansion over the centuries under Mongol and Qing dynasties extended China's influence over Tibet and parts of Central Asia (present day Xinjiang, an autonomous territory in Northwest China). On the other hand, India's boundaries shrank following the 1947 partition that broke up the subcontinent's strategic unity that went back to more than two thousand years to the first Mauryan Empire (322 BC — 185 BC). As a result of Chinese occupation of Tibet in 1950, India and China came into close physical contact for the first time and clashed. India's partition in 1947 and Chinese occupation of Tibet in 1950 have allowed China to extend its reach and influence into a region where it had, in terms of history and civilization, previously exercised no influence at all.

India was the first country in non-communist block to recognize China after it got independence on 1st October 1949 in the culmination of Chinese Civil War (1945-1949) and establish diplomatic relations with it. Pt. Nehru greeted the birth of communist China in October 1949 with great pomp and, in a rare gesture, India displayed excessive zeal in prompting China's membership in the United Nations. Pt. Nehru did not share the American perception that communism was a threat to world peace and stability. On the contrary, he believed that Western hatred of communism might boomerang, since nationalism in China was stronger than communism. He was convinced that Chinese nationalism played a far better important part than communism and that Chinese civilization was too old to succumb completely to Marxist dogma.

Pt. Nehru's belief seemed to be true as the early phase of India-China relations was marked by a close warm friendship, despite China's military takeover of Tibet in 1950 and India's providing asylum to Dalai Lama and his countless Buddhist followers. Although Indian government did not register a serious protest with Beijing, opposition leaders in parliament criticized Pt. Nehru's policy on the Tibetan issue but he remained unmoved and preferred to deal with monolithic China diplomatically by keeping it in check, and isolating it from USSR rather than coming into open confrontation with it. This strategy paid off and India was able to maintain peace and tranquility on its Northeastern borders for over a decade.

At Peking, in 29th April 1954, India and China signed an agreement on trade and intercourse between the Tibet region of China and India, and had an exchange of notes. India thus signed away all its inherited privileges in Tibet by virtue of earlier pacts. This agreement is also known as *Panchsheel.*

Panchsheel: It is also known as the Five Principles of Peaceful Co-existence, which were first formally enunciated in the Agreement on Trade and Intercourse between the Tibet region of China and India signed on 29th April 1954, which stated, in its preamble, that the two Governments have resolved to enter into the present Agreement based on the following principles:

(a) Mutual respect for each other's territorial integrity and sovereignty.

(b) Mutual non-aggression.

(c) Mutual non-interference.

(d) Equality and mutual benefit.

(e) Peaceful co-existence.

Two months later, during the visit of Premier Zhou Enlai to India, he and Pt. Nehru issued a joint statement on 28th June 1954 that elaborated their vision of *Panchsheel* as the framework, not only for relations between the two countries, but also for their relations with all other countries, so that a solid foundation could be laid for peace and security in the world. *Panchsheel,* as envisioned by its creators, gave substance to the voice of newly established countries who were seeking the space to consolidate their hard won independence, as it provided an alternative ideology dedicated to peace and development of all as the basis for international interaction, whether bilateral or multilateral. The two leaders also expressed the hope in the Joint Statement that the adoption of *Panchsheel* will also help in creating an area of peace which as circumstances permit can be enlarged thus lessening the chances of war and strengthening the cause of peace all over the world.

The vision of *Panchsheel* caught the imagination of the people of Asia and the world, and was incorporated into the Ten Principles of International Peace and Cooperation enunciated in the Declaration issued on 18th April 1955 at Bandung Conference of 29 Afro-Asian countries. The universal relevance of *Panchsheel* was emphasized when its tenets were incorporated in a resolution on peaceful co-existence presented by India, Yugoslavia and Sweden, and unanimously adopted on 11th December 1957, by the United Nations General Assembly. In 1961, the Conference of Non-Aligned Nations in Belgrade accepted *Panchsheel* as the principled core of the Non-Aligned Movement. Down the years, the ethos of *Panchsheel* continued to be reflected in the world events even if there was no conscious attribution, finding expression in the position of the developing countries in the North-South dialogue, and in other groupings. The timeless relevance of *Panchsheel* is based on its firm roots in the cultural traditions of its originators, two of the world's most ancient civilisations. The linkage that was established by the spread of Buddhism in China laid the historical basis for the formulation of the principles of Panchsheel by India and China.

The five Principles of Peaceful Coexistence and the Bandung Conference were highlights of India-China cooperation during the initial period of 1950s. However, by late 1950s, serious differences between the two states had begun to surface, particularly over the un-demarcated border. China refused to acknowledge the British demarcation of the India-China border, i.e., McMahon Line, which demarcates Arunachal Pradesh to be a part of India.

The first Premier of the People's Republic of China, Zhou Enlai refused to accept the McMahon Line as the final line of the border demarcation between India and China. To counter the Indian claim that Beijing had, in the past, never contested the legality of McMahon Line, China argued that Tibet was not a sovereign state and therefore did not have the power to conclude treaties with the British. Moreover, China regarded the disputed Aksai China area as part of the Chinese province of Sinkiang and not Tibet. Chinese maps showed some 65,000 sq. km. of the territory South of the Line as part of the Tibet Autonomous Region, known as South Tibet, in China. However, China recognized a Line of Actual Control which closely approximates McMahon Line in the Eastern part of its border with India, according to a 1959 diplomatic note by the Premier Zhou Enlai. To the contrary, India contested that Chinese maps had never shown Sinkiang to extend South of the Kuentun range, which separated it from Tibet. Ultimately, border clashes led to a full-scale India-China war in October 1962 and armed skirmishes in 1967 and 1987.

Between 1962 and 1969, India-China relations remained in a deep freeze. Cheered by its easy victory over India, China initiated a vitriolic and vituperative propaganda against India, which intensified India's suspicion over China even further. India's mistrust over China was further confirmed when China befriended Pakistan and started to extend military and political support to it. On the contrary, China saw Indo-Soviet friendship as an anti-China ploy. In the wake of humiliating defeat, when India accorded high priority to its armed forces, China accused India of militarism. When India sought support from the USA and Soviet Union for strengthening its armed forces, India was leveled as a stooge of the US imperialism and Soviet revisionism and social imperialism.

From the middle of 1966 onwards, the internal conditions of both the neighbours, India and China, were in a state of continuous flux. China was in the cobweb of socio-economic upheaval and acute leadership struggle during the Cultural Revolution phase of 1966-69. On the other hand, India was in the hand of a new Prime Minister, Mrs. Indira Gandhi who was an untried and untested leader. Besides she had to face many problems, like famines due to widespread drought. Parliamentary elections of

1967 severely weakened the central leadership, as Mrs. Gandhi returned to power with reduced majority. During the phase of Cultural Revolution, Chinese foreign policy remained dormant, but this did not stop the Chinese from extending its support to the so-called national liberation movement in the third world by exhorting them to replace the legitimate regimes. Accordingly, China started to exploit two basic weaknesses of the Indian administration.

(a) The inability to integrate the tribal people of the Northeast into the mainstream of India.

(b) The failure to ameliorate the condition of the rural peasantry and landless labours in the lower Ganges Valley.

Sensing the weaknesses of Indian administration as an opportunity, China openly supported Naga and Mizo insurgents and encouraged them to rise in revolution against India. The Naxalbari uprising in West Bengal catered a golden opportunity to the Chinese to recommend the Maoist path for the Indian revolutionaries. India-China relations further attenuated in June 1967 with the expulsion of two Indian diplomats from Beijing on alleged charges of espionage activities. On 11th September 1967, Chinese troops attacked Indian troops on the Sikkim border across the Nathu La and opened heavy mortar and artillery fire. After repeated Indian protest and proposal for ceasefire, by 15th September 1967, there was a virtual cessation of all hostile activities. Again, Chinese troops fired heavily on the Indian positions at Cho La on 1st October 1967 and both the sides suffered casualties. All these led to deterioration in the relations between the two countries. However, Mrs. Gandhi kept striving to normalize relations with Beijing and, by the end of 1967, in a discussion on external affairs she replied, "China continues to maintain an attitude of hostility towards us and carries anti-Indian propaganda not only against the Indian Government but also against the whole of our democratic functioning and even our national integrity. But, I would like to say that we do not harbor any evil intention towards the Chinese people, and we do hope that a day will come when they will also realize that it is in the interests of all the countries of Southeast Asia that we should be friends and that each country should be able to devote its strength to solving the very major problem of combating poverty and backwardness."

Mrs. Gandhi adopted a flex approach regarding relations with China and tried to establish healthy relations with it. In an address to parliament on 20th February 1970, the President of India Mr. V.V. Giri reiterated his government's desire to conduct its relations with China on "the principle of mutual respect of each other's sovereignty and territorial integrity and non-interference. We expect China to respect our rights to pursue own domestic affairs and foreign policy."

During the 1970s, China not only supported the military junta and its role in East Pakistan but also tried discreetly to moderate Yahya Khan's brutal policy towards East Pakistan. China alleged that "Weighted down with difficulties at home and abroad, the reactionary Indian government has embarked on a mad course of arms expansion and war preparations to carry out an expansionist policy towards its neighbor." It continued to step up friendly acts with Pakistan against India. Despite virulent anti-Indian Chinese propaganda, India played cool and maintained a low profile, and took the initiative to start dialogue with China, when its ambassador in Moscow met twice with his Chinese counterpart in May 1971, to discuss the terms of restoration of diplomatic representation to the Ambassadorial level. After a period of 14 years from India-China war, India's normalization of relations with Beijing ultimately resulted in the restoration of diplomatic relations with China in 1976. One of the senior members of the Indian Foreign Service, K.R. Narayanan who later became the President of India, was accredited India's Ambassador to Beijing in 1976. It was a pragmatic step towards putting India-China relations back on an even track.

The 1977 parliamentary elections paved the way for the formation of Janata Party-led government under the leadership of Morarji Desai, who was a strict disciplinarian and true Gandhian. Desai continued with the legacy of normalizing relations with China and sent his foreign minister, A.B. Vajpayee, to China in 1979 to carry forward the process of rapprochement. During the visit, Vajpayee broached the contentious border issue with Chinese leaders. Deng Xiaoping, Chinese revolutionary, politician, and paramount leader of the People's Republic of China from 1978 until his retirement in 1989, told Vajpayee to avoid bringing the issue on which both countries differed sharply into the discussion. Deng said, "We should have common ground while resolving differences. As for the boundary question, we can solve it through peaceful consultation. This question should not prevent us from improving our relations in other fields."

India-China relations entered into a new phase with the path-breaking visit of Prime Minister Rajiv Gandhi to Beijing on 19th December 1988. His visit saw a significant improvement in India-China relations, which became more cordial that at any time since mid-1950s. This visit was judged a success by both sides, because it was the first visit by an Indian Prime Minister to China since Pt. Nehru's 1954 visit and it helped balance the score in terms of summit visits. Rajiv Gandhi indicated India's willingness to increase consultation and cooperation with China on a range of international issues, such as the creation of a New International Economic Order, disarmament, and pollution. India's willingness to cooperate with China on such global issues represented acceptance of Chinese proposal that had been on the table since the early 1980s. The idea behind such macro diplomatic cooperation was that, as large developing countries with long histories, India and China shared many important characteristics and common interests. Moreover, by cooperating on these issues, the two countries could create an important atmosphere conductive to better bilateral relations.

During his visit, Rajiv Gandhi set the tone by declaring, "It is now time to look to the future, I have come to renew an old friendship". Deng Xiaoping responded by saying, "China and India should forget the unpleasant past and set their eyes on future." Premier Li Peng was Rajiv Gandhi's major interlocutor during the visit, and their discussion focused on the substantive issue of the border, Tibet, bilateral relations, and international situations. He also accepted an invitation to play a return visit to India.

During Rajiv Gandhi's visit the two countries had in-depth discussion on the India-China border questions and agreed to settle it through peaceful and friendly consultations. In December 1988, India and China decided to set up a Joint Working Group (JWG) on the boundary issue headed by Foreign Secretary on the Indian side and a Vice-minister of Foreign Affairs on the Chinese side. The JWG had following two important functions.

(a) The JWG was to make concrete recommendations for the overall solution of the boundary question.

(b) The JWG would ensure the peace and tranquility on the Line of Actual Control.

The two countries also agreed to develop relations in other fields and set up a joint group on economic relations and trade, as well as science and technology. They signed three accords on cultural, scientific, and technological cooperation as well as civil aviation.

Following Prime Minister Rajiv Gandhi's China visit, the Chinese Premier Li Peng paid a return visit to India on 11th December 1991. The joint statement issued at the end of the visit stressed that the boundary questions should not affect the development of bilateral relations. The JWG on the boundary questions should step up its work, and peace and tranquility should be maintained along the Line of Actual Control pending the final settlement of the boundary questions. Indian President R. Venkataraman paid a state visit to China in May 1992 and Vice-President K.R. Narayanan in October 1994. Between December 1988 and June 1993, six rounds of JWG meetings on the border issues were held.

Progress was made in reducing border tension through Confidence Building Measures (CBMs), including mutual troop reductions, regular meetings of local military officers and advance notification of military drills and exercises. After an interval of more than 30 years, border trade between India and China resumed in July 1992 and both the countries reopened their consulates in Mumbai and Shanghai on December 1992. Indian defense minister Sharad Pawar visited China on December

1992, when the two defense establishments agreed to develop academic, military, scientific and technological cooperation. In 1993, the two countries agreed to open an additional border trading post.

On September 1993, Prime Minister P.V. Narasimha Rao visited China and concluded an Agreement on Maintenance of Peace and Tranquility in Border Areas along the Line of Actual Control. In December, in the same year, a senior level Chinese military delegation made a six-days goodwill visit to India for fostering CBMs between the defence forces of two countries. In 1994, the two countries signed a number of agreements and MoUs, such as Agreement on Avoiding Double Taxation, Agreement for Cooperation on Health and Medical Science, MoUs on Simplifying the Procedure for Visa Application and Banking Cooperation, etc. In the beginning of 1994, Beijing announced that it not only favoured a negotiated settlement on Kashmir but also opposed any form of independence for the region.

President of the People's Republic of China, Jiang Zemin visited India in November-December 1996. This visit was notable for the agreement on CBMs in military field in the border areas along the Line of Actual Control, which covered troop reduction and weapons limitation along the borders. Both countries reaffirmed in the agreement that neither side would use force against the other by any means or seek unilateral military support for them. The leaders of both countries agreed to establish constrictive and cooperative partnership between India and China into 21st Century, on the principles of Panchsheel. Four other accords reached during the visit were those relating to maritime transport, cooperation in combating narcotic drug trafficking, improving communication across the border, and maintenance of the Consulate-General of India in Hongkong Special Administrative Region.

India-China Relations: Post-Pokhran-II

The sunshine period in India-China relations once again disappeared behind a dark cloud after Pokhran-II, which was the series of five nuclear bomb test explosions conducted by India at the Indian Army's Pokhran Test Range in May 1998. It was the second nuclear test conducted by India—the first test, code-named Smiling Buddha, was conducted in May 1974. In May 1998, Defense Minister George Fernandes made a remark that China was India's main threat, which caused once again, after the Sumdorong Chu incident in 1987 in Arunachal Pradesh, a setback to India-China relations. The atmosphere became tenser after the nuclear test. The Chinese saw the test as causing serious damage to the bilateral relations and took stronger objection to Prime Minister Vajpayee's letter to US President Clinton, justifying India's decision to test nuclear weapon by pointing to the threat from China, and asked for an Indian explanation for considering China as a threat. Beijing also joined the other UN Security Council member in passing Resolution No. 1172, which condemned the nuclear test by India and Pakistan. China cancelled its decision to participate in the pre-scheduled 1998 meeting of the JWG alternately held in each country to discuss CBMs.

China successfully exploded its first atomic bomb on October 1964, which opened up a new dimension in India-China relations—the nuclear dimension. In such a scenario, the Indian leaderships had to consider in the light of the latest development whether India should continue to be a non-nuclear weapons state. India had tried to appeal to the US and the UK for some form of protection from China's nuclear threat, but had failed to achieve any reassurance. Therefore, the threat of China's nuclear capability has continued to be an important driving force behind India's nuclear weapons programme to the present day. However, India remained in an ambiguous nuclear limbo, and had to choose between being a nuclear power and being a non-nuclear state. Although, India detonated its own nuclear device under Indira Gandhi's administration on May 1974, it maintained that the test was merely for peaceful purposes and it was reluctant to manufacture nuclear weapons. India's ambiguity towards developing nuclear weapons may have been seen as one strategic option for the Indian leaders, but it failed to come to terms with India's perceived threat arising from China's nuclear capability. By May 1998, India's deep-seated suspicions were reinforced by the possibility of China's nuclear coercion, China's clandestine support for Pakistan's nuclear weapons programme, and the enhanced international status China derived from nuclear weapons. The failure to achieve a satisfactory solution to its security concerns clearly spurred India's decision to move more surely down the road to nuclear weaponization. On May 1998, India finally discarded its traditional stance and proclaimed itself a nuclear weapons state after conducting a series of five rounds of nuclear tests. Unlike the 1974 tests, its rationale for exploding nuclear devices brought a new and more significant nuclear dimension to India-China relations.

India equipped with nuclear weapons presented a totally different challenge for China. India's possession of nuclear weapons altered the hard power structure and played a decisive role in building up a new military balance between India and China. Moreover, India's new identity as a nuclear power reshaped the ideational structure between India and China. Chinese leaders not only needed to reassess the implications of nuclear India's challenges to its security environment, but also needed to take account of India's enhanced international status derived from its possession of nuclear weapons. Meanwhile, China also had to deal with the "China threat" theory used by Indian strategic planners and to justify India's move against the international nuclear non-proliferation regime.

Before 1998, for China, the main concerns about a nuclear threat came first from the US and then the Soviet Union. Although, the hostile relationship meant that China became a potential nuclear threat to India, Chinese leaders did not feel it necessary to launch a nuclear attack against India, i.e., China's nuclear deterrent was not directed towards India. On the other hand, India has perceived a clear nuclear threat from China since 1964. There were three sources of concerns that had contributed to the construction of this perception.

(a) The scenario that China could use its nuclear capability to blackmail or coerce India.

(b) China's stance towards nuclear proliferation due to China's assistance to Pakistan.

(c) China's political and diplomatic status as a nuclear power.

Partly due to its possession of nuclear weapons, China edged out India and secured a higher international status. This undermined India's prestige and leadership among the Asian and developing countries. These concerns related to China's nuclear power motivated India to consider the nuclear option.

China's nuclear capability, its nuclear connection with Pakistan, and the nuclear-state status constituted an imperative incentive for India to develop its own nuclear weapons. However, India's nuclear weapons programme remained dormant between 1974 and 1998. The next two decades after the 1974 test saw India continue its efforts to keep disarmament in focus in international fora. India maintained an ambiguous stance, showing its nuclear capability and keeping the nuclear option without building a nuclear arsenal. The most controversial aspect of China's nuclear policy was its position towards non-proliferation. Only since the late 1980s has China adjusted its foreign policy operation to actively take part in the nuclear non-proliferation regime. China joined the International Atomic Energy Agency (IAEA) in 1985, more than two decades after going nuclear, and agreed to place its civilian nuclear facilities under IAEA safeguards in 1988. In 1992, it acceded to the Treaty on the Non-Proliferation of Nuclear Weapons (NPT). In addition, it joined the Zangger Committee in October 1997 and joined the Nuclear Suppliers Group (NSG) in June 2004. In September 2004, it officially submitted its application for membership of the Missile Technology Control Regime (MTCR). It was also among the first countries to sign the Comprehensive Test Ban Treaty (CTBT) in 1996.

As far as India-China nuclear relations are concerned, China's assistance to Pakistan's weapon programme has been a cause of grave concern for India's security. In the late 1970s, the media published evidence of China's aid for Pakistan's nuclear programme. Since then, apart from the conventional military equipment, China had been assisting Pakistan in developing its missile and nuclear capabilities to compensate for its deficit in weaponry vis-à-vis India. In 1983, China had transferred a complete nuclear weapon design and sufficient uranium to build a nuclear weapon in Pakistan. China also supplied nuclear-capable M-II missiles to Pakistan between 1992 and 1994. With Chinese assistance, Pakistan was believed to have moved towards serial production of solid-propellant Short-Range Ballistic Missiles (SRBMs), such as the Shaheen-I and Haider-I. China is also the 'mother' of Ghauri, Pakistan's Intermediate Range Ballistic Missile (IRBM).

Successive Indian governments had, over time, tried to restore the nuclear tests. According to former Indian Defence Minister (and later President), R. Venkataraman, India was ready with full preparations for an underground nuclear test in 1983, but was dissuaded from going ahead by external pressure. A similar attempt to carry out new nuclear tests was made in 1995, but the then American Ambassador to India, Frank Wisner, showed satellite photographs to Indian officials of India's preparations for nuclear tests and asked the Indian side to halt the programme. It was BJP, which won the general elections in 1998, that decided to end the long-standing ambiguity over the nuclear options. The reasons for the BJP government to go nuclear were mixed. To put it simply, three main factors were behind the decision—India's perception of its security needs, domestic political considerations, and the ambition to make India a world-recognised great power.

China might not have played a part in the domestic factor behind India's decision to develop nuclear weapons, but played a major part in shaping India's security perception, and found itself relevant in India's pursuit of becoming a major world power. This reflected India's perception and assessment of the post-cold war security environment—the end of the Cold War had done little to ameliorate India's security concerns, and China was seen as the major contributor in destabilizing India's security environment. Defence Minister George Fernandes termed China as India's "potential threat number one", stressing that the potential threat from China was greater than that from Pakistan because India was encircled by Chinese military and naval activity—China had extended eleven airfields in Tibet, which posed a threat to India's security, and had set up electronic surveillance installations on the Coco islands, 40 km off the northern tip of the Andaman and Nicobar islands, to observe Indian missile trials and other exercises. Fernandes' comments on China had evoked sharp criticism from China, which had officially protested to India twice in less than a month. China's Foreign Ministry spokesman described Indian defence minister's utterances as "ridiculous and not worthy of refutation", but his statements had seriously sabotaged the atmosphere for improving relations.

Despite the furor created in China by India's nuclear test, a thaw between the two sides eventually emerged. The nuclear issue featured as an irritant in India-China relations for some time, which really put the bilateral relationship in a limbo. In order to mend relations, the Indian side took several initiatives to placate the Chinese. First was the statement by Brajesh Mishra, the Principal Secretary to the Prime Minister, who said that India wanted to have the best of relations with China and urged China to return to dialogue. This was followed by Vajpayee's statement that some misunderstanding between China and India had been created only by the distorted version of statements appearing in the media. However, China expected a more credible commitment from India. In February 1999, Indian officials were sent to Beijing in an attempt to urge their counterparts to restart the dialogue on the boundary question. The official visit brought about a positive result with an announcement by the Chinese Foreign Minister Tang Jiaxuan just a few weeks later that the Chinse side had recently acknowledged the statements issued by Indian leaders that China posed no threat to India. Tang's announcement came as the first positive signal of China's desire to put behind the bitterness that had arisen in the wake of India's nuclear tests. Finally, both countries were able to resume talks once again after a span of nine months when, in June 1999, the Minister of External Affairs Jaswant Singh visited China. Both the sides reached a consensus that the prerequisite for restoring and developing India-China relations, and it was assured that neither side will regard the other as a threat. President K.R. Narayan visited China on May 2000, when his Chinese counterpart, Jiang Zemin, proposed a four-point proposal concerning the development of bilateral relations in the 21st century. After all these initiatives, the two neighbouring giants enhanced the level of bilateral personnel visits to increase mutual understanding and trust; expanded trade and economic cooperation; strengthened coordination and cooperation in international affairs; and properly handled issues left over from the past in the spirit of seeking common ground while reserving differences.

Following the trend to restore the pre-Pokhran-II relationship, at the twelfth Joint Working Group (JWG) meeting on the boundary problem in April 2000, India and China agreed to resume high-level military interactions, which had been suspended after India's nuclear tests. Chinese Foreign Minister Tang Jiaxuan visited India in July 2000, followed by Lt. General Tian Shugen, Vice-President of the Academy of Military Science, in August 2000. It was the first exchange between the two armies after the People's Liberation Army Chief of General Staff Fu Quanyou had visited India during April to May 1998. Subsequently, two Indian naval ships paid a goodwill visit to China in September 2000. Thus, there was a positive shift in the tone and content of the bilateral relationship between India and China. A comprehensive dialogue mechanism was formed with the aim of promoting an improvement of and a development in bilateral relations through dialogue. Despite the existing negotiation mechanism on boundary problem, a security dialogue was established in June 1999 during External Affairs Minister Jaswant Singh's visit to China. Three rounds of the dialogue were held between March 2000 and September 2002. An India-China Eminent Persons Group was constituted during President K.R. Narayanan's state visit to China during May-June 2000, and the first meeting of this group took place in New Delhi on 17th-18th September 2001. The group was expected to serve as an important advisory agency for the two governments. The India-China dialogue mechanism on counter terrorism was established during Chinese Premier Zhu Rongji's visit to India in January 2002 to address concerns in the wake of the September 11 events. The first meeting was held in New Delhi on 23rd April 2002.

The dialogue mechanism appeared to be a new feature of India-China relations in the post-Pokhran era, but there was still doubt whether both sides could make use of it to enhance mutual understanding and further strengthen bilateral relations. During Prime Minister Atal Bihari Vajpayee's visit to China from 22nd to 27th June 2003, both sides issued a declaration on Principles for Relations and Comprehensive Cooperation, which stated, "The two countries are not a threat to each other. Neither side shall use or threaten to use force against the other." However, the so-called "constructive partnership of cooperation oriented towards the twenty-first century" had not worked out as satisfactorily as hoped since its proclamation.

India and China showed a willingness and a capability to manage the diplomatic aftershock of India's nuclear tests, however, suspicions and distrust still remained. With India's emergence as a nuclear power in its neighbourhood, for the Chinese, a more significant question that needed to be answered was whether a nuclear India would undermine China's security. In fact, China had not ignored India's military power in assessment of India-China relations. In assessing India's nuclear weapons programme, the major concern for China was that China lost most of its nuclear superiority against India. No matter how credible India's nuclear weapons were, China perceived India's nuclear weapons as an unpleasant factor in its security environment. The quantitative and qualitative improvement of India's nuclear forces has led to an increased perception of threat in China. As a result, China is still very reluctant to recognize India's status as a nuclear state and tries to underline the illegitimacy of India's nuclear weapons programme.

Since India had taken China's and Pakistan's nuclear capability as the main security imperative in the development of a nuclear weapons programme, the implication was that India intended to use its nuclear weapons to counterbalance China's strength. In other words, India's possession of nuclear weapons had made an impact on China's strategic environment. China had become a member of the nuclear club decades before India and its nuclear weapons programme remained many years in advance of India's. However, India's decision to go down the route of developing nuclear weapons has neutralized China's perceived superiority in terms of military strength. Now, China will no longer be able to use nuclear blackmail and coercion against India, because India is also equipped with nuclear strike ability, i.e., with India being a nuclear power, China would not like to antagonize India beyond a certain point.

One element of India's nuclear doctrine is that it unequivocally renounces the first use of nuclear weapons. The commitment to no-first-use has explicitly underscored India's lack of any intention to use nuclear weapons as a tool of pre-emptive policy and its intention to use them instead simply to dissuade attempts by any state at nuclear blackmail. Though it is tempting to dismiss the no-first-use commitment as a mere boilerplate, and although the efficiency of the no-first-use policy is also questioned by some analysts, the deterrent nature of India's nuclear doctrine appears clear. The primary role of India's nuclear force is to protect the nation from the prospect of nuclear blackmail and coercion at the hands of nuclear powered countries such as China and Pakistan. Since, China also claims that it will not be the first to use nuclear weapons, the no-first-use principle has become a set of double safety valves between India and China to avoid a nuclear clash. Therefore, even though the two countries are equipped with nuclear weapons, a nuclear war between India and China remains less likely.

India-China Relations: Border Disputes

India is China's second largest neighbor sharing a little over 4000 km. land border which stretches from the barren Aksai Chin plateau in the west (administered by China but claimed by India as part of the Ladakh district of Jammu and Kashmir) through the former kingdom of Sikkim in the middle section, and across to the eastern Indian state of Arunachal Pradesh (administered by India but claimed by China as 'South Tibet').

The origins of border dispute stem from a combination of difficult terrain, nascent survey technology, the absence of

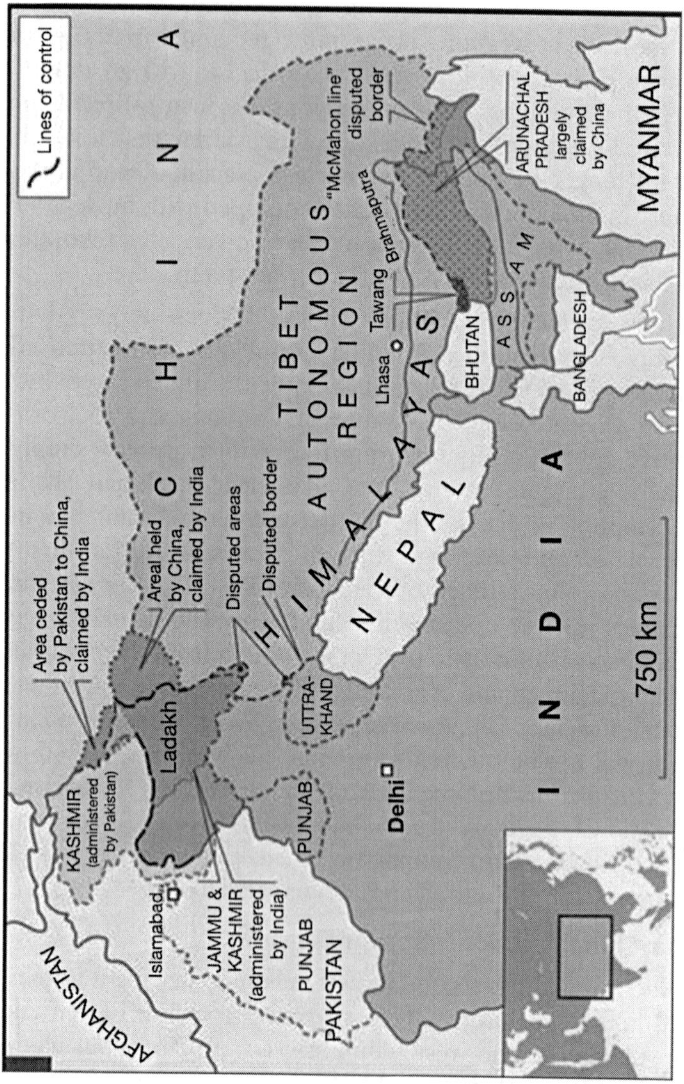

a functioning Tibetan state and the craft of British Imperial map, making writ large. In 1914, at the Anglo-Tibetan Shimla Conference, the British colonial authorities drew the McMahon Line (named after the chief negotiator Sir Henry McMahon), which established the boundary between British India and Tibet. Although, Chinese representative were present at Shimla, they refused to sign or recognize the accords on the basis that Tibet was under Chinse jurisdiction and therefore did not have the power to conclude treaties.

Currently, India and China dispute over a land area of about 125000 sq. km., which can be divided into the eastern, middle and western sectors. The eastern sector includes the McMahon Line which runs from the tri-junction between India, China and Bhutan from the west to Brahmaputra River in the east, largely along the crest of the Himalayas. This section is now called the Indian State of Arunachal Pradesh and occupies about an area of 90000 sq. km. having a population of over a million people. The middle sector starts from the tri-junction between the Southwestern of Ngari Prefecture, Tibet, La Dvags and Punjab to the tri-junction between China, India and Nepal. It length is about 450 km. long, with about 2000 sq. km. of land under dispute. The disputed area in the middle sector on the other hand is much smaller, involving only several pockets. The western sector starts with the pass of Karakoram in the North to the tri-junction between Tibet's Ngari Prefecture, La Dvags and Himachal Pradesh, running along 600 km. The disputed area, known as Aksai Chin, occupies about 33500 sq. km. of land and is now controlled by China. India's claim to the area is largely based on the "Johnson Line". In 1846, Great Britain annexed Kashmir which played a critical role in the British strategy for securing the northern frontiers of India. To advance its border claims, in 1865, W.H. Johnson, a civil servant with the Survey of India who was sent to survey the area, proposed the "Johnson Line", putting Aksai Chin in Kashmir. While Aksai Chin is a virtually uninhabited bleak barren plateau, it is of high strategic value to China as it is a vital passage point between Tibet and Xinjiang.

India-China border disputes are complex historical issues. As both countries cannot agree on border delimitation, the India-China border has never been officially drawn. When India came under British rule, it began to advance the two countries' traditional border to the Chinese side. During the 1913-1914 tripartite conference involving a Tibetan delegate, a representative of Chinese central government, and Sir Henry McMahon, a foreign secretary of the British Indian government, a secret bilateral agreement was signed with the Tibetan representative on a new border line, also known as the McMahon Line. The Chinese central government rejected the accord and their plenipotentiary, and the Tibetan government later disputed the legality of the McMahon Line. Furthermore, the McMahon Line was initially rejected by the British-run Indian government as incompatible with the 1907 Anglo-Russian Convention. However, the British began using the McMahon Line on the Survey of India maps in 1937, and officially published the Shimla Accord in 1938. During the Second World War and immediately after that, the British made extensive effort to expand their control towards the claimed McMahon Line. By the time India gained independence on 15th August 1947, the McMahon Line had become India's Northeast border.

India inherited the British territorial policy, including the McMahon Line as the legitimate border. After the newly established People's Republic of China took over Tibet in 1951, India felt threatened by the Chinese military presence in Tibet and quickly extended administrative and military control in the eastern sector. In the same year, India took control of the Tawang, a centre of Tibet's Buddhist culture with one of the biggest Tibetan monasteries outside Lhasa. It is also a holy site as it was the birthplace of the sixth Dalai Lama in the seventeenth century. While the Tibetan government fiercely protested against India's move, the Chinese central government remained silent on the issue and this silence was perceived by India as an indication that the newly founded People's Republic of China (PRC) was willing to accept the McMahon Line.

After taking control of Tawang, the India-China border became quite again, and both the countries had undertaken substantial efforts in building infrastructure roads and check-posts, and sending out patrol and survey teams. In 1954, two countries signed an agreement on trade and intercourse across Tibetan borders. This was the first document whereby both India and China enunciated the so-called "Five Principles of Peaceful Coexistence". In the agreement, India surrendered various rights and privileges over Tibet, which the British had induced Tibet to grant, without any mention of the border issue in the agreement. While China back then felt it was better to postpone discussions on the border issue, India's interpretation of the agreement was very different, believing that the two countries had agreed that there was no border dispute between them. However, from China's perspective, there was no trade-off between Tibet and the border, real or imagined, and the Chinese position has steadfastly remained that India's recognition of China's sovereignty over Tibet, and China's acceptance of the former colonial McMahon Line were not connected issues.

But, later on, Pt. Nehru announced that the two countries' borders were drawn and there should be no further disputes on the border issue. He recommended a system of check-posts to be set up along the entire border. Furthermore, after establishing a presence in the border areas, India claimed that certain sections of the McMahon line should be modified, placing it further north into China's side. This eventually led to first India-China military clash in August 1959 at Longju. Yet both countries' border dispute did not start in the eastern sector along the McMahon Line. Instead, the first border dispute occurred in the middle sector in 1954 when India occupied several posts. In 1958 China's ambassador to India at the time sent two memos to the Indian Foreign Ministry calling for an immediate withdrawal of Indian troops from the disputed areas and the resumption of negotiations. Later, greater tensions occurred in the western sector because, between 1953 and 1957, China had undertaken massive projects for road construction to support its presence in Tibet. One important project started in 1953 was to convert the old caravan route in Aksai Chin from Xinjiang into a motorable road, which was finally completed in September 1957.

On 18th October 1958, India sent a memo to the Chinese government, officially claiming Aksai Chin as Indian territory. In this memo to Zhou Enlai, the first Premier of the People's Republic of China, Pt. Nehru wrote, "There can be no question of these large parts of India (shown as within China on the Chinese map) being anything but India and there is no dispute about it". In January 1959, Zhou's reply highlighted following points.

(a) Both countries' borders had never been formally demarcated.

(b) Border disputes do exist between India and China.

(c) Aksai Chin was China's land and had always been under Chinese jurisdiction.

(d) Through the McMahon Line was illegal, China would consider accepting it if it could legitimize the McMahon Line while India waived or sharply modified its claim to Aksai Chin.

The proposal of Zhou was rejected by Pt. Nehru who insisted on sending Indian troops into all territories claimed by India. After Kongka Pass incident, Zhou visited India hoping to solve the border disputes peacefully through negotiations. During the meeting, Zhou made China's proposal explicit for the first time—reciprocal acceptance of present actualities in both sectors and constitution of a boundary commission. However, India rejected the proposal, claiming that there should be no compromise, no standstill agreement and no negotiations. After the failed summit, while India began to implement its Forward Policy between 1961 and 1962, China for its part attempted to increase its military forces in the disputed areas by setting up check-posts and enhancing border patrols. Tensions continued to rise in all sectors of the India-China border. On 20th October 1962, China launched a pre-emptive offensive marking the start of India-China border war. During the month-long war, Chinese forces advanced deep into Indian territory in Ladakh and Arunachal Pradesh, before withdrawing back to their previous positions along the Line of Actual Control. The war ended with China's victory with ceasefire on 22nd November 1962. China voluntarily withdrew its army to position 20 km. behind the Line of Actual Control that had existed in 1959, and proposed that officials of the two sides hold meetings immediately. The Chinese made three proposals—to stop the border conflict, to reopen negotiations, and to settle the India-China boundary question. In order to create a good atmosphere for reconciliation between the two countries, China released more than 600 Indian personnel and returned the equipment that had been captured during the war.

India-China war proved Pt. Nehru's friendly policy towards China, such as granting recognition, the Bandung conference and accepting China's claim over Tibet, a failure. The Indians felt that they had been betrayed by the Chinese. On the other hand, the Chinese blamed India for the hostile developments. As a point of diplomatic history, it seems likely that the border war will be symbolic of the tortuous nature of India-China relations. All the euphoria about the India-China brotherhood dissipated. Both sides' inability to find a mutually acceptable proposal impeded the improvement of India-China relations. Haunted by the border war, India-China relations since 1962 have been characterized by mutual antagonism, rivalry, distrust, and hostility. Throughout the Cold War and in the post-Cold War era, the border dispute remained an indelible mark in India-China relations and China and India continued to hold each other responsible. The military clash is still deeply inscribed in the memory of strategic decision-makers and analyst, and has acted as an aggravating factor whenever India and China prepare to engage each other.

China tried to build up an image of being keen to settle the boundary problem by peaceful negotiation, the implication being that if the boundary negotiation between China and India failed, China should not be blamed. India's suspicion of China deepened in the wake of China's first nuclear test in October 1964, barely two years after the India-China border war. It placed great pressure on India and tensions continued as there were border skirmishes in 1965 and 1967. India's annexation of Sikkim during 1973-1975 raised another diplomatic confrontation between the two countries.

After the war, the borders became quiet, but India still refused to negotiate with China on border issues, and India-China relations remained frozen until the late 1970s. In 1971, India renamed North East Frontier Agency (NEFA), the disputed eastern sector. NEFA became the Union Territory of Arunachal

Pradesh, which was subsequently granted full statehood on 20th February 1987. However, Arunachal Pradesh was never recognized by China. Despite various constraints, both countries undertook efforts to normalize bilateral relations and restored ambassadorial relations in 1976. India was willing to resolve the border disputes through peaceful negotiations. In 1979, during India's foreign minister's visit to China, Deng Xiaoping put forward a package plan for both countries—advocating "mutual understanding and mutual accommodation" for the negotiation of the rival claims. But, India rejected the plan and insisted that the Chinese withdrew their troops from India's claimed territories as the precondition for mutual negotiations. Xiaoping also suggested that China and India could adopt a "one package deal" to solve the border dispute when Indian Foreign Minister Atal Bihari Vajpayee visited Beijing in 1979. He said that the package deal meant China would accept the border claimed by India in the eastern sector, namely, the McMahon Line, in return for Indian acceptance of the status quo in the western sector. Since then, the package deal has become one of China's basic principles to settle the longstanding border dispute between the two countries. On the other hand, India refused to accept the package deal and supported a separate negotiation of each sector's border, taking into account the specific aspects of each. The Indian side insisted on minor territorial adjustments in the eastern sector and China's unilateral concession in the western sector. India was more concerned with the effect of the border dispute on its security environment, insisted that a settlement of the border issue was a necessary precondition for improving bilateral relations, and rejected the package proposal of Deng Xiaoping.

India's border policy changed slightly under Rajiv Gandhi's leadership. Now, India no longer insisted that the Chinese withdraw their troops from India's claimed territories as the precondition for both countries to negotiate. In 1981, China's Vice Premier and Foreign Minister Huang Hua visited India, which led to both countries deciding to hold talks on border issues. Since each side merely reiterated its well-known position on the border problem and then dispersed, the eight rounds of border talks at the vice minister level between 1981 and 1987 did not lead to a breakthrough or even substantial progress being made in the solution of the border dispute. The only achievement was that both sides agreed to maintain stability and tranquility along the border and that the border dispute should be resolved through peaceful negotiations and friendly consultations. However, between 1986 and 1987, a severe military standoff occurred between India and China at the Sumdorong Chu Valley. Fortunately, this military conflict did not lead to another India-China war.

The visit by Prime Minister Rajiv Gandhi to China in December 1988 broke the impasse in India-China relations leading to the re-commencement of border negotiations and the ongoing border talk between the two countries was raised to a higher level. For resolving the boundary problem, the two countries decided to set up a Joint Working Group (JWG) on the boundary issue to work out a mutually acceptable resolution.

With frequent visits from leaders of both countries, bilateral relations improved throughout the early 1990s. During June 1989 and August 2001, fourteen sessions of the JWG meetings were held. In September 1993, Prime Minister Narasimha Rao visited to China and an India-China Diplomatic and Military Expert Group was created as a subgroup of the JWG. The Expert Group, which was designed to deal with technical details at the deputy director-general/undersecretary level, met fourteen times between February 1994 and June 2002. However, these meetings made little progress in reaching a concrete solution on the border problems, but they were instrumental in establishing a mechanism for regular discussions. More importantly, unlike the previous border talks held between 1981 and 1987, the JWG and Expert Group meetings proved successful in maintaining peace and tranquility in troubled areas along the India-China border, i.e., to some extent, the dialogue mechanism itself was a kind of confidence building measures (CBMs), which tied both sides to the negotiation table, to avoid the need to resort to extreme measures.

Since early 1990s, some CBMs were proposed and followed by India and China to secure the peace along the disputed boundary areas. After Chinese Premier Li Peng's visit to India in 1991, the two countries agreed to regularize the meetings between border personnel, which would be held at Bum La in the eastern sector and in the Spanggur Gap area in the western sector in June and October every year. They also agreed to establish telephone links to facilitate communication between border personnel. Transparency, communication, and constraint measures were on the agenda, and the discussions focused on the mutual transparency of the location of military positions, prior notification of military exercise, prevention of air intrusion, and redeployment of forces along the Line of Actual Control (LAC).

The visit of Prime Minister Narasimha Rao in September 1993, provided the setting for the codification of the work done by the JWG meetings. The two countries signed the Agreement on the Maintenance of Peace and Tranquility along the LAC in the India-China border areas. The issues included in this agreement were troop reduction, conflict avoidance measures, notification measures, and the establishment of the Expert Group comprising diplomatic and military representatives from both sides to assist the JWG. Being the first CBMs agreement between the two countries, the deal was described as a "positive breakthrough" in India-China relations. After Prime Minister Narasimha Rao's visit to China, the JWG and the Expert Group worked toward the 1993 CBMs Agreement's implementation. A further step in that direction was taken with the signing of the Agreement on the Confidence Building Measures in the military field along the LAC in the India-China border areas during Chinese President Jiang Zemin's four-day state visit to India in November 1996, the first by a Chinese head of state since the two countries had established diplomatic relations in 1950. In this agreement, both the countries advanced beyond agreeing on declaratory principles and proposed more detailed implementation measures. For example, they set a ceiling on the scale of any military exercises and created a "no-fly zone" along the border areas. However, despite agreeing to limit the respective military forces to "minimum levels compatible with the friendly and good neighbourly relations between the two countries", India and China still could not reach an accord on the method of troop reductions. Furthermore, the 1996 CBMs Agreement was held up by a discussion over provisions for communication and constraint measures, and the lack of any means to verify and monitor. Like the 1993 CBMs Agreement, the 1996 CBMs Agreement functioned more as a conflict avoidance measure. However, it cannot be denied that the signing of the agreement was another new political initiative to help ease tensions along the India-China border. Even if the two countries were still unable to narrow their differences on troop reductions along the border, yet both sides expressed satisfaction with the results of the two CBMs agreements, and the border has since remained peaceful. Furthermore, both countries tried to marginalize the boundary dispute to make sure that the overall development of India-China friendship and cooperation would not be hijacked by the boundary issue.

The JWG mechanism has helped to build a CBMs regime along the disputed India-China border and to stabilize the LAC, but the difficulty of delineating the LAC made India believe that the boundary problem should be solved from a political perspective, rather than in a historical, technical, or legal manner. Again, it was India that proposed the new initiative to find a concrete solution of India-China border problem. During the visit of Prime Minister Vajpayee to China from 22nd to 27th June 2003, a new mechanism for border talks was set up. India and China agreed to raise the level of negotiators to a higher political status by appointing their respective Special Representatives as the key negotiators to explore the framework of a boundary settlement from the political perspective of the overall bilateral relationship. To show its seriousness on the initiative, India appointed its National Security Adviser as the Special Representative for India-China boundary problem. As it was India that had taken the decision to upgrade the level of talks, however, China accepted the overture reluctantly. Initially, China desired to appoint a secretary level official as its special envoy, but India had no intention of making the special representative a sequel to the JWG meetings, and, therefore, favoured a more senior leader with sufficient political clout. Then China appointed its Executive Vice Foreign Minister, Dai Bingguo as Special Representative. Apparently, the political level of Vice Foreign Minister is below that of National Security Advisor, but India believed the change of formalities for the boundary talks would help resolve the problem.

The first meeting of the Special Representatives held in Delhi on 23rd-24th October 2003. By August 2009, thirteen rounds of Special Representative meetings had taken place on the basis of their mandate to evolve a framework for a boundary settlement and address the problem from the political perspective of the overall bilateral relationship, i.e., India and China decided to stop the process of focusing on technical problems, and prioritized the identification of common principles as the first task for solving the boundary problem. In general, there were two stages for meetings. During the first phase, the aim of the meeting was to hammer out a methodology to resolve the boundary dispute. Whereas during the second phase, the focus was on devising a framework agreement for resolving the dispute on the basis of the "political parameters and guiding principles". The special representative mechanism was compatible with China's strategy towards the boundary dispute. According to Chinese Premier Wen Jiabao, it was important that the two sides "bear in mind the large picture, expand exchanges and cooperation in all areas, and properly settle questions left over from history".

After five rounds of talks, the meetings of Special Representative led to the conclusion of the Agreement on Political Parameters and Guiding Principles for the Settlement of the India-China Boundary Questions, which was signed on 11th April 2005 during Chinese Premier Wen Jiabao's visit to India. The Guiding Principles Agreement reveals that the two sides have reduced the differences in perception on the approach to the boundary problem. For instance, India had earlier insisted on a sector-by-sector approach for solving the border dispute while China wanted a package deal. India has now agreed to discuss the problem on a sector-by-sector basis, but to announce the agreement once the differences on all the sectors are sorted out. Thus, the Guiding Principles Agreement was an achievement of meetings of the Special Representatives. However, this positive development did not imply that all obstacles had been cleared and that a mutually acceptable solution could be reached any sooner. The conception behind the Special Representative meetings was that both sides first identified the principles and terms of reference on the basis of which the settlement of the boundary issue could be established. Then, both sides would apply such principles to construct a framework, which would be used to delineate the actual boundary on the ground, i.e., the conclusion of the agreement on Guiding Principles in fact marked the beginning of the second phase of negotiations under the mechanism of Special Representatives.

Achievements on Boundary Talks: For India, a symbolic achievement on the boundary talks in the post-Pokhran era was the Sikkim issue. Earlier, China had steadfastly questioned the legality of Sikkim's merger with India in 1975. But, in July 1994, the Chinese Vice Premier and Foreign Minister, Qian Qichen, stated that China was dropping its opposition to Sikkim's accession to India. China's decision at the third Expert Group meeting in March 1995 to hold border personnel meetings with India at Nathu La in the Sikkim sector implied its acquiescence that Sikkim was under India's rule. The former Chinese ambassador to India, Cheng Ruisheng also revealed that China was considering recognizing Sikkim's merger with India. Despite these signals, China did not formally recognize Sikkim as a state of Indian Union. China's inflexibility on the Sikkim issue was due to fact that China saw the Sikkim issue as a bargaining chip to be used in the boundary problem. However, during Prime Minister Vajpayee's visit to China in 2003, India successfully persuaded China to change its position and to accept the reality that Sikkim is the part and parcel of India. Both the countries signed a bilateral agreement about opening a point in Sikkim for border trade. India had recognized China's take-over of Tibet by signing the 1954 agreement, so it was expected that China would recognize Sikkim by signing the border trade agreement. In return for recognition, India agreed to China's terms on the status of Tibet as being an equivalent concession.

China had rejected any suggestion that it had recognized India's sovereignty over Sikkim, without even waiting until Prime Minister Vajpayee and his party were in China. Chinese Foreign Ministry spokesperson said that the political status of Sikkim was historical baggage and would still require to be solved in a gradual manner. China's reluctance to recognize India's annexation of Sikkim was seen as a surprise and embarrassment to the Indian side. China saw the Sikkim issue as part of the broader border negotiations, and as a means to deny India the possibility of taking advantage of the Tibet issue. However, China was also worried that India might withdraw its endorsement of the new discourse on Tibet if China continued to reject India's claims over Sikkim. As a result, China assured India in a low-profile way that the Sikkim issue would cease to be an irritant in India-China relations and that China wanted to build a long standing, stable, and healthy relationship with India amid the fast-changing global scenario. Then the Chinese Foreign Minister deleted a webpage from its official website, which had showed Sikkim as a separate country in Asia, ahead of Chinese Premier Wen Jiabao's meeting with his Indian counterpart, Prime Minister Vajpayee, on the sidelines of the ASEAN summit at Bali in Indonesia.

Later Chinese Consul General in Kolkata Mao Siwei admitted that China had already recognized Sikkim as part of India during Prime Minister Vajpayee's visit to Beijing in 2003. However, China was reluctant to openly assert that it had already recognized Sikkim as part of India. When Chinese Premier Wen Jiabao visited India in 2005, the Chinese side finally presented to India a newly printed official map that showed Sikkim as being part of India. The joint statement issued by two sides clearly speaks of Sikkim as a state of the Republic of India.

Following this positive development, in July 2006, the two countries reopened border trade across the 15000 feet Nathu La Pass in addition to the Shipki La Pass, opened in 1993 and the Lipulekh Pass, opened in 1992. Border trade between the two countries in fact did not contribute much to the overall volume of trade between the two countries, partly due to restrictions in tradable items, but in this instance, it was an indication of a broader rapprochement.

However, the Tibet-Sikkim border was to play a further role in the boundary controversy and became a new point of contention. During 2005-2008 close to four hundred Chinese intrusions took place into Indian territory in Sikkim. This time, the Indians were tormented with anxiety by China's claims over the so-called 2.1 sq. km. "Finger Area" in northern Sikkim. China further threatened to demolish existing stone structure there. India strongly rebutted these claims, lodged an official protest, and barred the Chinese troops from entering the area. This was after China had protested against other troop deployments in Sikkim resulting from the relocation of Indian troops from the western border. Due to this diplomatic discord, road construction near the area was halted. During External Affairs Minister Pranab Mukherjee's visit to China in June 2008, the Chinese reportedly tried to corner India by raising the issue of the "Finger Area".

Repeated incursions into Sikkim along with other disputed areas by the Chinese have been a cause of concern for India. From India's point of view, China's act was provocative and irritating, and in some cases, the intrusions were extremely provocative. For example, in April 2008, 10R Chinese troops came 12 kms inside Maja in Arunachal Pradesh. An incursion event along the LAC in the western sector of the India-China boundary at Demchok, northeast of Ladakh, nearly led to a major confrontation between the patrol teams of the two sides, but conflict was averted by the timely intervention of senior officers from Indian side. China has always used ill-defined LAC to disturb India. The absence of a mutually accepted LAC being physically demarcated on the ground and on military maps means China will continue to make use of these lacunae. In response, Indian officials were compelled to announce in public the plan to upgrade the strategically located helipads in Arunachal Pradesh, including the eight of these located in the Tawang district. India had also to reinforce its positions and construct pathways in the area. With no demarcation of the border, India has to station over three lakhs of soldiers in the disputed India-China border areas.

Tawang Problem: Till now, not much headway has been made in the talks over China's claim to Tawang in Arunachal Pradesh. Obtaining Tawang forms part of China's package proposal, although Tawang is situated well to the south of the Indian side of the LAC. It is assumed that China would recognize India's sovereignty over Arunachal Pradesh while it would insist on taking over Tawang. This proposal is strategically unacceptable to India because Tawang is close to the north-eastern states and Bhutan.

Chinese claim on Tawang is based on the fact that Tibet had traditionally exercised administrative control over the region and, moreover, Tawang was the capital of the Monyul district, which is the birthplace of the Sixth Dalai Lama. The Chinese argued that ceding the area to foreigners would hurt the feelings of the Tibetans. China believed that it would fail to conciliate Tibetans if it were not able to repossess Tawang. The other reason behind China's intention to take over Tawang is that it wants to negate the McMahon Line. China's claim over the Tawang region of Arunachal Pradesh is an irritant to India. China has also indicated that India should be prepared for substantial adjustments on the LAC, which refers to China's claim on Tawang as well as other adjustments in the disputed areas. To deal with these issues, in the Guiding Principles Agreement, India successfully secured the following significant clauses, "In reaching a boundary settlement, the two sides shall safeguard the due interests of their settled populations in the border areas". For India, this clause implied that the status quo of the disputed populated areas, like Tawang or even the whole of Arunachal Pradesh, would be maintained. However, China showed little interest in sharing the same idea. Just before Chinese President Hu Jintao's visit to India in November 2006, the Chinese Ambassador to India, Sun Yuxi, declared that the whole Arunachal Pradesh, including Tawang, is China's territory. India reacted to this promptly and External Affairs Minister Pranab Mukherjee asserted that Arunachal Pradesh is an integral part of India and it was made clear that there could be no discussion on the issue.

Border Disputes in the Larger Context of India-China Relations: Neither India nor China has allowed the bilateral ties to be hijacked by the border disputes alone. In the post-Cold War world, political leaders in both countries have realized that India and China share many common interests at the bilateral, regional, and global levels. Both countries have understood that they have a similar, if not completely identical task of sustaining strong economic growth and development in order to reduce poverty and improve the living standards of their respective growing populations. The prerequisite for either party to focus on its internal socio-economic advancement is to have a stable and peaceful border region. This is the reason why both countries have managed to set up various stabilization measures to handle their border disputes through negotiations. They have even initiated regular defence consultation meetings and joint military exercises, even though the exercises are small in scale and limited to low sensitivity areas. Due to both sides' strategic thinking that prioritizes overall stability, trade has over recent years grown at a phenomenal rate, significantly benefitting bilateral ties in trade and other economic aspects.

On the other hand, at the regional level, India and China are involved in a complex strategic rivalry—both sides have avoided actions that jeopardise the fundamental strategic interests of the other party. Since late 1990s, China has attempted to adopt a more balanced policy towards India and Pakistan—the two South Asian countries that have been embroiled in hostility for decades. China's growing presence in the Indian Ocean, also termed as string of pearls strategy, was aimed at protecting China's trade and energy interests in the region. On the other hand, because of its long tradition of non-alignment and the desire to sustain national autonomy in its relations with other major powers of the world, India has decided not to strategically align itself with the US in what China's fear is a US-driven containment policy against China. India has also not actively responded to the invitations from Japan to form an "arch of democracies" or a "diamond of democracies" among Japan,

India, and Australia, which China argues is part of a policy of 'encirclement' against itself. To be sure, China will continue to be wary of India's strategic dominance in South Asia, and India will continue to seek to undermine any Chinese effort towards a China-centric regional order in East Asia. However, there are currently no indications that the two Asian giants are heading towards a strategic contest that will dampen bilateral ties. On the contrary, both China and India have expressed interest in the Regional Comprehensive Economic Partnership (RCEP) initiative spearheaded by ASEAN. It means that both the countries seem to be interested in participating in regional integration in East Asia.

At the global level, India and China have numerous very tangible and long-term common interests. Both the countries believe that the world should become multi-polar and emerging powers should play a more important role in international affairs. They also have very similar views on global policy responses on issues such as climate change, international trade and finance, and non-intervention in the domestic affairs of other countries. They have strengthened their cooperation in the context of the G20 and the BRICS, and other newly emerging multilateral institutions, in order to contend with Global Super Powers for global influence and decision-making power. However, India-China relations at the global level are not without problems. For example, China has always opposed India's bid for a permanent membership in the UN Security Council.

India-China Relations: The Tibet Issue

Historically India and Tibet were very close to each other. It was easier and convenient to go to Beijing from Lhasa via India and sea route than by land route. The Anglo-Tibetan agreement of 1904 had granted India military, communication, postal, trading and other rights in Tibet and at the same time recognized the Chinese suzerainty over Tibet. However, the changes in the geopolitical situation due to Chinese occupation of Tibet in 1950 made India to redefine its relationship with the China. India protested the use of force by China in dealing with Tibet and hoped that Tibet would be granted genuine autonomy.

India recognized Tibet as a region of China and signed the first agreement in 1954 with the China after protracted negotiations. This agreement aimed at developing a good neighbourly relationship between the two countries and conduct border trade between India and Tibet. Trusting China's friendly gestures, India surrendered the special rights it had inherited from the British government according to the 1904 agreement. The agreement of 1954, in addition to recognizing Tibet as a part of China, can be considered as the first confidence building measure between the two countries as it had for the first time laid five principles of peaceful coexistence that could still be considered a model for conducting relationship between any two sovereign countries. Besides establishing trade agencies in India and Tibet, specifying markets for trade, designation of traditional passes and routes, the 1954 agreement also accredited traditions and customs for pilgrimages from India and Tibet to each other's places. However, this agreement did not last for more than eight years due to strained relationship between India and China caused by the subsequent events in 1950s like Khampa rebellion, riots in Tibet and the Dalai Lama's exiled to India along with his followers, and border clashes.

China's Tibet policy has been influenced either by hardliners or moderates at different times over the years. China's domestic policies and its external environment have equal impact on its Tibet policy. Its Tibet policy has five discernible phases of different approaches.

Phase-1 (1951–1959): The 1951 agreement granted full autonomy to Tibet in the matters of governance, religion, language and culture, and preserving the traditional religious and administrative institutions like the institutions of the Dalai Lama and Panchen Lama within the geographical boundaries of Tibet and vesting the foreign and defence matters with the Chinese central government. However, as a young communist nation, China was in great hurry to introduce communist reforms in Tibet. It was a sudden and painful experience for the people of Tibet who had been leading an almost isolated different system for several centuries, away from external interference. Tibet was a neutral during the World War-II, which alienated the Tibetan people and their leadership. Due to this, riots and rebellion broke out in Tibet many times between 1952 and 1957, with certain external support. In February 1957, Mao had said that conditions in Tibet were not ripe for reforms and, therefore, the implementation of reforms be postponed till 1962; and offered to reduce the Han cadres in Tibet. Mao's policy of moderation and gradualism had the support of Dalai Lama and the elite Tibetans, but it was not implemented in practice. This phase was ended with the exodus of Dalai Lama and his supporters to India in 1959.

Phase-2 (1959–1976): This phase was dominated by the hardline policies and internal power struggle in China. The 'Great Leap Forward' and 'Great Proletarian Cultural Revolution' brought unparallel turmoil within China. The involvement of Communist Party of China (CPC) members in Tibet like attack on religious institutions, culture and language, and increasingly strained relationship with India only further alienated the people of Tibet. China reorganized Tibet by making U-tsang as Tibet Autonomous Region and merging Kham and Amdo regions with Yunnan, Sichuan, Gansu, and Qinghai provinces.

Phase-3 (1978–1986): In this phase, Deng Xiaoping adopted soft policy to handle Tibet issue and proposed to talk with Dalai Lama. However, this step also ended in failure, but a communication line was set up for the first time between Dalai Lama and the Chinese leadership.

Phase-4 (1987–2001): After failure of Deng's soft policy, China adopted a different approach to solve Tibet issue through economic development instead of focusing on political solution alone. This policy had some success as Dalai Lama diluted his demand from independence to autonomy, but Chinese leadership had not taken much interest in carrying any negotiations with the Tibetan leadership.

Phase-5 (2002– ...): Current phase is marked by realistic handling of Tibetan issue, which combines winning Tibetans through economic development and conducting dialogue with the Tibetan leadership in exile in India. China has proposed that since Tibet has already been liberated and integrated into the big Chinese family, Dalai Lama and other Tibetans who had left Tibet should come back and take part in the development of Tibet.

China considers Tibet issue its internal matter in which no foreign countries have any right to interfere. Since India has officially recognized Chinese claims over Tibet since 1954 when the two countries signed an agreement regarding trade and intercourse between the Tibet region and India, China believes that India should adhere to the Five Principle of Peaceful Coexistence and the Tibet issue will not come up in the agenda of India-China relations. However, the interactions over the last decade seemed to be against such an expectation as India's sincerity in honouring its commitment is frequently questioned by China, which has repeatedly expressed concerns about the anti-China activities of exiled Tibetans in India.

India cannot always conform to China's demand to stand away from the Tibet issue as, more significantly, it is identified as strategic leverage against China. Since India has security threat from China, the Tibet issue is one of the bargaining chips India can use when dealing with China. India's particular role in the Tibet issue, especially India's hosting of the Tibetan leader, Dalai Lama, and thousands of his followers, gives India a say in the matter. Therefore, China is not satisfied with India's dealing on and attitude to the Tibetan question, but it expects to marginalize the Tibet issue in India-China relations in order to avoid India's involvement. China's continued suspicion about India's sincerity and interactions on the Tibetan question has contributed to the formation of a culture of distrust between the countries, which is also one of the features of India-China relations. Unless China and Tibet reach a final agreement on Tibet's relations with China, India's role and involvement in the Tibetan question will still be seen as a thorn by China, and a source of mistrust.

China's liberation of Tibet in the early 1950s appeared the only issue that might worsen India-China relations. In October 1950, China dispatched troops into Tibet to liberate the region. Then the Tibetan authority was compelled to send representatives to Beijing to negotiate its status and relationship with the new

China. On 23rd May 1951, the Chinese and Tibetan deputations signed the Seventeen-Point Agreement for the Peaceful Liberation of Tibet. The agreement stated that the Tibetan people would return to "the big family of the Motherland", and Beijing would not alter the existing political system in Tibet and promised that the Tibetan people would have the right to exercise national regional autonomy under the leadership of China's Central Government. However, China's military action against Tibet came as a shock to the Indians. When India became independent in 1947, it inherited, the existing treaty rights and obligations of British India regarding Tibet. It also wanted to continue British policy towards Tibet, namely, treating Tibet as an autonomous buffer region between India and China, while recognizing Chinese suzerainty, but not sovereignty over Tibet. Therefore, India soon branded China's military actions against Tibet as an "invasion" and sent several notes to the Chinese government to lodge protest. However, despite these diplomatic gestures, India was not willing to confront China over the issue. On 12th February 1951, Prime Minister Pt. Nehru said in Parliament that he would not allow the event to affect India's policy or desire to maintain friendly relations with China. Even he had no intention of letting the development affect India's China policy in general and the policy regarding the entry of China into the United Nations in particular.

India's policy of non-intervention in the Tibet issue was strengthened when China's takeover of Tibet was legalized by the conclusion of the Seventeen-Point Agreement. India accepted China's claim over Tibet by refusing to sponsor the Tibetan appeal to the United Nations against the People's Liberation Army's invasion. In order to solve India's inherited historical rights regarding Tibet, such as the deployment of military guards, India and China began negotiations in December 1953. Finally, the two countries signed the agreement regarding trade and intercourse between India and Tibet in April 1954, setting up the legal framework for India's relations with the post-liberated Tibet; and India accepted China's sovereignty over Tibet while using the term the "Tibet region of China".

India's reluctant attitude and caution could not prevent Tibet becoming a controversial issue between India and China, and the Tibet issue continued to test India-China friendship. In May 1959, the People's Liberation Army moved into Lhasa to quell the most serious revolt since the peaceful liberation, and there were rumours among the Tibetans that the Army would harm Dalai Lama. As a result, Dalai Lama and his associates decided to escape from Tibet. Dalai Lama with his associates fled to India and asked for political asylum. India soon granted asylum to the Dalai Lama and his followers. Indira Gandhi was given the task of setting up an all-party Central Relief Committee for the Tibetan refugees. However, India was still not willing to challenge China over Tibet issue, therefore, India abstained from voting on the United Nations General Assembly resolution that criticized the Chinese, of violating of human rights in Tibet. India hoped that such an abstention would facilitate eventual conciliatory efforts towards a peaceful solution of the Tibetan problem.

To solve Tibet issue, Pt. Nehru tried to play the role of mediator and requested China to send Panchen Lama, the second highest ranking leader in Tibet, or any other Chinese representatives to come to India to discuss the situation of Tibet with Dalai Lama. However, China rejected the proposal by saying that Tibet issue was entirely an internal issue, and China was not prepared to allow a third party to become involved. As China saw India's sheltering Dalai Lama as a breach of the spirit of the Five Principles of Peaceful Coexistence to interfere in China's internal affairs, Tibet issue began to shatter the mutual trust between China and India. In retaliation to India's Tibet policy, China encouraged the Naga and Mizo rebellions in northeast India.

Although, India remains very concerned about China's takeover of Tibet, from Pt. Nehru's administration onward, the Indian government has clearly acknowledged the fact that Tibet is under China's control and it is very difficult for India alone to help Tibet split from China. In addition, India needs to take account of its own domestic situation if it wants to accommodate

Tibet's independence. Like China's far-flung communities of Tibet and Xinjiang, India's Northeast and Kashmir are its weak spots. China was sponsoring Naga and Mizo insurgencies in India's Northeast by the late 1970s. It also backed Pakistan's stand on the Kashmir issue. Any Indian public support for Tibetan independence would possibly result in China taking revenge by interfering in India's domestic discord, especially the agitation in Kashmir and the Northeast region. In any way, China will not allow the secessionist movement of the Tibetans to succeed and weaken its hold on Tibet. Even if making Tibet a security buffer would serve India's interests, India has to be very cautious about any mention of Tibet's independence. Therefore, although India has a particular role and special relationship with Tibet, the Indian government has had no intention of supporting Tibetan independence in public.

China's cautious treatment of the Tibet issue in India-China relations signals that it would like to develop relations in other fields while shelving the differences between India and China. On the other hand, it also hopes to encourage India to extricate itself from the Tibet embroilment while stressing that common interests outweigh the differences. For China, overemphasis on India's role in the Tibet issue would only give India greater leverage against China and contribute to the internationalization of the Tibet issue. The continuous effort to reduce the significance of the Tibet issue in India-China relations were found during Prime Minister Narasimha Rao's visit to China in 1993. The Tibet issue received a relatively perfunctory treatment in the talks of Prime Minister Narasimha Rao and the Chinese leaders as they focused on the border talks. Similarly, in 1996 when Chinese President Jiang Zemin visited India, Tibet issue was raised only during the meeting between Chinese Foreign Minister Qian Qichen and his Indian counterpart Inder Kumar Gujral. These developments reflected that India and China shared the common aspiration to marginalize the Tibet issues while improving relations in other fields.

India-China Relations: Water Diplomacy

Tibetan plateau, known as Water Tower of Asia, is the origin of ten major river systems of Asia, including the Indus,

Brahmaputra, Sutlej, Yellow, Yangtze, Mekong, and Salween. These rivers traverse eleven countries and support two billion people stretching from Afghanistan to India in South Asia, and to Vietnam in Southeast Asia. Both the Indus and Brahmaputra rivers flow downstream from China into India. China is the source of more transnational water flows than any other upstream power in the world. However, despite the wealth of water in Tibet, China faces an emerging water crisis further aggravated by overuse and pollution. In 2004, China's available water per capita was one of the lowest in the world for a populous country, just one-third of the average for developing countries, one-fourth of the world average, and one-fifth of the US average. The comparison indicates a 23 percent decrease in China's available water per capita over the past 20 years. But, the demand for water is growing more than 10 percent annually in Chinese cities and more than five percent annually for its industries. The decline in available water resources has worsened an already critical shortage in drinking water for China's huge population. More than 25 percent of Chinese population are without access to drinking water and almost half of China's 668 largest cities are short of water with 108 identified as serious and 60 as critical. According to Chinese government, by 2030, China's annual freshwater shortage will reach 200 billion cubic meters. China's worsening water shortage is exacerbated by increased pollution on a historic scale. More than 90 percent of China's underground aquifers, which supply 70 percent of the country's drinking water, are polluted. More than 75 percent of surface water flowing along China's rivers is unsafe for drinking or fishing, and 30 percent is unsuitable for agriculture and industry. China's water problem has a stark regional dimension as well—the Southern part has the preponderance of water while the Northern part has the higher demand. This has created a significant regional disparity that is getting worse with time. While 45 percent of China's population and 60 percent of its agriculture are in the Northern part, the region has only 13.8 percent of the fresh water. In per capita terms, the amount of available water in the Northern part is about 25 percent of that available in the Southern part.

On the other hand, water resources are scarcer in India, yet the country does not have a water supply problem, but rather poor water management practices. India will suffer from water scarcity unless it acts to alleviate demand-side pressures and expand its water supply. It receives a large amount of rainfall during its monsoon season, but it lacks the infrastructure to store this water. Its poor water management stems from an agriculture sector that consumes the vast majority, about 90 percent, of its available water supply. Climate change threatens to affect monsoon intensity and frequency, which would prove detrimental to agricultural production and significantly affect Indian food security. Part of India's water scarcity can be attributed to poor surface water storage capacity which is one-eleventh of the size of China's. Rapid population growth, urban expansion and significant industrialization all compounded India's water scarcity. By 2030, India's demand for water is expected to surpass supply by 50 percent. By 2050, India's population is expected to reach 1.6 billion, therefore, the country must enhance its water storage capacity, particularly as rapid urbanization is proving detrimental to India's aquifers and surface waters.

Thus, due to multiple causes, both India and China are stressed for water, which has contributed to tensions between the two neighbouring countries. Climate change, depleting aquifers, rapid population growth and urbanization are placing pressure on scarce water resources within the two countries. Tibet has remained an underlying issue that has an impact on India-China relations. Coupled with on-going border disputes over Arunachal Pradesh, tension over water has continued to strengthen since China began constructing dams upstream.

India is the middle riparian country between China and Bangladesh on the Brahmaputra river, which is also known as the Yarlung Tsangpo in China and has its headwaters in Tibet, and flows 2900 kms from China, through India and Bangladesh where it meets the Ganga river before draining into the Bay of Bengal. The river's unruly, braided physical flow through the three countries parallels a tricky political configuration. The river originates in troubled Tibet, a recurring source of India-China discord since the Dalai Lama fled to India in 1959. It flows through land that is still contested by China and India following a 1962 border conflict and is the basis of an evolving competitive-cooperative relationship. The river serves as both a socio-economic resource and occasional threat to livelihoods in Northeast region of India. And finally, Brahmaputra becomes a critical lifeline for Bangladesh, whose Indian centric historical origins and land, as well as riparian connections, create fraught relations. India's middle riparian position provides it with a whole-of-basin perspective. But its discrete, distinct interests and troubled relations with its upper riparian and lower riparian neighbours, combined with the domestic dynamics of center-state relations in Northeast India, pull India's concerns, drivers and cooperative and competitive activities in complex, inconsistent directions, shaping India's intense debate and mixed policies regarding the Brahmaputra river.

Strategic Interests along the Brahmaputra River: India and China are faced with increasing water demands from their rising middle-class population and urbanization. Irrigated framing, while attempting to ensure food security, uses large amounts of water along with the growth of water intensive industries. Climate change is also adding significant pressure to regional water and food security. Glacial melt in the Himalayas is threatening future water security not only for India and China, but for the majority of South and South-East Asia.

Now, the global competition for energy resources is driving the need for hydropower which is a clean alternative source of energy and will enhance the economic growth of the country. China is giving greater attention towards hydropower generation which will reduce the income gap between its eastern and western provinces. Also, hydropower technology is facilitating greater regional engagement with countries such as Thailand which purchases electricity from China.

China is exploring the possibility of the Grand Western Water Division plan at the Great Bend to divert water to its arid northern region. The proposed rerouting of the Brahmaputra at the Great Bend will significantly decrease the quantity and quality of water flowing into India. Salinity will increase, posing a threat to agriculture, aquatic life, and livelihoods downstream. The Brahmaputra makes up 30 percent of India's water

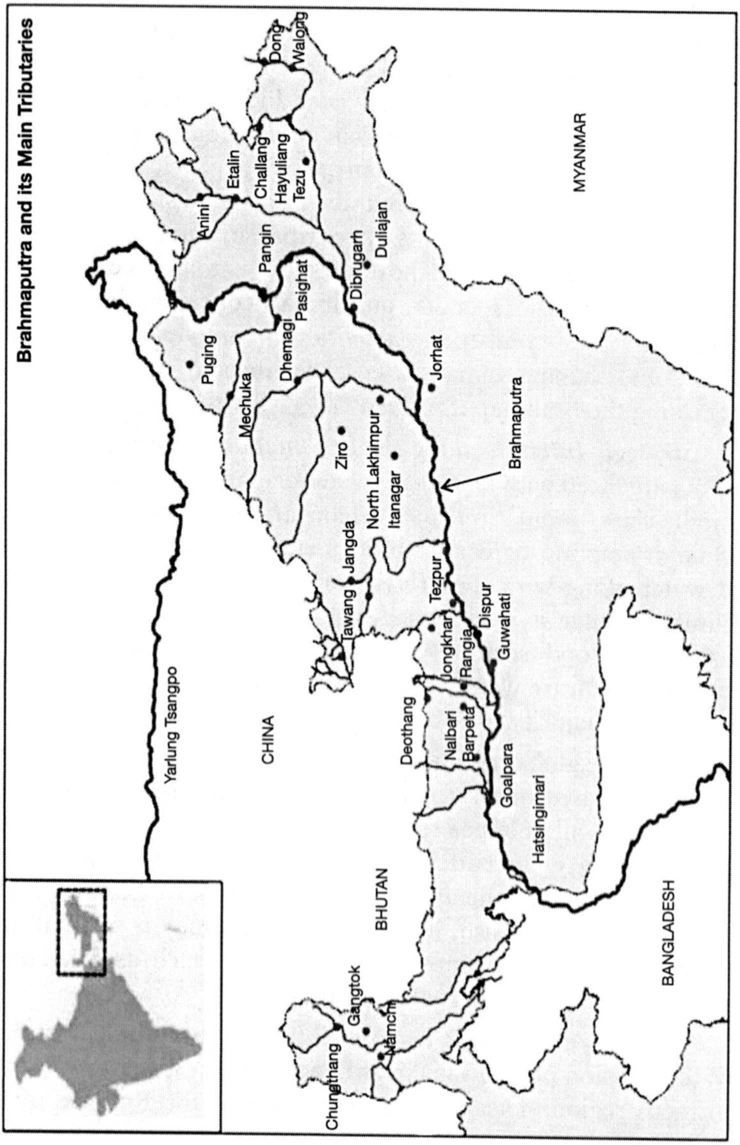

supply. If China proceeds with its water diversion plan, water flow will be reduced by 60 percent, enough to create serious consequences downstream. However, China has dismissed its plans as economically and environmentally unfeasible, but great suspicion exists within India about the project. China has claimed that it does not want to antagonize India, but China's historical tendency to withhold hydrological information has created an air of mistrust between the two countries.

China can use water as a potential political tool. Chinese damming and potential hydro-diversion projects are an imminent threat to water security in India. In November 2014, the first unit of China's US$ 1.2 billion Zangmu Hydropower Station on Brahmaputra River at Gyaca, Tibet Autonomous Region of China, became operational. The dam is located in the middle reaches of the river and has the capacity to generate 2.5 billion kilowatt hours of electricity per year. Five other generating units of the project have been completed in 2015. China has assured that it will continue to liaise with its downstream riparian, following Indian concern that the dam could disrupt downstream water supply. If it is taken seriously by both countries, the potential for conflict would be reduced.

Water Scarcity and its Ties to Conflict: Water security is defined as the availability of an acceptable quantity and quality of water for health, livelihoods, ecosystems, and production, coupled with an acceptable amount of water-related risks to people, environment, and economies. This concept of water security includes the negative effects of having too little water or water scarcity, and damage from having too much water such as floods, contamination, erosion, and epidemics. We can survive diseases and natural catastrophes, but we cannot survive without water. Unfortunately, fresh water is an increasingly scarce and precious resource. Less than 2.5 percent of all water on earth is fresh water, and more than half of it is trapped in polar ice and high-altitude glaciers around the world. This precious-little amount is declining due to increasing consumption, pollution, and climate change. Global per capita freshwater availability is continuously declining for more than a century, plummeting more than 60 percent since 1950 alone. According to a study, approximately 66 percent of the world's population, or more than four billion people, live in areas under severe water scarcity. Of these four billion people, one billion live in India and 900 million live in China, the majority of their populations thus live in areas of sever water scarcity. In 2006, a World Bank Working Paper on water scarcity revealed that China will soon become the most water-stressed country in East and Southeast Asia.

The glaciers in Tibet region are melting at a faster rate and coupled with growing water scarcity and a widening North-South regional water gap, China is facing increasing pressure to implement a controversial upstream water diversion plan in its western provinces. This project will threaten India since the downstream portion of the Brahmaputra river flows through a disputed area with strong implications for national sovereignty. Then, both the countries will increase their security postures in an already heavily militarized border region. Thus, China's established and planned hydropower and water diversion projects along the Brahmaputra river are a security concern that has the potential to impact on India-China relations.

China is not a signatory to any multilateral treaties on water resources, nor did it sign the 1997 United Nations Watercourses Convention that set the legal framework for rules and cooperation between more than 100 nations and their relevant international watercourses. Given its control over the source of most of Asia's rivers, China is in a unique position to unilaterally secure its water supply and future needs. On the other hand, India's damming of the Ganga river has reduced river flow in Bangladesh, which has increased soil salinity and affected agriculture, forcing many Bangladeshis to relocate to Northeast India. The influx of Bangladeshis has initiated ethnic conflicts in Assam. If upstream damming were to have an effect on the flow of the Brahmaputra, the potential for ethnic tension in India and Bangladesh could increase. Chinese activity in upstream has the potential to exacerbate water scarcity downstream, which, in turn, could lead to mass migration that will affect the entire region in Bangladesh. As the upstream riparian of the Brahmaputra, China has an advantageous position. It can choose to withhold hydrological information and build infrastructure to intentionally prevent water from flowing downstream. However, China is one of India's primary trading partners and India exports raw materials and imports Chinese electronics and manufactured goods. Also, India and China are arguably the largest powers in the region, as well rising global powers. Therefore, given their interdependence, the potential for conflict could be seen as relatively low.

China's relatively higher position in the international order could encourage it to use water to gain leverage over India. China sees the strategic partnership between the United States and India as a threat to its power within the region. Chinese apprehension towards a deepening military connection between the United States and India may cause China to use its upstream advantage over India in the future. Given China's desire to be global power, the improving relationship between India and the United States could increase the likelihood of China engaging in destructive upstream activity. However, the potential for conflict remains low, because China is increasingly demonstrating a willingness to cooperate with downstream riparian. But, China's willingness to engage with transboundary water issues remains susceptible to its political climate and still has the potential to be used as a tool for negotiation. Many of the major rivers originating in Tibet are the sources of water needed for agriculture and livelihoods downstream in many Asian countries. Any attempt by China to redirect the flow of rivers would be provocative and risky; and would increase the geopolitical tension. Since, China is not party to any international agreement on water resources that it is obliged to comply with, it appears that lower riparian will be significantly affected by its hydro-activity and its dam-building activities may destabilize the region and will result in a zero-sum game.

India's Policies Regarding the Brahmaputra River: The poor state of India-China relations generally and the fact that the Brahmaputra runs through disputed territory drive India's anxieties. Three most important drivers that influence India's policies regarding the Brahmaputra are China's plans to dam

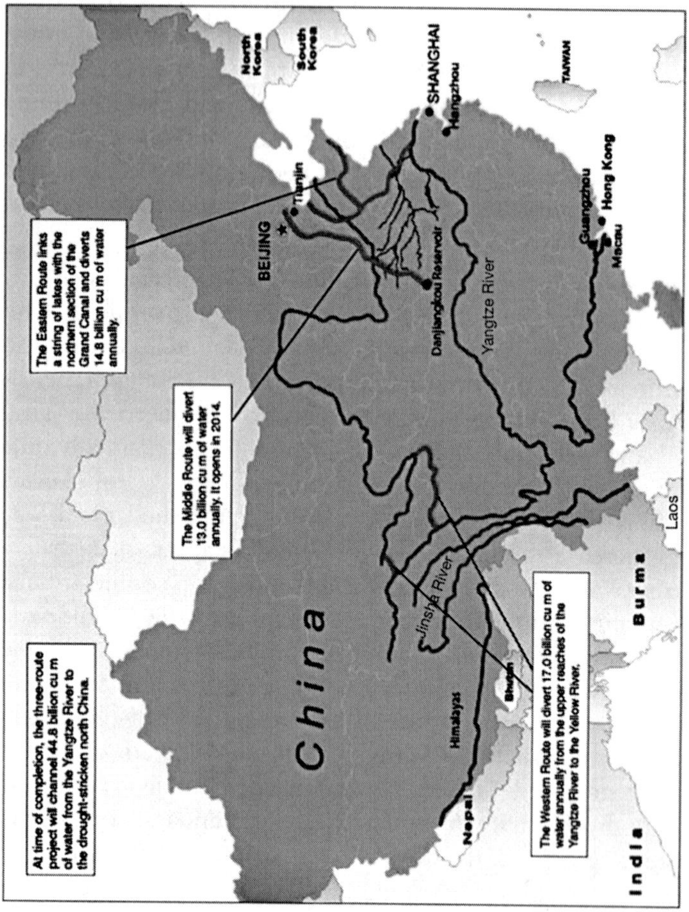

and possibly divert the river; India's desire to uphold user rights on the river and consolidate its existing hold on territory; and India's need to manage flooding and soil erosion in its Northeastern states.

China's Damming and Possible Diversion of the Brahmaputra: India's most important concern is China's damming and possible diversion of the river to meet the needs of Northern and Western regions of China that are more populous, agricultural, industries, and/or urban than remote, under-populated Southern Tibet. Its anxiety over China's upper riparian activities increased in 2005 following publication of the book Tibet's Water Will Save China, by Li Ling, an officer of the 2nd Artillery Corps. The book suggests various options for diversion of river water in the amount of 200.6 billion cubic meters, of which the Brahmaputra would account for the overwhelming share at 118.8 billion cubic meters. Soon after publication of the book, India began to undertake numerous cross-ministry and -agency studies to investigate and respond to Chinese activities. On the other hand, India continues to pursue incremental and limited riverine cooperation with China, but it is unable to influence China to cease dam construction.

India's User Rights and Consolidating its Hold on Disputed Territory: One of the most important priorities for India and China has been establishing their riparian rights. In 2008, India established a Technical Expert Group (TEG) headed by the joint secretary level in the Ministry of Power which includes representatives of the Ministry of Water Resources, Department of Road Transport and Highways, Ministry of Environment and Forests, Ministry of External Affairs, and Arunachal Pradesh state government, to draw up an Action Plan for establishing India's user rights on Brahmaputra and its tributaries coming from China. Technical Expert Group's first recommendation was that "in order to establish the First User Rights, the first priority would be to complete Lower Subansiri ... the Lower Siang ... and Demwe Lower ...". The second recommendation was for state government of Arunachal Pradesh to expeditiously allot at least one major project in these basins as close to the international border as possible, and get them implemented promptly, in order to quickly and more firmly establishing "Existing User" rights.

India's anxiety about asserting its riparian rights on the Brahmaputra has not steamed from a legal or political challenge to these rights by China as there is no evidence that China has ever challenged these rights. More likely, its anxiety comes from the objective of consolidating India's rights to the territory where the transboundary Brahmaputra flows rather than to the water of the river per se. India has taken it as a prudent course of action given the disputed territory through which the river flows and China's international efforts to challenge India's claims to the territory. In March 2009, China had opposed a nearly US$ 3 billion Asian Development Bank loan to India because it included funding for a US$ 60 million flood management and hydro program in Arunachal Pradesh.

In India, dam building is an extremely slow and limited process, largely due to political and civic opposition to dam construction but also because of financial and technical constraints. On the other hand, China is robustly building dam on its portion of the upper Brahmaputra river. India has plans to build several dams to consolidate its hold on territory and further establish riparian rights, control flood and soil erosion, develop hydro-electric power, and contribute to the overall development of the Northeast region.

Managing Flooding and Soil Erosion: Soil erosion is a major feature in the catchment area of Northeast India. According to the Brahmaputra Board of India's Ministry of Water Resources, "Due to heavy deposition of silt, the river has frequently changed its course. Excessive silt deposition has also given rise to braiding and meandering pattern in the alignment of the river system". High siltation arises from many factors, including landslides due to heavy rainfall in the area, earthquake shocks, and manmade actions such as changes in cultivation patterns and exploitation of forest resources in the hills above the valley through which the river runs. But flooding is the cause that directly initiated India's cooperative outreach to China, resulting in the current ongoing dialogue and limited hydrological data sharing agreements. India-China bilateral discussions on cooperation about the river began in the early 2000s as a result of the flooding concerns. Hydrological data sharing between China and India has gone hand in hand with a more unilateral Indian approach to controlling floods, i.e., by building dams. However, the number of dams actually being built still appears to be extremely limited. Thus, the need to control flooding and soil erosion, along with the threat of China's dams and possible water diversion, and India's need to establish user rights and consolidate a hold on territory, appears to be a key driver of India's activities vis-à-vis China regarding the Brahmaputra.

Co-operation along the Brahmaputra—Steps to Avoid Conflict: A major flood in Northeast India took place in June 2000 when a natural dam that had formed due to a landslide on a tributary of the Brahmaputra in Tibet, broke. Due to this, 3-4 billion cubic meters of water poured into Arunachal Pradesh and Assam, killing 30 Indian nationals and leaving 50,000 homeless. It is believed that China withheld hydrological data that could have prevented the disaster—this led to friction in India-China relations.

Concerning floods in Northeast India, India and China have established a series of agreements to share hydrological data. In April 2002, China agreed to provide India with hydrological data from three monitoring stations on the Brahmaputra between 1st June and 15th October of each year, corresponding to the annual flood season. During visit of Chinese president Hu Jintao to India in November 2006, the two countries agreed to establish an expert-level group to discuss hydrological data and emergency response measures. Further, in 2013, India and China signed a Memorandum of Understanding, recognizing that transboundary rivers are an important asset to the development of all riparian. Both countries agreed to strengthen communication and strategic trust. China agreed to provide more hydrological information to India at the start of the flood season. It has also extended the data-sharing period from 15th May to 15th October.

India-China cooperation related to the Brahmaputra is likely to be limited by two factors—ongoing border dispute and mutual distrust. Contested ownership of Arunachal Pradesh means that China and India will probably be unable to reach a major accord on transboundary river rights and objects, such as a water-sharing treaty. There are no signs that this dispute is set to abate in the near to medium term. While mutual distrust may be a factor at the official level, it may be more pronounced within civil society in both countries. Nevertheless, there may still be opportunities for a modest expansion of India-China cooperation on Brahmaputra issues. This is most likely on narrow technical subjects that can be separated from the border dispute. Specifically, China may be receptive to cooperation in areas such as disaster management, environmental protection and river safety, or on scientific topics, such as the effects of climate change on long-term river flow. Some of these issues may be discussed at an official level, such as between the water resource ministries of both countries, while others may be more usefully deliberated initially at the Track 2 level, perhaps involving specialists from Indian and Chinese government-funded research institutes. Following are some of drivers that could promote enhanced cooperation on these issues.

(a) A positive overall direction in India-China relations, symbolized by fruitful high-level exchanges and economic agreements, could remove obstacles and set the stage for cooperation on transboundary river issues.

(b) China may be able to draw on its own initiatives related to the Brahmaputra to portray itself as a responsible upper riparian. For China, modestly enhancing outreach on water security challenges could be a relatively low-cost way to foster diplomatic goodwill with India.

(c) Additional progress may be facilitated if initiatives are proposed and encouraged by India.

A conflict may arise and escalate if either India or China falsely believes it is under threat from the other. Fear has been created in India because of previous tendencies where China has been unwilling to provide details of its hydro-projects, and when it did, gave contradictory information. There is a need for both countries to develop mutual goodwill. Undertaking joint research projects in the region and sharing water data more extensively could foster stronger bilateral relations. Therefore, developing an understanding of shared water resource challenges will help limit the potential for conflict. Also, implementing efficient water management policies will reduce the severity of future food and water crises and reduce the risk of conflict. Poor water resources management and underdeveloped infrastructure undermine food and water security in India. Water should be conceptualized as a scarce and strategic resource. In case of China, pollution and unequal natural water allocations threatens its food and water security. Therefore, efficient water management is essential to food security, economic growth, population health and social stability; and managing water as a scarce resource with holistic ramifications is essential to reducing the potential for future wars on water.

China's role as a water hegemon should involve soft power as the primary use of negotiation and diplomatic actions. Its communication is essential to reassure riparian of its hydro-intentions and reduce the potential for conflict caused by mistrust. In the interest of regional stability, it is crucial that no country feel it is under threat of acute water insecurity as a result of upstream damming or diversion projects. Therefore, China should change its strategy from "responsive diplomacy" to "preventive diplomacy", where it should be responsible for proactively engaging with riparian to avoid disputes. Only a combination of bilateral cooperation and strong leadership with demand and supply side management can influence the future and reduce the potential for an India-China conflict on water.

India-China Relations: Regional Competition and Cooperation

India and China, two oldest civilization-states and once great powers of the world, are back as claimants to preeminence in Asia and the world. Now, both are contributing a greater part in the global economy and possess nuclear powers with expanding military capabilities to match their growing ambitions. However, they have a paradoxical and challenging relationship, where growing cooperation goes hand in hand with mounting rivalries. Only during the last few years, they have begun to shed their wariness toward each other by initiating measures to stabilize their relationship, including regular high-level visits. This rapprochement is based on a mutual need to focus on social and political stability, and strong economic growth and a sense of security, so each of them can avoid the perils of stagnation or decline.

During a visit to India in 2015, Chinese Premier Wen Jiabao said that there is enough space in the world for the development of both China and India. This statement clearly highlights that the two countries have developed a shared common conception of their role on the global stage. As two large developing countries, India and China are aware of each other's role in the process of promoting the establishment of a new international political and economic order. They are supportive of the democratization of international relations and multilateralism, establishment of a new international political and economic order that is fair, rational, equal and mutually beneficial, and promotion of North-South Dialogue and South-South Cooperation. They have also agreed at the time that the United Nations should undergo comprehensive reform, with emphasis on increasing the representation of developing countries.

The incipient India-China entente has the potential to radically alter these countries security environment and restructure Asian geopolitics. However, India-China ties remain fragile and as vulnerable as ever to sudden deterioration as a result of misperceptions, unrealistic expectations, and eruption of unresolved issues. Internal issues of stability and the external overlapping spheres of influence forestall the chances for a genuine India-China rapprochement. The issues that bind these two countries are also the issues that divide them and fuel their rivalry. With their ever-expanding economies and widening geopolitical horizons, the bilateral relationship between the two rising Asian giants could be characterized more by competition than cooperation. As India and China are moving ahead simultaneously on their relative power trajectories, geopolitical equations and power relations in Asia are bound to undergo significant realignment. Despite growing interaction at the political, cultural, and economic levels, the gulf between the two countries, in terms of their perceptions, attitudes, and expectations of each other, has widened over the years. China has a deep distrust over India and it does not want to see India play a role beyond South Asia or emerge as a peer competitor. It has made its displeasure known over Southeast Asian countries' recent attempts to draw India into the region. In the power competition game, China has clearly surged far ahead of India by acquiring potent economic and military capabilities and the existing asymmetry in power and status serves China's interests very well. Therefore, China has very limited expectations from India which can be described by its "five No's" principles.

(a) Don't peddle—China threat theory.

(b) Don't support Tibet or Taiwan's independence.

(c) Don't object to the China-Pakistan strategic partnership.

(d) Don't align with the United States and/or Japan to contain China.

(e) Don't see or project yourself as an equal of China or as a nuclear and economic counterweight to China in Asia.

Based on these principles, China is trying to make relationship with India as part of its friendly neighborhood strategy. China would be happy if India's relations with the United States and Israel cool off and lose the momentum that was developed in the transfer of advanced weaponry such as the Phalcon airborne early warning system to India.

On the other hand, for India, emotions range from the euphoria of misperceived India-China brotherhood in the 1950s, to the bitterness of India's 1962 military defeat by China, and back again to the euphoria of imagined togetherness in the twenty-first century. With its current focus on economic progress, China is seen as a restrained power interested in managing, if not resolving, conflict. Guided by this perception, India hopes that intensifying trade and commerce would facilitate a resolution to their protracted boundary dispute. India also believes that a sound India-China relationship will help induce Pakistan into a negotiated settlement of the Kashmir dispute.

Though, India and China are competitors for power and influence in Asia, they also share common goals of maintaining regional stability, maintaining access to capital and markets, and benefiting from globalization. Cooperation will allow them to balance the influence of United States and increase their negotiating positions with the sole superpower.

Continued hostility between India and Pakistan, China's involvement in the India-Pakistan conflicts, and competition between the superpowers had turned South Asia into a significant area for rivalry between India and China. In the wake of the

1962 India-China war and the China-Soviet split, China chose to go with Pakistan to counter India, as well as to retain its influence in South Asia. Thus, China became involved in India-Pakistan conflict. As the competition for regional leadership remains a significant element in post-Cold War India-China relations, the regional competition has contributed a culture of rivalry between India and China. Also, India-China interaction on regional issues reveals both the country's asymmetrical perceptions of threat. India tends to be mired in the traditional security concept that China is seeking to enclose India in a South Asian straitjacket by engaging other South Asian states. On the other hand, China appears comparatively confident about threats from India although it is mindful of India's relations with ASEAN states and Japan.

Over the years bilateral relations between India and China have improved, but they still have misgivings about each other's engagement with their neighbours. India keeps a wary eye on China's ties with its South Asian neighbours, especially Pakistan. Both India and Pakistan saw threats emanating from each other as being major threats to their security. China and Pakistan still see each other as reliable partners whenever India-Pakistan relations sour. As a result, China-Pakistan relationship, especially China-Pakistani arms nexus, has been a cause of grave concern for India. China also encouraged other smaller South Asian states such as Nepal and Bangladesh to stand up to India's aspiration to dominate South Asia. India's longstanding conflicts with other South Asian states would drain and weaken India and, thus, serve China's strategic interests. However, from the Indian point of view, China has consistently sought to constrain Indian power and confine it essentially to the region of South Asia.

On the other hand, China is concerned with India's increasing efforts to extend its influence eastward and is conscious of the ongoing deep engagement between India and other Asian countries. While China has issues with some of its marine neighbours over the South China Sea, India has embarked on a "Look East" policy to engage the ASEAN states of Japan, South Korea and Taiwan. In addition to the traditional antagonism in South Asia, Southeast Asia emerges as a new area of India-China competition. Thus, along with the competitive dimension, there is linkage between the perception of threat and cooperation in India-China relations. In fact, India and China have reasons to cooperate even over regional issues. In addition to geopolitical competition, sub-regional economic cooperation and anti-terrorism campaigns have been added to the agenda of India-China relations in recent years. These developments, along with China's cautious neutrality towards the India-Pakistan conflict, shows that India and China are willing to scale down their enmity. Hence, from a regional perspective, India and China are not always bound to clash in their journey from regional to global power. They are acting as both competitors and partners in regional affairs. India-China relations are a mixture of competition and cooperation, although the latter might be somewhat less noticeable.

The Pakistan Factor—China's Balanced Policy Towards the India-Pakistan Conflicts: India has projected the China-Pakistan relationship as a strategic convergence against India, where Pakistan is acting as the proxy of China to counter Indian influence in the region. China has characterized its ties with Pakistan as an "all-weather friendship", implying that the two countries have developed a strong partnership that has indeed weathered the changes that have taken place in the domestic and international scenario. The China-Pakistan friendship reflects the saying that "an enemy's enemy is a friend". It implies that the China-Pakistan bonhomie is based upon their common bitter relationship with India.

China has acknowledged India's dominant role in South Asia, but at the same time it has ensured that Pakistan remains a strong military counterweight to India. The China-Pakistan "special relationship" is a part of China's grand strategy that molds the Asian security environment. The China-Pakistan military alliance, in particular the nuclear and missile nexus, has ensured that the South Asian military balance of power is neither pro-India nor pro-Pakistan but is pro-China. China shares Pakistan's deep mistrust of India's strategic ambitions and sees India as a rising power that must be balanced. China believes that as long as Indian military is preoccupied with Pakistan on its western frontier, India cannot focus on China and East Asia. China thinks that if India cannot sway the subcontinent, its influence in the larger arena becomes moot.

Pakistan cannot be a threat to India without China's military support just as Taiwan cannot be a threat to China without United States support. China's nuclear assistance to Pakistan is considered as the root cause of "deficit of trust" between the two countries. However, China has made it clear that it will not improve ties with India at the cost of Pakistan. On a cost-benefit analysis, the combined strategic and political advantages that China receives from its alliance with Pakistan, and through Pakistan other Islamic countries, easily outweigh any advantages of a closer relationship with India. Pakistan is vitally important to China's energy security (by providing access to and naval bases in the Persian Gulf), military security (by keeping India's military engaged on its western frontiers), geopolitics (given its geostrategic location at the intersection of South Asia, Central Asia and the Middle East), national unity and territorial integrity (maintaining control over Tibet and Xinjiang), maritime strategy in the Indian Ocean, and as a staunch diplomatically (in international forums, including the Islamic world), a buyer and supplier of conventional and unconventional weaponry, and above all, as a powerful bargaining chip in China's relations with India and the United States. However, China has also advised Pakistan against embarking on military misadventures and flirting with terrorism and religious extremism to further its geopolitical interests in Afghanistan and Kashmir.

China's approach towards India-Pakistan conflicts in the post-Cold War era was determined by its motivation to launch economic development at home and supported by the change in the security environment in South Asia. It favours a stable peripheral environment conductive to its domestic economic development. In a shift from unequivocal support to Pakistan, it no longer thinks India-Pakistan conflicts are in its interest and is now reluctant to side with either country in any dispute between them. Under the good neighbourly policy, China is trying to establish a more balanced relationship with India and Pakistan than the complicated equation in the past. As a result, China has shifted from a focus on exploiting the India-Pakistan conflict to a policy designed to help stabilize the region. In an attempt to relieve India's concerns, China stresses that the China-Pakistan friendship has no animus against any third country. It has emphasized that its relationship with Pakistan is "normal" and not directed towards India. This more balanced policy also indicates that China seems to think it possible to develop a parallel close relationship with both India and Pakistan. In order not to irritate Pakistan, China stressed that the improvement of India-China relations would not be the detriment of a third party, nor would it affect China's existing friendly relations with other countries. China also wants to enhance the scope of a "constructive cooperative partnership" with India and, at the same time, it wants to remain engaged with Pakistan.

China's Shift on the Kashmir Dispute: China's stand towards the Kashmir issue probably best describes the change of its stance towards the India-Pakistan conflict. It has had a role to play in the Kashmir issue because of its alliance relationship with Pakistan, and also because it obtained a piece of Kashmir under the 1963 China-Pakistan border treaty. Being the close ally of Pakistan, it has openly backed Pakistan's claim to all of Kashmir after China-India relations deteriorated. However, contrary to the traditional impression, China has not always supported Pakistan's stance over Kashmir. Ever since the late 1980s, China has tried to approach the Kashmir issue on its own merits and appeared to avoid taking sides with Pakistan in tune with increasingly warm relations with India. After the end of the Cold War, in 1994, China even pressured Pakistan to withdraw a resolution, tabled at the United Nations Human Rights Commission in Geneva, condemning India for human rights violations in Kashmir.

China's altered attitude towards the Kashmir issue has also been contributed by serious nationalist unrest in Xinjiang. Since 1980, China has distanced itself from its support for Pakistan's position to hold a plebiscite to decide the future of Kashmir.

China has also declined to intervene in the Kashmir issue by emphasizing the need for India and Pakistan to resolve the problem through dialogue. China thinks that an independent state of Kashmir would inspire Muslim separatists in Xinjiang to seek independence. According to China, Kashmir issue is a legacy from the British Empire and involves conflicting territorial claims, religion, ethnicity and other complex factors. China has supported Pakistan's stand that the sovereignty of Kashmir has not been defined and that it is the "core issue" in India-Pakistan relations, in contrast to the Indian position that Kashmir has always been a part of India. However, China has agreed that the dispute is steeped in history and India and Pakistan should seek an effective solution to the Kashmir conflict through peaceful dialogue, implying the issue should be decided by India and Pakistan bilaterally. This position of China is against Pakistan's hope to internationalise the Kashmir issue, and meets India's demands. The China referred to the United Nation Resolution on Kashmir in the context of solving the problem after India's nuclear tests of 1998, but then went back to insisting that a peaceful negotiated settlement between India and Pakistan should be made possible. Clearly, China is determined to insulate itself from the ups and downs of India-Pakistan ties, such as the Kashmir dispute, while improving its relations with both India and Pakistan.

However, dealing with India-Pakistan conflicts is a key question regarding China's western geo-political strategy and frontier security. The Kargil crisis of 1999 had put China's balanced approach to the test. Although Pakistan approached China for support, China appeared to have taken a position of cautious neutrality and did not give any special diplomatic favours to Pakistan. China repeatedly stated the need for restraint by both India and Pakistan, and the importance of resolving the problem through peaceful negotiations. This balanced posture was due to China's mounting concern about a major military conflict between India and Pakistan. Cheng Ruisheng, the former Chinese Ambassador to India, even claimed that China has a traditional friendship with Pakistan, but China's policy is not to side with Pakistan on the Kashmir issue. China refused to give Pakistan "carte blanche". Thus, China's position in the Kargil crisis confirmed the trend that China was determined to follow, specifically, a calibrated balanced policy in navigating the turbulence arising from India-Pakistan relations. China's moderate posture towards the India-Pakistan conflict altered the traditional impression of Chinese support for Pakistan and gave India some relief in its dealings with Pakistan. In addition to the demonstrated neutrality in the latest India-Pakistan confrontation, another significant development has been China's demonstration of its desire to play a more positive role to damp down the India-Pakistan conflict, rather than keeping the India-Pakistan tension at a distance. Even Pakistan has appealed to China to play an active role in South Asia to maintain a regional strategic balance and to settle the Kashmir issue, but during Chinese Premier Zhu Rongji's visit to India in January 2002, China assured India that it had neither any intention of mediating between India and Pakistan nor would it play any mediatory role between them.

India's Look East Policy: Feeling pressure from China's engagement with South Asian states, India has been able to take some balancing initiatives to counter its perceived encirclement by China. For example, it has tried to strengthen its engagement with China's neighbouring states, such as the countries in East Asia, to put pressure on China's security environment and, thus, distracting China. In the early 1990s, when India began to undertake economic reforms, there was an appraisal of India's policy towards the countries in East Asia. The steady economic development of the region, especially before the financial crisis, attracted much of India's attention. Against this backdrop, P.V. Narasimha Rao's government unveiled the "Look East Policy" to revive India's relations with East Asia, particularly ASEAN states. During the initial phase, this policy had gained favourable results on the economic and trade fronts, and in 1992, India became a Sectoral Dialogue Partner of ASEAN. The two sides had identified four broad sectors for cooperation—trade, investment, science and technology, and tourism—that had the aim of contributing to a closer economic link between India and ASEAN countries. Japan, Korea and ASEAN countries also emerged as a lucrative export market and source of foreign investments for India.

As India embarked on the Look East policy to reach out to countries in East Asia, it showed its ambition to extend its influence beyond the sub-continent and identified Southeast Asia as its "extended neighbourhood" with strategic implications for India and wished to maintain the momentum of the Look East Policy to forge a closer partnership with ASEAN countries. It can be seen that geography inevitably predetermines India as having close and cooperative relations with countries of ASEAN and the Asia-Pacific region. This policy could be seen as one of India's successful geo-strategies because India's relations with the countries in the region have since improved significantly. This policy also provides a possible approach for India to challenge China's status in the region. On the other hand, China is closely monitoring India-ASEAN ties to prevent the formation of an anti-China collaboration in the region.

Security Dimension of Look East Policy: The economic interactions between India and ASEAN countries might have slowed down with the Southeast Asian economic meltdown, but India changed its previous perceptions of ASEAN countries and so tended to attribute more significance to relations with ASEAN countries. As a result, in October 2003, India joined the Treaty of Amity and Cooperation in Southeast Asia. In November 2004, India and ASEAN further concluded the "India-ASEAN Partnership for Peace, Progress and Shared Prosperity". This signifies India's commitment to work with ASEAN countries in maintaining regional peace and stability. In 2005, India was also allowed to take part in the East Asia Summit. Meanwhile, the economic and trade fronts remain as important elements of the relations between India and ASEAN countries. In 2003, India and ASEAN signed the Framework Agreement on Comprehensive Economic Cooperation, which aimed to establish a free trade area by 2011. An India-ASEAN Free Trade Agreement (FTA) in goods was signed in August 2009, besides India has been actively conducting bilateral FTA negotiations with the countries in the region. For example, India signed a bilateral FTA agreement with Thailand in July 2003, and the Comprehensive Economic Cooperation Agreement with Singapore in June 2005. India has also concluded trade-related institutional arrangements with Vietnam, Philippines, Laos, Myanmar and Malaysia. With the conclusion of such arrangements, India is poised for greater economic integration with ASEAN countries and the region.

The Look East Policy of India was premised on trade and economic interaction with Southeast Asian nations, but subsequently it expanded to other areas of common interest. Despite the economic engagement, during India's search for an association with new friends in the region, security ties and military cooperation have been identified as being among the areas of India-ASEAN cooperation. However, the motivation for the Look East Policy was primarily economical, but the political relations and security ties between India and the ASEAN nations have also gradually progressed. On security and political front, India joined the ASEAN Regional Forum (ARF) in 1996, which is an organization aimed at fostering dialogue and consultation on political and security issues of common interest and concern, and at making significant contributions to efforts towards confidence-building and preventative diplomacy in the Asia-Pacific region. In 1996, India was accepted as a full dialogue partner of ASEAN and participated for the first time in the Post Ministerial Conference (PMC) of ASEAN in Jakarta. The first India-ASEAN summit was held in 2002 and India became the fourth country, after China, Japan and South Korea, to establish the summit mechanism with ASEAN.

India has also shown interest in strengthening military cooperation with ASEAN nations by offering training slots to ASEAN nations and holding joint military exercises with them, which have over the years increased in scope and content, and at the same time enhanced interoperability. Conducting the exercises has been institutionalized between India and Singapore, and joint patrols continue with Indonesia and Thailand. In addition, India has also made military relations with Vietnam and Myanmar. For example, during the Indian Defence Minister George Fernandes' visit to Vietnam in March 2000, the two countries signed a wide-ranging agreement paving the way for greater military cooperation, which included the sale of advanced military light helicopters, assisting in the repair and overhaul of Vietnam's mainstay MiG fighters and raising the level of military contacts.

Due to its common border with India and China, Myanmar has traditionally sought to maintain a balance between these two neighbours. But, both India and China want to have Myanmar as their ally against the other state. India sees China's aid to Myanmar as China's intention to infiltrate its military strength as far as the Indian Ocean. For example, with China's help, Myanmar is expanding its naval facilities in Great Coco Island, which is the site of a major signals intelligence facility situated near India's Andaman and Nicobar Islands. To counterbalance China's strategic link, India has also increased its cooperation with the Myanmar Military Junta. Particularly, there has been a substantial increase in bilateral defence cooperation between the Indian Army and the Myanmar Army in training and other fields. There have been exchanges of high-level visits, such as that of the Indian Chief of the Army Staff to Myanmar and the Commander in Chief of the Myanmar Navy to India. India is also willing to expand the ambit of military cooperation between the two countries, including military transfers, and has promised to give a favourable response to the Myanmar Government's request for military equipment. In April 2007, the Indian and Myanmar security forces had conducted joint military operations along the 1643 km India-Myanmar border to neutralize insurgent groups. Thus, India's impulses to continue "Look East Policy" are not only dictated by the economic engagement, but also are grounded in the consideration of geopolitics.

The expansion of India's profile in the defence sector has created interests among the regional powers in partnering with India. China thinks that ASEAN nations welcome Indian military presence in this region because they consider that India could contribute to maintain the balance of power. This is why ASEAN nations did not follow the United States or Japan's example in criticizing India's nuclear tests of 1998. China interpreted the mild response by ASEAN nations as their acknowledgement of India as a rising political power that has near-parity with China and a balance against its influence. India has gradually revealed its potential as an economic power and now it is ASEAN nations that are turning to India. The region sees India as one of its growing partners in trade and as a major source for future investments.

There are two major drives behind India's Look East Policy.

(a) The essence of this policy is the recognition that India's aspirations for a larger global role cannot be realized while its foreign policy and national security preoccupations are limited to the subcontinent. It is a necessary step if India wishes to achieve the goal of being a world power. India has also to establish closer contacts with the relevant region to prevent marginalization in the context of the trend towards regionalism. In other words, this policy is part of India's grand strategy for securing global-power status.

(b) This policy became one of India's ploys to counter China's "omnidirectional pressure". The presence of India's navy in the South China Sea was a particular source of concern to China. India's navy stayed in the South China Sea even after concluding a joint military exercise with Singapore, Vietnam and so on. Given the territorial disputes between China and some ASEAN nations, it was argued that India's attempt to maintain a substantial military presence in the South China Sea would have a profound and long-term implications for China's policies towards the region.

India commands the geo-strategic location at the heart of the world's vital commercial shipping lanes in the Indian Ocean and can play a significant role in the safety of the "new silk route", which extends from the Persian Gulf and straddles the Indian Ocean till it enters the Strait of Malacca, the gateway to South-East Asia. Given the high stakes involved in the uninterrupted flow of commercial shipping, India's area of interest extends from north of the Arabian Sea to the South China Sea. The overlapping claims over the sovereignty of the oil-rich Spratly

Islands in the South China Sea have placed additional pressure on China's security. China do not want to see countries in the region working together with outside powers against China over the South China Sea issue, therefore it has a deep concern about the propensity of India to extend its areas of operation and interests eastward to the South China Sea. China, looking at the South China Sea as its special domain, does not like India's presence in the area. The improvement in India-ASEAN relations and the establishment of a cooperative partnership have made China's security environment more complicated, putting pressure upon China's western and southern regions, challenging China's maritime security, and increasing its difficulty in solving the boundary problem and the territorial claims in the South China Sea.

Nuclear Proliferation and Military Competition: China's nuclear and missile proliferation is one of the most important source of contention for India. It is the adversarial nature of the India-China relationship that has driven India's and Pakistan's nuclear weapons program. Majority of Western powers have grudgingly acknowledged India's de facto nuclear status, but China shows no sign of softening its demand that India should initiate a complete rollback of its nuclear weapons program and unconditionally participate in the Comprehensive Test Ban Treaty (CTBT) and the Nuclear Non-Proliferation Treaty (NPT) as a Non-Nuclear Weapons State. China always objected India's entry into the exclusive Nuclear Five Club and distanced itself from any move that would acknowledge, legalize, or legitimize India's status as a Nuclear Weapons State. It has also consistently rejected India's proposals for bilateral nuclear confidence-building measures (CBMs). It has also objected India's call for a "common nuclear doctrine for India, China and Pakistan based on no-first-use (NFU) pledge". The idea of a common nuclear doctrine, though impractical and unrealistic given their different security imperatives, talks of "credible, transparent, and verifiable CBMs in treaty form to minimize the risk of nuclear and missile conflict with China or Pakistan". China has withdrawn its NFU pledge to India in 1995 when it amended its nuclear doctrine to make the NFU pledge applicable only to

NPT member-states. Since neither China nor Pakistan follows a policy of NFU of nuclear weapons vis-à-vis India, India wants to bind them to a NFU pledge.

It is ironical that China demands India's denuclearization, but itself is continuing to proliferate in violation of its legal commitments under the NPT. China has also offered nuclear reactors to Pakistan despite growing international concern over Pakistan's troubling nuclear proliferation record. On the positive side, a regular security dialogue has begun, and navies of India and China have conducted their first search and rescue exercise in November 2003. In March 2004, the two countries agreed to enhance bilateral defense relations and, for the first time, granted observer status to military officers at each other's exercises. India and China have supported Europe's challenge to American space supremacy by investing Euro 300 million and 200 million respectively in the Galileo global satellite navigation system. Both see the Galileo project as a real alternative to the de facto monopoly of the American Global Positioning System (GPS) and the Russian GLONASS system.

However, Indian and Chinese militaries view each other as future rivals and each points to threatening trends and behaviour in the other. Both countries keep a close watch on changes in military doctrines, defense spending, capabilities and related activities and remain committed to neutralizing perceived security gains of the other side. They support nuclear disarmament but continue to expand their own nuclear arsenals and capabilities. Possession of nuclear arsenals may be vital to preserving strategic autonomy for India and China, but it also raises the stakes in their competitive relationship.

Energy Security to Maritime Rivalry: India and China are facing growing demand for energy and are locked in fierce competition for stakes in overseas oil and gas fields in Russia, Myanmar, Iran, Iraq, Sudan, Vietnam and Libya. For example, a US$ 600 million acquisition in Angola by Indian oil company was won after a fight with a Chinese bidder. Competition between India and China has also intensified in Central and Southeast Asia as both view these regions as vital sources of natural resources and markets for their goods. But China has a lead over India both economically and diplomatically, and each has put forward its own proposals for multilateral cooperation that exclude the other. Nearly 70 percent of China's trade is through the Strait of Malacca, the Indian Ocean, and the Suez Canal. The predominance of the United States and Indian navies along these sea-lanes of communication is viewed as a major threat to Chinese security. To protect its long-term economic security interests, China is now laying the groundwork for a naval presence along maritime chokepoints in the South China Sea, the Malacca Straits, the Indian Ocean, and the Strait of Hormuz in the Persian Gulf through acquisition of naval bases in Cambodia, Myanmar, Bangladesh, and Pakistan. On the other hand, India has countered by promoting defense cooperation with Iran, Oman and Israel in the west while upgrading military ties with Myanmar, Singapore, the Maldives, Thailand, Vietnam, Taiwan, Philippines, Australia, Japan and United States in the east. Its new naval doctrine is to influence events around the Indian Ocean and beyond. Maritime competition is likely to intensify as Indian and Chinese navies show off their flag in the South China Sea and the Indian Ocean with greater frequency.

India and China in the Middle East: India and China have long lasting commercial ties with the Middle East. However, it is only in 1993, as China became a net oil importer country, that the Middle East countries took a strategic importance, and that China gave up its ideological foreign policy for a more pragmatic approach based on its internal development and stability. Today, both India's and China's relationships with the Middle East are mainly, but not exclusively, based on energy. To meet their increasing energy requirements, both countries have become increasingly dependent on the supply from the Middle East countries and their energy diplomacy has been playing a crucial role in their global foreign policy. First, on an economic point of view, the economic growth of India and China opened the Middle East countries to new export markets for their oil and investors, at a time where the West started losing its economic attractiveness. Secondly, it has counterbalanced the United States' hegemony over the region—on the one hand giving a new importance to countries such as Iran, which remained in the shadow of the American sanctions, and on the other hand putting Western companies in direct competition with Asian firms in countries such as Saudi Arabia which were considered as part of the Western sphere of influence.

Indian and Chinese policies in the Middle East are rather characterized by fragmented, bilateral relations, and their relations with the Middle East countries are based on the mutual respect for sovereignty and non-intervention in internal affairs, and consequently mainly about mutual economic interests. However, it does not mean that they are excluding all political or strategic considerations.

In spite of adopting similar approaches towards their relations with the Middle East countries, India and China remain competitors, in a region already faced by fierce international competition. First of all, they compete for oil. Both have encouraged their state-owned companies to acquire so called "equity oil" contracts at premium prices in order to be able to control the production and the prices. This approach has exposed them to criticism from the West, which considers it to be a distortion of market mechanisms and which repeatedly encouraged them to respect the rules of the international market. In this competition, Chinese companies have so far proven to be more efficient than Indian ones, who lost several contracts against their Chinese competitors. Yadavaran oilfield in Iran seems to be a perfect illustration of the ongoing India-China competition, but also potential cooperation. In Yadavaran oilfield, Indian companies have 20% stake whereas their Chinese counterpart has 50% stake.

Thus, India has succeeded in developing a real strategic relationship with Iran while maintain a good working relationship with the United States. India has been developing a defence and military cooperation with Iran since 2001. This can be explained by the geographical position of Iran at the Western border of Pakistan, and by the strategic interest of India to have allies within the Muslim world which could support it in case of war over Kashmir. Concerning the China-Iran relationship, it has been suffering of the consequences of the American pressure on China during the Iranian crisis, which has leaded China to officially stop supporting Iranian nuclearization since 2006.

If India-Iran partnership is on a better track than China-Iran one, China on the contrary is in a better position in Saudi Arabia, which has replaced Iran as China's major supplier in 2009. On the other hand, politically the relations between India and Saudi Arabia have been not so good due to the Saudi support to Pakistan, and financing of Islamic schools in India at a time of increasing internal interreligious conflicts. Yet India considers Saudi Arabia as a possible counterweight to Pakistan in the Islamic world.

The most important and strategic issue of competition between India and China is the control of the Indian Ocean, of the main Sea Lanes of Transportation, and of the Straits of Hormuz through which 80 percent of the oil passes, and of Malacca through which 70 percent of Chinese oil passes. India and China worry that a blockade of these chokepoints would lead to supply disruption. The Indian Ocean region, through which most of the oil passes, is considered by India as its natural zone of influence, and by China as a strategic zone that needs to be controlled. Therefore, a fierce competition exists between China which considers India's claim as illegitimate as illustrated by the quote of the Chinese General Chi Haotin according to which the Indians must understand that "it is Indian Ocean not India's Ocean", and India which sees itself encircled from all sides by the Chinese construction of ports. While India has engaged itself in modernization of its navy, in which it has been supported by the United States in the framework of the Indo-US defence cooperation agreement signed in 2005, China has been leading a policy called by the United States and India "The String of Pearls Strategy", consisting in participating in the construction of infrastructure in strategic ports in countries along the Sea Lanes of Communication, in order to secure their oil supply. China has been building ports in Myanmar, Cambodia, Bangladesh, and the most important is the Deep-Water Sea Port at Gwadar in Pakistan, 400 Km from the strait of Hormuz, which can be used as a means to avoid the Malacca Strait and to diminish the cost of sea transportation, by transporting the oil and gas through land to China.

As a response to Gwadar Port, India has collaborated with Iran to build the Port of Chabahar, which is also very strategically located and would represent both a strategic point for alternative routes of transportation, and a strategic point in case of a war with Pakistan. The Iran-Pakistan-India pipeline projects, which is so far victim of poor India-Pakistan relations, Pakistan's internal security, and American pressure in favour of the alternative Turkmenistan-Afghanistan-Pakistan-India pipeline, is another sign of the well-functioning Indo-Iranian cooperation.

Thus, there is a tough competition for transportation routes, which gives to the Indian Ocean and Central Asian regions a strategic importance. In these sectors, the role of the United States and of Pakistan is central, and the evolution of their positions will have an essential influence on future developments. The Indo-American cooperation seems to place India in a comfortable position in the Indian Ocean, while the Sino-Pakistan cooperation could give China an advantage once the Gwadar port will really be operational.

Due to competition for energy markets between China and India within the Middle East, the prices of oil and gas had increased. To deal with such situation, in 2005, India and China had developed a dialogue on energy cooperation under Indian initiative. In the same year, they signed the Sino-Indian partnership for peace and prosperity and have since then conducted several joint military exercises in the Indian Ocean. These developments, if one can doubt whether they really reflect the reality of the India-China relationship, illustrate the reciprocal awareness of the needs for cooperation in areas where both have mutual interests. For example, Chinese and Indian oil companies jointly purchased shares of 36 Syrian oilfields. The Syrian joint venture was their first common acquirement of oil assets.

Regional Cooperation between India and China: Common interests between India and China far outweigh their differences, so both countries could focus on expanding cooperation rather than fighting over differences. As far as the geographic proximity is concerned, it not only generates competition between India and China, but also presents an opportunity for cooperation in some areas. According to Chinese President Jiang Zemin, geographic proximity could be an advantage for China-India cooperation, along with the vast land masses, rich natural resources, large populations and huge markets. Unfortunately, in the past, border disputes have prevented both sides from exploring the possibility of benefiting more from their geographic proximity. In order to move forward India-China relations away from the notion of competition and towards cooperation, both countries are seeking opportunities to make use of the geographical advantages, rather than focusing on the disputes. In a development likely to forge more benign interactions, India and China are working to place the issues regarding regional cooperation on their agenda, with the expectation of imparting additional momentum to improve their relations.

Anti-Terrorism Cooperation: India and China have a common concern over malignant cross-border activities. During Chinese President Jiang Zemin's visit to India in 1996, India and China signed an agreement on combating drug trafficking. The common willingness to combat Islamic militancy and fundamentalists emanating from Central Asia and Afghanistan is likely to provide a fillip to the India-China relationship. Although both the countries have worked hard to repress the terrorist activities in their respective regions, the internal-external linkage has created difficulties. External sympathetic groups in Central Asian states, Afghanistan, and Pakistan have provided sanctuary, support, and training for the terrorists. Therefore, seeking international cooperation to block extremist movements inside their own territories and cut the links across the border is a fundamental aspect of China's and India's policies to combat cross-border terrorism.

China has expressed its willingness to share intelligence with India on terrorism in Kashmir and unrest in Northeast in exchange for India's intelligence on the Uighur separatists. The first India-China counter-terrorism dialogue took place in April

2002 and the second was held in June 2003. However, the extent to which the dialogue mechanism can bring India and China closer remains debatable. The key to further cooperation on counter-terrorism will depend on whether the two countries can reconcile their differences over the definition of terrorism. China tends to equate religious extremists and national separatists with international terrorists. Therefore, according to the Chinese definition, there is no difference between Uighur and Tibetan separatists and both should be crushed without mercy. But it is difficult for India to accept this sort of concept in view of fact that India still provides sanctuary to the Dalai Lama and his government-in-exile.

China has claimed that it opposes all forms of terrorism, no matter when, where or in what form terrorism strikes, and no matter against whom it is directed. But this definition finds China difficult to assent to India's definition regarding international terrorism, particularly its accusations about Pakistan. China has dismissed the charge that Pakistan has rendered training to the Uighur terrorists, and will not agree to expand the war on terrorism to include Pakistan. Chinese sensitivity to the issue is evident from the fact that the Chinese officials play down the significance of this dialogue mechanism on countering terrorism. Such differences could exacerbate divisions between India and China and limit the scope of cooperation. Since both India and China insist that there should be no double standards in addressing the issue of terrorism, they have to forge a consensus on the definition of terrorism. However, the common course of anti-terrorism has provided a platform for the two countries. The armies of two countries conducted the first-ever India-China Joint Anti-Terrorism Training Code named "Hand-in-Hand 2007" in December 2007 in Kunming, China's Yunnan province. It was followed by the "Hand-in-Hand 2008" joint military training and exercise at Belgaum in Karnataka, India.

The Kunming Initiative: The improved relations between India and China since the late 1980s and the introduction of India's economic reform have provided a new setting for stronger economic engagement. By focusing on economic development, China has been keen to promote sub-regional economic cooperation by adopting an opening-up policy towards its neighbouring countries. For example, back in 1991, Sichuan's officials had publicly demanded that the entire region of Southwest China should be open up for India, along with Myanmar, Bangladesh, Pakistan, Thailand and Malaysia. Similarly, Yunnan's officials said they wanted to make the province an "international hub" for transport through Southeast Asia and the South Asian subcontinent. Like Southwest China, India's Northeast region comprising the seven states of Assam, Arunachal Pradesh, Manipur, Meghalaya, Mizoram, Nagaland and Tripura, is interested in engaging with contiguous regions of Bangladesh, Myanmar, Bhutan and Tibet. Economic backwardness of Northeast India has contributed to the development of various insurgencies and other riot activities, making it one of the most volatile and sensitive regions of India. The fact that this region shares less than two percent of its borders with the rest of India reflects the importance of opening it up for its neighbouring countries. Therefore, exchanges between the two land-locked sub-regions, Southwest China and Northeast India, should be increased to boost the economy. In order to transform geographic proximity into an economic advantage, some initiatives have been taken. Since, there is no common border between the two sub-regions, it was decided the engagement had to be carried out in a multilateral framework, involving a third party, such as Myanmar. The proposal centered round the theme of transportation infrastructure links and the development of a sub-regional economic integration forum, because the lack of transportation links was chiefly responsible for the sluggish growth of foreign trade between Southwest China and India.

Sub-regional economic integration is a major initiative that involves China's Sichuan and Yunnan provinces, and India's Northeastern states, Myanmar and Bangladesh. This track-II Kunming initiative, named after the capital of China's Yunnan province, came out of an academic symposium called the "Conference on Regional Cooperation and Development among China, India, Myanmar and Bangladesh". The "Kunming Initiative" was discussed and signed by the leaders of the four delegations. The main thrust of the exercise was to exhort the governments concerned to establish a forum for sub-regional economic cooperation comprising China, India, Myanmar, and Bangladesh. It was believed that the economies in the sub-region can be strengthened significantly through increased cooperation by the quadrangle.

Doklam—Interpreting India-China Relations: The recent standoff between India and China on the Doklam plateau which lies at a tri-junction between the India, China, and Bhutan, is the latest in an increasingly long history of conflicts along the border. It has turned into the biggest military standoff between the two armies in years. Although, the latest incursion by Chinese forces occurred in the Doklam region along Bhutan's border with China, and not the India-China border, Indian personnel responded in kind to back up their Bhutanese neighbours.

The relationship between India and Bhutan, in many ways, is a model relationship and they enjoy strong political, development, economic, and military relations. Following China's adoption of communism and its incorporation of Tibet, Bhutan distanced itself from its northern neighbour China. India encouraged Bhutan to join the United Nations and establish diplomatic relations with other countries. Militarily, without an air force, Bhutan depends on Indian air support. It opts not to maintain official relations with China, although there are ongoing border talks between the two countries. Since 1984, twenty-four rounds of talks have occurred between Bhutan and China over their disputed border without a clear solution.

The standoff in Bhutan's disputed Doklam region occurred near the tri-junction of India-China-Bhutan, and just east of the Sikkim border. Doklam also lies close to the Indian Siliguri Pass, which is also known as "Chicken's Neck" in the Northeast region of India. This narrow region, flanked on two sides by Bangladesh and Nepal, is the only land access to the Northeast. Therefore, Chinese incursions so close to this area provoke a strategic threat to India as well as Bhutan. The incursion began in mid-June of 2017 when People's Liberation Army (PLA) personnel entered the disputed territory and began construction

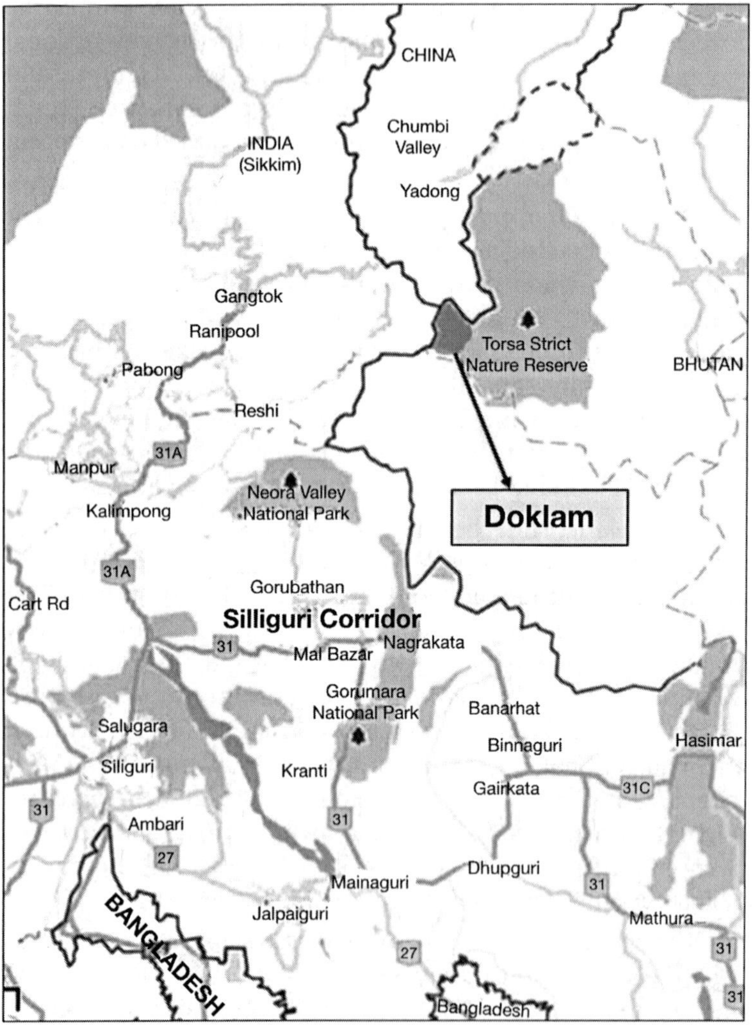

of a road. Bhutanese security forces requested their withdrawal from the disputed land, and India subsequently responded by sending troops to backup Bhutan's position. Later, China accused Indian troops of entering in its territory and India accused the Chinese of destroying its bunker (PLA bulldozed an old bunker of the Indian army stationed in Doklam). Thereafter, China stopped the passage of pilgrims heading toward Kailash-

Manasarovar through the Nathu La pass in Sikkim. However, no loss of life occurred, but there could have been a more intense military flare-up.

The recent incursion in Doklam appeared more brazen than other recent actions. Chinese mass media served up fiery rhetoric around the dispute and were dismissive of Indian complaints. Tensions were partly diffused when disengagement took place towards the end of August and preceding the 9th BRICS summit held in Xiamen, China. Although the situation has cooled down, the India-China border faces constant tension and the seventy-one-day engagement in Doklam is proof of the need for concerted diplomatic communication to prevent such instances.

India-China Relations: In the Global Context

The future of India-China relations is believed to be a crucial factor in shaping the international order. India and China with their huge population are rising players in the international

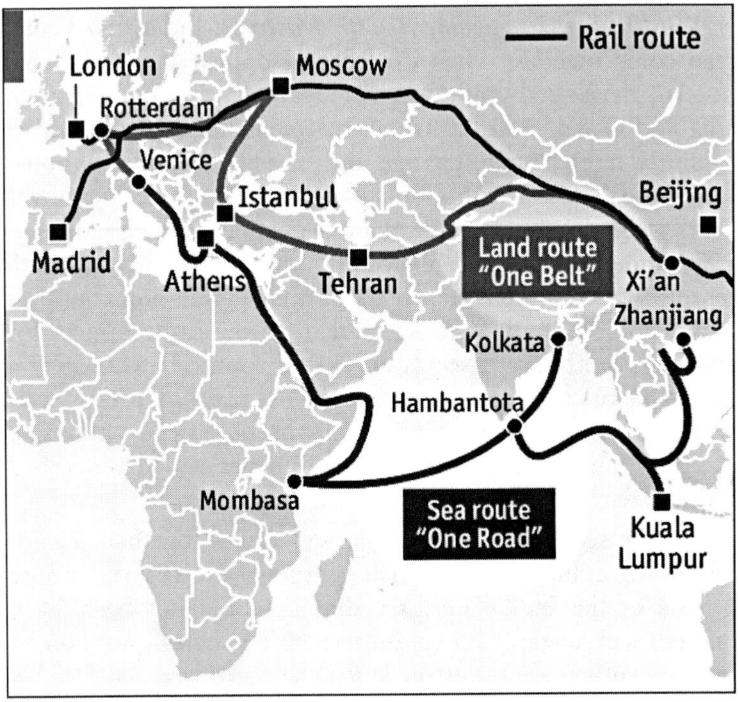

arena and, therefore, their interactions not only affect the two countries, but also international society. The India-China relation has gone beyond the bilateral context and acquired a global dimension. Therefore, a stable, normal and friendly relationship between India and China not only conforms with the fundamental interests of the two countries, but also helps promote peace, stability and development not only throughout Asia, but also in the world as a whole. On the other hand, if India and China work to counterbalance each other, it will serve the interests of the so-called "hegemonist". There are several possibilities regarding how India-China interactions could shape the international order. Of these, the most noticeable are Indo-American alliance against China, an India-China-Russia strategic triangle against the United States, and "Chindia" as a dominant player in international society. These in fact are related to two different strategies of reducing threat perception—balancing and bandwagoning.

Multilateral Engagement with Mistrust: India and China often come together when it comes to oppose demands from western, developed countries. For example, in climate policy, India and China signed a five-year agreement in October 2009 to jointly fight climate change and to negotiate international climate deals using common positions. This agreement was made prior to the United Nations' climate change summit in Copenhagen in December 2009. India and China, both members of G20, consistently argue that developing countries should not be required to set and meet the same targets for reducing greenhouse gases as developed countries who carry a greater historical responsibility for the increase in atmospheric greenhouse gases. They rejected calls by developed nations to set legally binding targets, and both countries signed a modified Copenhagen Accord in March 2010.

On the economic arena, India and China together did not consent to a bilateral Free Trade Agreement (FTA) because of fears of the Indian industry that it would not be able to compete with cheap Chinese imports. Nonetheless, an indirect arrangement came into effect in 2010, when an India-ASEAN

FTA and a China-ASEAN FTA was signed, respectively. India and China have also joined hands in the World Trade Organisation (WTO). In 2008, at the Doha Development Agenda (DDA) trade talks in Geneva, the main cleavage was between the developed countries led by the United States and the European Union, and BASIC (Brazil, South Africa, India and China). After years of negotiation, and after almost reaching an agreement, talks broke down after the United States refused to discuss "special safeguard agreements" in agriculture as India has requested. China backed India's stand. Although this mutual support drew widespread criticism from not only developed countries but also from Brazil, the joint position of the two neighbouring countries has continued ever since.

In multilateral forums, both Asian giants share a geo-strategic interest, but the seemingly strong solidarity between India and China vanishes when it comes to what both assume to be their own respective backyards. The Shanghai Cooperation Organisation (SCO) is a group of Central Asian Countries, Russia and China dominated by the latter two nations, while the South Asian Association for Regional Cooperation (SAARC) is a regional forum dominated by India. India and China tried to keep each other out of their respective denominations to contain greater regional influence by the other. But pressure from the other countries within the SAARC and SCO who have friendlier ties with the respective regional power eventually gave India SCO observer status in 2005 and as part of the deal China also became an observer in the SAARC. For India, as the economically and politically weaker party of the India-China power struggle, multilateral engagement can be a good tool to contain China's dominance outside the areas of India's interests.

Indo-American Alliance: Relations between India and the United States have continued to witness intensive engagement regarding a qualitative transformation over the past few years. Both the countries want to strengthen their ties further and develop a strategic partnership. They have been involved in institutional dialogues and interactions on issues of mutual concerns and interests—from the issues of defense, combating international terrorism to trade, and science and technology. They have also increased the number of military exchanges and have conducted joint exercises on a regular basis. However, Indo-American relations was affected by India's nuclear tests of 1998. In addition to postponing President Clinton's visit to India, Washington also put economic sanctions on India to force it to join the non-proliferation regime. But, India has since successfully repaired its relations with the United States by conducting formal consultations and resuming high-level visits. Indo-American relations came to a climax when President Clinton resumed his delayed visit to India and Pakistan in March 2000. He spent five days in India, but only five hours in Pakistan. During his visit, India and the United States signed a document entitled "India-US Relations: A Vision for the 21st Century", pledging to deepen the partnership through institutionalized dialogue and engagement in regular consultations. India and the United States were referred to as partners in peace, with a common interest in and complementary responsibility for ensuring regional and international security. Although the two countries failed to reach an agreement on nuclear non-proliferation, an issue that President Clinton termed important to realise the full potential of the Indo-American relationship, there is no denying that Indo-American relations have improved significantly.

Although the war against terrorism made the United States restore US-Pakistan strategic relations, the role of India has also been well-recognised by it, i.e., it does not treat India on par with Pakistan, but does accept that India has much more strategic importance in the region. In an important manifestation of the qualitative change in India-US relations, the President George W. Bush and Prime Minister Vajpayee announced the Next Steps in the Strategic Partnership (NSSP) in January 2004, which covered cooperation in four areas—civilian space, civilian nuclear energy, dual-use items, and missile defence. Unlike its concerns over China's rise, the United States administration considered the rise of India as adding value to its strategic plot.

China was carefully observing the adjustment of the United States' policy towards India. The United States had soon waived economic sanctions upon India and Pakistan after the events of 11th September 2001 to seek the two countries' support. More significantly, the military cooperation between India and the United States also gained momentum after the September 11 terrorist attacks. In April 2002, India signed a US$ 146 million deal with the United States to purchase eight AN/TPQ-37 Fire finder weapon locating radars. This was the first major government-to-government weapons transaction in more than three decades between India and the United States. The United States Defense Department statement read, "This sale will contribute to the foreign policy and national security interests of the United States by helping to improve the security of a country that has been and continues to be a force for political stability and economic progress in South Asia". This significant improvement in the India-US military ties might not be directly aimed against China, but the development had cast a shadow on China's security environment.

The rise of China is one of the major factors that influence the United States' policy towards India. After the demise of the USSR, China has been a possible challenger to the United States in the future, and the United States has watched China's rise in international society and its military modernization with misgivings. It is thought that the United States would like to contain China by establishing an anti-China alliance. The perception of China's growing threat has made the United States lean more towards India. As China's military grows more formidable, there might be a greater coincidence of interests between India and the Western powers in thinking about a more effective balance to manage China. In pursuit of a shared objective of dissuading China from aggressive actions, India's counterbalance against China is seen as a visible interest in broadening the ambit of US-India defence cooperation. The Indo-US joint manoeuvres can be seen as efforts by a democratic coalition to contain the rise of China. The India-US nuclear deal can be seen as a significant step in this direction. The Indo-US strategic nexus is likely to continue and to be reinforced further with the growing rift between the United States and China or India and China.

China is keenly observing the increasing closeness of Indo-US relations, especially on issues concerning military cooperation. It seems to be increasingly worried about the formation of Indo-American strategic cooperation, which suggests a pattern of alliance-building activities that it cannot ignore. From China's perspective, the coming together of the United States and India could well serve the United States' plans to contain China's growing economic and military might in Asia. The shared security concerns regarding China's rise can be an incentive to boost relations between India and the United States. However, China does not believe that India will join the United States in confronting China. It deems that India will not blindly follow the lead of the United States. The considerations within the Chinese leadership are whether it should maintain some relations with India or let India unite with the United States on the international stage. Understanding the significance, China will engage with India if it senses that India would unite with the United States at the international level. It is believed that the difficulties in the relations between China and the United States will play an important role in encouraging the Chinese leadership to accelerate the process of normalizing relations with India.

It is believed that the United States' global security interests take priority over India's hope to become an independent power, i.e., the United States wants to help India to become a power to fulfil Washington's own strategic goals, not to fulfil those of India. Therefore, the United States has been opposing the Iran-India-Pakistan pipeline project, which is important for India's energy security. Pakistan-US relations and nuclear issues are also creating obstacles in developing a closer Indo-American friendship. The United States had no intention of developing Indo-American relations while ignoring Pakistan, no matter what kind of government was in power. However, India and the United States may also believe that the improvement of their bilateral relationship could generate greater foreign policy leverages for each other. The United States may use India's growing economic and military might to meet its strategic needs in Asia and to limit further Chinese influence in the region. No matter how China perceives India-US military relations, India wants to maintain good relations with the United States. Also, it is not in India's interests to spoil relations with China, i.e., India is not ready to behave like Japan, a reliable ally of the United States in East Asia. Therefore, sometimes India jumps on the bandwagon with the United States, and sometimes it acts in pursuit of its own goals.

India-China-Russia Strategic Triangle: The idea of establishing a strategic triangle consisting of India, China and Russia was first proposed by the then Russian Prime Minister Yevgeny Primakov during his visit to India in December 1998 and since then, the idea of establishing a India-China-Russia strategic triangle and its implications surface occasionally, as people are concerned with the possibility that the three countries will transform the potential for an alliance into a formal alliance. Ties between the three nations have since grown dramatically and a series of bilateral pacts have been signed to define the direction of the relationship.

China has initiated "partnership diplomacy" with many countries and regions. As far as Russia-China relations and India-China relations are concerned, in 1994, Russia and China established a constructive partnership looking towards the 21st century and then a "partnership of strategic coordination" in April 1996, while India and China set up a "constructive cooperative partnership oriented towards the 21st century" in November 1996 and a "strategic and cooperative partnership for peace and prosperity" in April 2005. India and Russia have also continued the special relationship founded in the former Soviet Union era. An India-Russia strategic partnership was established in 1997, and the strategic partnership agreement was concluded in 2000. Therefore, it is believed that it would be neither strange nor difficult for these three countries to transform their declared bilateral strategic partnership into a triangular format.

Among the world's seven declared nuclear nations, three are India, Russia and China, and they combined have one-third of the world's population. Russia and China have already secured permanent membership of the United Nations Security Council while India is widely tipped to gain a new seat in the expanded United Nations Security Council. The combined strength of these three countries will increase and this group could act as a counterweight to the United States on the international arena. A strategic triangle alliance may bring about a new world order where the United States does not have such a preponderance of power. Even if they do not build up a strategic partnership to counterbalance the United States, they will find common areas for cooperation. As cooperation among these countries increases, so will their weight in international affairs. However, despite intense discussions among the three countries involved and the international community, the concept has not yet become a reality due to various constraints.

India-China-Russia cooperation has a rich and positive potential because they advocate a multi-polar world order and the establishment of a just and fair new international order, and object to the hegemonism and the United States dominated international order in the post-Cold War era. Thus, the similar viewpoints shared by India, China and Russia on major international issues can be seen as the basis for further development of their trilateral relationship and they are likely to work together in the international field in order to promote the establishment of an international order and a multi-polar world.

Policies of the United States provided a good setting and opportunities for India, China and Russia to voice their joint concerns about the global order. The concept of the strategic triangle came at a time when the United States and Britain launched the bombardment of Iraq, bypassing the United Nations Security Council. The need for such strategic triangle felt because of the unilateral nature of the United States' operation. Russia sensed the need to take countermeasures to check the United States' geopolitical "offensive" in Eurasia, such as NATO's eastward expansion right up to its borders. In sharp contrast to the concept of an Indo-American strategic partnership to counter China's increasing power, the idea of India-China-Russia strategic triangle reflected the thinking about the need to check the growing dominance by the United States.

Russia is engaged in bilateral ties with India and China along with actively promoting the trilateral cooperation among them. While, at the beginning, India and China demonstrated a relatively lukewarm attitude towards the strategic triangle. However, obstacles remain in moving towards a trilateral strategic partnership, but unilateral tendencies on the part of the United States are encouraging the three countries to move closer to each other. Attitudes of India and China have changed towards the triangle proposal after the military action in Kosovo in 1999. The Kosovo war reminds the three countries that they share common interests in international affairs. As a result, the idea of establishing a strategic triangle has been raised again and it won more positive responses from India and China.

The "strategic triangle" dilemma facing India, China and Russia is that they need a trilateral relationship with strategic significance to counterbalance the United States' unilateralism, but they do not want to provoke the United States needlessly. To deal with this dilemma, these countries have changed the phraseology for the concept—the term "trilateral coordination and cooperation" is now used to describe the efforts to promote the trilateral relationship, instead of the somewhat contentious "strategic triangle" phraseology. Under "trilateral coordination and cooperation", the trilateral interaction between India, China and Russia has vigorously developed in recent years, and an intensive political dialogue has been established. They have begun to conduct an informal consultative exercise to make sure that they can create and maintain the necessary coordination in international affairs. Since 2002, the Foreign Ministers of these countries have often held trilateral meetings on the sidelines of the United Nations General Assembly session in New York. Now, the trilateral meetings have evolved into a gathering of heads of state. In July 2006, the first India-China-Russia summit was held in St. Petersburg, Russia, to formulate the common agenda, the possibilities of joint cooperative actions to deal with issues such as terrorism and other global threats, energy security, and health and related matters. These countries then promptly held the second summit in New Delhi and issued a Joint Communique concerning their shared desire to work together on energy, terror, security and trade. Although China flatly refuses to describe its relationship with India and Russia as an alliance partnership, it has been keen to conduct joint manoeuvres. In October 1999, China and Russia held their first joint naval exercises in the East China Sea. Such an event had not been seen even during the 1950s when China adopted a "lean-to-one" policy of aligning with the Soviet Union. Similarly, for the first time in the history of relations between India and China, the India-China naval exercises took place in November 2003. Now it is the matter of time when the three countries will hold a trilateral exercise.

"Hindi-Chini Buy, Buy"—The Concept of Chindia: The term "Chindia", which refers to the combination of China and India, was coined by the then Indian Minister of State for Commerce Jairam Ramesh in 2004. The fact that India and China declared the year 2006 as the "Year of India-China Friendship" was hailed as a realization of the Chindia concept and the resurrection of "Hindi-Chini Bhai Bhai". The expectation behind this concept was that India and China would emerge as the fastest growing economies and the economic cooperation would act as the driving force and the focal point of bilateral ties.

Growing middle classes in India and China want to consume high quality goods for affordable prices in a secure environment. War and insecurity are not an option for them and if there are conflicts they should be solved peacefully because securing the prosperity of the nation and its citizens through peaceful means is the main objective of the state. Rising trade has itself contributed to an easing of the border issues. For example, China's recognition of Sikkim as part of India enabled an agreement to open the Nathu La and Jelep La Passes in Sikkim as trading links in 2004. Closed since 1962, the Nathu La pass finally reopened in July 2006. However, trade through the pass, once the route for 80 percent of bilateral trade, has been limited, primarily benefiting areas in close proximity to the pass. While the opening of the pass has been broadly interpreted as a goodwill gesture, there is still mutual mistrust. Both sides have placed restrictions on items that can be traded across the pass.

China is one of the largest trading partners of India, but the trade comes with a frustrating deficit for India as it is difficult to sell Indian made products in China, while Chinese goods are flooding the Indian market. India wants to reduce the dominance of primary products and raw materials, like iron ore, in India's export basket by including manufactured goods therein. For India it is very important to solve these issues with China because the trade deficit is a factor in the depreciation of the Indian currency. It has also put enormous pressure on India to attract foreign investment. The trade imbalance shows that India's manufacturing infrastructure is still weak and that Indian manufacturers are not capable to produce high quality goods which consumers like to buy, like their Chinese counterparts. Indian firms are pressuring the Indian government to protect them from Chinese dumping prices. But this policy might backfire and hurt the economy as well as the Indian consumer. The pros and cons of a stronger Chinese engagement in the Indian market is a matter that the Indian government and the Indian public must evaluate themselves. Economic stability and profit are the main motives for India and China to work together. They have signed a draft bilateral investment promotion and protection agreement during President Hu Jintao's visit to India in November 2006. The agreement was one of thirteen trade pacts signed between India and China during the official visit and provides an institutional and legal framework for increased foreign investment flows between them. They have also agreed to encourage cooperation in oilfield bidding and exploration and the development of hydrocarbons in third countries. For example, in Sudan both countries work together—India drills the oil and China provides the infrastructure by building the pipe lines. This is an example where Chindia happens.

It is believed that if India and China join together they would be able to resolve global challenges, such as climate change or energy issues. They are also two of the biggest oil consumers. If they work together they could put great pressure on the oil producing countries along with G7 states. This is the basic concept of Chindia and this term is often used for the possible synergies in the IT sector or business in general, where China produces the hardware (manufacturing) and India provides the software (service).

However, Chindia is not limited to the economic aspect, but is also being applied to broader political issues. It reflects the optimistic expectations about the coming together of India and China, and is seen as a prelude to the emergence of a World Commonwealth. Thus, despite their bitter experiences and differences over disputes, it is believed that India and China will stand together in international affairs as a powerful combination. Indeed, there is a possibility that both countries can enhance cooperation in the establishment of a new international order. A certain convergence of views on the international order enables them to project a distinctive developing countries' perspective on global affairs. On the other hand, their viewpoints on international issues are not always identical or compatible, which also restrains India and China from expanding cooperation.

CHAPTER 1

Agreement between The Republic of India and The People's Republic of China on Trade and Intercourse between Tibet Region of China and India

Peking, 29 April 1954

The Government of the Republic of India and The Central People's Government of the People's Republic of China, Being desirous of promoting trade and cultural intercourse between Tibet Region of China and India and of facilitating pilgrimage and travel by the peoples of China and India, Have resolved to enter into the present Agreement based on the following principles:

1. mutual respect for each other's territorial integrity and sovereignty,
2. mutual non-aggression,
3. mutual non-interference in each other's internal affairs,
4. equality and mutual benefit, and
5. peaceful co-existence. And for this purpose have appointed as their respective Plenipotentiaries:

The Government of the Republic of India,

H.E. Nedyam Raghavan, Ambassador Extraordinary and Plenipotentiary of India accredited to the People's Republic of China;

the Central People's Government of the People's Republic of China, H.E. Chang Han-fu, Vice-Minister of Foreign Affairs of the Central People's Government, who, having examined each other's credentials and finding them in good and due form, have agreed upon the following: Article I The

High Contracting Parties mutually agree to establish Trade Agencies:

1. The Government of India agrees that the Government of China may establish Trade Agencies at New Delhi, Calcutta and Kalimpong.
2. The Government of China agrees that the Government of India may establish Trade Agencies at Yatung, Gyantse and Gartok. The Trade Agencies of both Parties shall be accorded the same status and same treatment. The Trade Agents of both Parties shall enjoy freedom from arrest while exercising their functions, and shall enjoy in respect of themselves, their wives and children who are dependent on them for livelihood, freedom from search. The Trade Agencies of both Parties shall enjoy the privileges and immunities for couriers, mail-bags and communications in code. Article II The High Contracting Parties agree that traders of both countries known to be customarily and specifically engaged in trade between Tibet Region of China and India may trade at the following places.
3. The Government of China agrees to specify (1) Yatung, (2) Gyantse and (3) Phari as markets for trade. The Government of India agrees that trade may be carried on in India, including places like (1) Kalimpong, (2) Siliguri, and (3) Calcutta, according to customary practice.
4. The Government of China agrees to specify (1) Gartok, (2) Pulanchung (Taklakot), (3) Gyanima-Khargo, (4) Gyanima-Chakra, (5) Ramura, (6) Dongbra, (7) Pulang-Sumdo, (8) Nabra, (9) Shangtse and (10) Tashigong as markets for trade; the Government of India agrees that in future, when in accordance with the development and need of trade between the Ari District of Tibet Region of China and India, it has become necessary to specify markets for trade in the corresponding district in India adjacent to the Ari District of Tibet Region of China, it will be prepared to consider on the basis of equality and reciprocity to do so.

Article III

The High Contracting Parties agree that pilgrimage by religious believers of the two countries shall be carried on in accordance with the following provisions: (1) Pilgrims from India of Lamaist, Hindu and Buddhist faiths may visit Kang Rimpoche (Kailas) and Mavern Tso (Manasarovar) in Tibet Region of China in accordance with custom.

1. Pilgrims from Tibet Region of China of Lamaist and Buddhist faiths may visit Banaras, Sarnath, Gaya and Sanchi in India in accordance with custom.

2. Pilgrims customarily visiting Lhasa may continue to do so in accordance with custom. Article IV Traders and Pilgrims of both countries may travel by the following passes and route: (1) Shipki La pass, (2) Mana pass, (3) Niti pass, (4) Kungri Bingri pass, (5) Darma pass and (6) Lipu Lekh pass. Also, the customary route leading to Tashigong along the valley of the Shangatsangpu (Indus) River may continue to be traversed in accordance with custom. Article V For travelling across the border, the High Contracting Parties agree that diplomatic personnel, officials and nationals of the two countries shall hold passports issued by their own respective countries and visas by the other Party except as provided in Paragraphs 1, 2, 3 and 4 of this Article.

3. Traders of both countries known to be customarily and specifically engaged in trade between Tibet Region of China and India, their wives and children who are dependent on them for livelihood and their attendants will be allowed entry for purposes of trade into India or Tibet Region of China, as the case may be, in accordance with custom on the production of certificates duly issued by the local government of their own country or by its duly authorised agents and examined by the border check-posts of the other Party.

4. Inhabitants of the border districts of the two countries who cross the border to carry on petty trade or to visit friends and relatives may proceed to the border districts of the other Party as they have customarily done heretofore and need not be

restricted to the passes and route specified in Article IV above and shall not be required to hold passport, visas or permits.

5. Porters and mule team drivers of the two countries who cross the border to perform necessary transportation services need not hold passports issued by their own country, but shall only hold certificates good for a definite period of time (three months, half a year or one year) duly issued by the local government of their own country or by its duly authorised agents and produce them for registration at the border checkposts of the other Party.

6. Pilgrims of both countries need not carry documents of certification but shall register at the border checkposts of the other Party and receive a permit for pilgrimage.

7. Notwithstanding the provisions of the foregoing paragraphs of this Article, either Government may refuse entry to any particular person.

8. Persons who enter the territory of the other Party in accordance with the foregoing paragraphs of this Article may stay within its territory only after complying with the procedures specified by the other Party. Article VI The present Agreement shall come into effect upon ratification by both Governments and shall remain in force for eight (8) years. Extension of the present Agreement may be negotiated by the two Parties if either Party requests for it six (6) months prior to the expiry of the Agreement and the request is agreed to by the other Party. DONE in duplicate in Peking on the twenty-ninth day of April, 1954 in Hindi, Chinese and English languages, all texts being equally valid.

(Sd.) NEDYAM RAGHAVAN
Plenipotentiary of the Government
of India

(Sd.) CHANG HAN-FU
Plenipotentiary of the Central
People's Republic of China

Notes Exchanged

Peking, April 29, 1954

NOTE: Your Excellency Mr. Vice-FOREIGN MINISTER, In the course of our discussions regarding the Agreement on Trade and Intercourse Between Tibet Region of China and

India, which has been happily concluded today, the Delegation of the Government of the Republic of India and the Delegation of the Government of the People's Republic of China agreed that certain matters be regulated by an exchange of notes. In pursuance of this understanding, it is hereby agreed between the two Governments as follows: (1) The Government of India will be pleased to withdraw completely within six (6) months from date of exchange of the present notes the military escorts now stationed at Yatung and Gyantse in Tibet Region of China. The Government of China will render facilities and assistance in such withdrawal.

1. The Government of India will be pleased to hand over to the Government of China at a reasonable price the postal, telegraph and public telephone services together with their equipment operated by the Government of India in Tibet Region of China. The concrete measures in this regard will be decided upon through further negotiations between the Indian Embassy in China and the Foreign Ministry of China, which shall start immediately after the exchange of the present notes.

2. The Government of India will be pleased to hand over to the Government of China at a reasonable price the twelve (12) rest houses of the Government of India in Tibet Region of China. The concrete measures in this regard will be decided upon through further negotiations between the Indian Embassy in China and the Foreign Ministry of China, which shall start immediately after the exchange of the present notes. The Government of China agrees that they shall continue as rest houses.

3. The Government of China agrees that all buildings within the compound walls of the Trade Agencies of the Government of India at Yatung and Gyantse in Tibet Region of China may be retained by the Government of India. The Government of India may continue to lease the land within its Agency compound walls from the Chinese side. And the Government of India agrees that the Trade Agencies of the Government of China at Kalimpong and Calcutta may lease lands from the Indian side for the use of the Agencies and construct buildings thereon. The

Government of China will render every possible assistance for housing the Indian Trade Agency at Gartok. The Government of India will also render every possible assistance for housing the Chinese Trade Agency at New Delhi.

4. The Government of India will be pleased to return to the Government of China all lands used or occupied by the Government of India other than the lands within its Trade Agency compound walls at Yatung. If there are godowns and buildings of the Government of India on the above mentioned lands used or occupied and to be returned by the Government of India and if Indian traders have stores, godowns or buildings on the above-mentioned lands so that there is a need to continue leasing lands, the Government of China agrees to sign contracts with the Government of India or Indian traders, as the case may be, for leasing to them those parts of the land occupied by the said godowns, buildings or stores and pertaining thereto.

5. The Trade Agents of both Parties may, in accordance with the laws and regulations of the local governments, have access to their nationals involved in civil or criminal cases.

6. The Trade Agents and traders of both countries may hire employees in the locality.

7. The hospitals of the Indian Trade Agencies at Gyantse and Yatung will continue to serve personnel of the Indian Trade Agencies.

8. Each Government shall protect the person and property of the traders and pilgrims of the other country.

9. The Government of China agrees, so far as possible, to construct rest houses for the use of pilgrims along the route from Pulanchung (Taklakot) to Kang Rimpoche (Kailas) and Mavam Tso (Manasarover); and the Government of India agrees to place all possible facilities in India at the disposal of pilgrims.

10. Traders and pilgrims of both countries shall have the facility of hiring means of transportation at normal and reasonable rates.

11. The three Trade Agencies of each Party may function throughout the year.

12. Traders of each country may rent buildings and godowns in accordance with local regulations in places under the jurisdiction of the other Party. (14) Traders of both countries may carry on normal trade in accordance with local regulations at places as provided in Article II of the Agreement. (15) Disputes between traders of both countries over debts and claims shall be handled in accordance with local laws and regulations. On behalf of the Government of the Republic of India I hereby agree that the present Note along with Your Excellency's reply shall become an agreement between our two Governments which shall come into force upon the exchange of the present Notes. I avail myself of this opportunity to express to Your Excellency Mr. Vice-Foreign Minister, the assurances of my highest consideration.

(Sd.) N. RAGHAVAN
Ambassador Extraordinary and
Plenipotentiary of the Republic of India

His Excellency Mr. CHANG HAN-FU, Vice-Minister of Foreign Affairs, Central People's Government, People's Republic of China. April 29, 1954

Your Excellency Mr. AMBASSADOR:

I have the honour to receive your note dated April 29, 1954 which reads: [Not reprinted] On behalf of the Central People's Government of the People's Republic of China, I hereby agree to Your Excellency's note, and your note along with the present note in reply shall become an agreement between our two Governments, which shall come into force upon the exchange of the present notes. I avail myself of this opportunity to express to Your Excellency,

Mir. Ambassador, the assurances of my highest consideration.

(Sd.) CHANG HAN-FU
Vice Minister, Ministry of Foreign Affairs

People's Republic of China.

H.E. NEDYAM RAGHAVAN,

Ambassador Extraordinary and Plenipotentiary, Republic of India.

(Original in English.) NOTES REGAIMING RATIFICATION Peking, the 17th August, 1954

EXCELLENCY, I have the honour to state that WHEREAS an agreement between the Government of the Republic of India and the Central People's Government of the People's Republic of China on trade and intercourse between Tibet region of China and India was signed at Peking on the 29th Day of April, 1954, by the respective plenipotentiaries of the two Governments, namely, For the Government of the Republic of India. His Excellency Nedyam Raghavan, Ambassador Extraordinary and Plenipotentiary of India, For the Central People's Government of the People's Republic of China, His Excellency Chang Han-fu, Which Agreement is reproduced, word for word, in the Annexure hereto,

AND WHEREAS the Government of the Republic of India has ratified this Agreement on the 3rd June, 1954. I request you to convey information of the said ratification to the Central People's Government of the People's Republic of China. I avail myself of this opportunity to renew to you, Excellency, the assurances of my highest consideration.

NEDYAM RAGHAVAN. Ambassador of the Republic of India.

His Excellency Mr. CHOU EN-LAI, Minister for Foreign Affairs, Central People's Government of the People's Republic of China, Peking. (Original in Chinese.)

EMBASSY OF THE PEOPLE'S REPUBLIC OF CHINA IN INDIA (Translation) No. M/680/54 17 August, 1954

EXCELLENCY,

I have the honour to inform you that the Agreement between the People's Republic of China and the Republic-of India on Trade and Intercourse between Tibet Region of China and India, which was signed at Peking on the 29th of April, 1954, by Chang Han-fu, Vice-Minister, Ministry of Foreign Affairs, Central People's Government of the People's Republic of China, for the central People's Government of the people's Republic of China and Nedyam Raghavan, Ambassador Extraordinary and Plenipotentiary of the Republic of India to the People's Republic, of China, for' the Government of the Republic of India, was subsequently ratified on the 3rd June, 1954, by the Central People's Government of the People's Republic of China. I hereby request you to convey information of the said ratification to the Government of India.

The Agreement is reproduced, word for word, in the annexure hereto. I avail myself of this opportunity to renew to you, Excellency, the assurances of my highest consideration.

(Sd.) YUAN CHUNG-HSIEN
Ambassador Extraordinary and
Plenipotentiary of the People's
Republic of China

His Excellency
PANDIT JAWAHARLAL NEHRU,
Minister for External Affairs,
Government of Republic of India,
New Delhi

CHAPTER 2

Trade Agreement between The Republic of India and The People's Republic of China

New Delhi, 14 October 1954

The Government of the Republic of India and the Central People's Government of the People's Republic of China, animated by the common desire to develop trade between the two countries and to strengthen further the friendship that already exists between the Governments and the peoples of India and China have, on the basis of equality and mutual benefit, reached agreement as follows:

Article I

The two contracting parties being desirous of adopting all appropriate measures for the expansion of trade between the two countries agree to give the fullest consideration to all suggestions for the promotion of such trade.

Article II

The two contracting parties agree that all commercial transactions between the two countries shall be carried out in accordance with the Import, Export and Foreign Exchange Regulations in force from time to time in their respective countries.

Article III

The two contracting parties agree to accord, subject to the laws and regulations of the two countries for the time being in force, facilities for the import and export of the commodities mentioned in the attached Schedules "A" and "B".

Article IV

The present Agreement will not preclude the two contracting parties from facilitating trade in commodities not mentioned in attached Schedule 'A' and 'B'.

Article V

The Trade between the Republic of India and the Tibet Region of the People's Republic of China will be conducted in accordance with the provisions of the Agreement between the Republic of India and the People's Republic of China on Trade and Intercourse between Indian and the Tibet Region of China signed in Peking on the 29th April, 1954.

Article VI

The Government of the Republic of India agree that on request by the Government of the People's Republic of China, they will, subject to the regulations in force, accord reasonable facilities for the entry into the Port of Calcutta, and subsequent movement to the Tibet Region of the People's Republic of China, of such commercial goods as cannot be obtained in India. These facilities will be accorded only to goods of Chinese origin.

Article VII

All commercial and non-commercial payments between the Republic of India and the People's Republic of China may be effected in Indian rupees or in pounds sterling as may be mutually convenient. For the purpose of facilitating such payments, the People's Bank of China will open one or more account(s) with one or more commercial bank(s) in India authorised to deal in Foreign Exchange to be called account(s) "A". In addition, the People's Bank of China will, if necessary, open another account with the Reserve Bank of India to be called account "B". All payments between the two countries will be made through account(s) "A". Account "B" will be used only for replenishing the balance(s) in account(s) 'N' whenever necessary. Payments to be made by residents of India to residents of the People's Republic of China will be effected by crediting the amounts of such payments to the above-mentioned account(s) "A". Payments to be made to residents of India by residents of the

People's Republic of China will be effected by debiting the said account(s) "A". The account(s) "A" will be replenished as and when necessary by one of the following methods, namely:

(i) by transfer of funds from another account "A" of the People's Bank of China with another commercial bank, or from account "B" with the Reserve Bank of India;

(ii) by sale of sterling to the bank concerned. Account "B" will be replenished either by sale of sterling to the Reserve Bank of India or by transfer of funds from account(s) "A".

2. Article VII of this Agreement covers the following payments: (i) Payments for the commodities imported or exported under the present Agreement; (ii) Payments connected with commercial transactions and covering insurance, freight (in case of shipments of goods by the ships of either country), port charges, storage and forwarding; (iii) Payments for distribution of films, for incomes and expenses of cultural performances and other exhibitions (iv) Payments of expenses on account of tours of delegations of commercial, cultural, social or official nature; (v) Payments for the maintenance of the Embassy, Consulates and Trade Agencies of the Republic of India in China and for the maintenance of the Embassy, Consulates and Trade Agencies of the People's Republic of China in India; (vi) Other non-commercial payments on which agreement is reached between the Reserve Bank of India and the People's Bank of China.

3. Any balances on the credit side of the account(s) "A" or Account "B" maintained by the People's Bank of China will be convertible on demand into sterling at any time at the usual Bank's selling rate for sterling as fixed from time to time by the Indian Exchange Bank's Association. The above mentioned balances will be convertible into sterling even after the expiry of this Agreement.

4. Payments for Border Trade between the Republic of India and the People's Republic of China, however, will be settled according to the customary practice.

Article VIII

The two contracting parties agree to consult with each other on questions that may arise in the course of the implementation of the present Agreement.

Article IX

This Agreement will come into force from the date of its signature and will remain valid for a period of two years. This Agreement can be extended or renewed by negotiation between the two contracting parties to be commenced three months prior to its expiry.

DONE in duplicate in New Delhi on the fourteenth day of October 1954, in Hindi, Chinese and English languages, all texts being equally authentic.

(Sd.) KUNG YUAN
On behalf of the Government of the
People's Republic of China

(Sd.) H.V.R. IENGAR
On behalf of the Government of
the Republic of India

SCHEDULE A

Goods Available for Export From China to India

1. Cereals. (1) Rice. (2) Cereals other than rice. (3) Green beans. (4) Soyabeans—green and black.

2. Machinery. Including Planning and shaping machines, Drilling Machines, Other machine tools, inclinable notching press, Steam Engines, Harvester, Road Roller (Road Marshall), Electric Pump, Air Compressor, Concrete Mixer, Rock Crusher, Printing Machinery, Moulding Machine, Trandormers, Pump, Motors Electric, Sowers, Gear Grooving machines, Cotton Textile Machinery, Jute Textile Machinery, Telephone Exchange Control, Rubber Insulated Wire, Ventilator, Equipments for Steam Generator, D.C. and A.C. Welder, Medical Apparatus.

3. Minerals. (1) Antimony, Crude and Regulus. (2) Gypsum. (3) Graphite. (4) Fluorspar. (5) Sulphur. (6) Realgar (Munsell). (7) Orpiment. (8) Borax. (9) Naphathalene Refined. (10) Clay. (11) Arsenolite (Arsenic Oxide).

4. Silk and Silk piece goods. (1) White and Yellow Raw Silk, Steam Filature. (2) Spun Silk. (3) Tussah Silk (Wild Silk).

(4) Douppion Silk. (5) Silk piecegoods. (6) Fuji Silk piecegoods. (7) Tussah Silk piecegoods.

5. Animal Products. (1) Wool. (2) Skins and Hides. (3) Duck Feathers, Goose Feathers. (4) Woollen Yam. (5) White Wax. (6) Honey.

6. Paper and Stationery. (1) Newsprint. (2) Mechanical Pulp free printing paper. (3) Packing paper. (4) Stencil paper. (5) Blotting paper. (6) Fountain pen. (7) Pencil. (8) Ink. (9) Printing ink. (10) Numbering machine.

7. Chemicals. (1) DinitrochlorD-Benzene. (2) Sodium Phosphate. (3) Carbolic Acid (Phenol). (4) Potassium Carbonate. (5) Mono-chloro@benzene. (6) 666 Insecticide. (7) Bleaching Powder.

8. Oils. (1) Tung Oil (Wood oil). (2) Cinnamon Oil. (3) Peppermint Oil.

9. Miscellaneous. (1) Camphor. (2) Cassia Laignea. (3) Musk. (4) Nutgall. (5) Aniseed start (start anise). (6) Menthol Crystal. (7) Apricot Kernel. (8) Galangal. (9) Resin. (10) Vegetable Medicinal substances. (11) Hair not. (12) Fluorescent tubes. (13) Paint. (14) Bicycles. (15) Sports goods. (16) Porcelain. (17) Glass and glassware. (18) Printed matter and books. (19) Canned goods. (20) Torch lights. (21) Vacuum flasks. (22) Buttons. (23) Lacquer ware. (24) Fire crackers. (25) Hosiery needles. (26) Stitching needles. (27) Fish and sea products. (28) Dried fruits. (29) Vegetables and vegetable products. (30) Garlic. (31) Vern-deelli. (32) Chinese film (exposed).

SCHEDULE B

Part I

Goods Available for Export from India to China including Tibet

Food Products and Tobacco. (1) Grams, Rice and Pulses. (2) Kyanite Ore. (3) Tobacco unmanufactured.

Raw materials and articles mainly unmanufactured Ores and Concentrates. (1) Chrome Ore. (2) Kyanite Ore. (3) Manganese Ore. (4) Tin and Zinc concentrates.

Oils, Vegetable. (1) Groundnut oil. Oils,

Essential. (1) Lemon grass oil. (2) Sandalwood oil.

Textile and fibre. (1) Cotton raw. (2) Wool raw.

Wood and Timber. Sandal wood. Hides and skins—Raw goat skins and sheep skins of heavier variety and hides and skins tanned. Miscellaneous: (1) Myrobalan and Myrobalan extracts. (2) Paraffin wax. (3) Art Shellac.

Articles mainly manufactured Chemicals, chemical products and drugs and medicines:

(1) Chemicals (Bichromates, Calcium Chloride, Chromic Acid, Glycerine, Magnesium Chloride, Magnesium Sulphate, Naphthalene, Potassium Bromide, Potassium Nitrate, Sodium Bromide, Sodium Sulphide, Sodium Sulphite). (2) Electric lamps. (3) Processed dyes. (4) Shark liver oil. Instruments, apparatus and appliances: (1) Clinical thermometers. (2) Electric lamps. (3) Electric insulating materials. (4) Electro-medical apparatus. (5) Mathematical instruments. (6) Surgical instruments. (7) X-Ray equipment. (8) Telephone. (9) Electric Fans. Machinery: (1) Ball and Roller bearings. (2) Generators. (3) Motors. (4) Textile Machinery including Spindles, ring frames, carding engines, looms and finishing machinery. (5) Boilers. Machine Tools: including Centre Lathe, Drilling Machine, Shaping Machines, Slotting Machines, Planing Machines, Hack sawing machines, Mechanical Power Presses, Lathe Chuks, Drill Chucks, Lathe Centres and Lathe mandrills, Machine Vices, Plain Drill Sleeves, Wood Thiclmess Planers, Round Collects, Acetylene Generators, Round seaming machines, Power operated belt driven guillotine shearing machines, Live Centres, Hand Presses and Foot Presses, Treadle guillotine shearing machines, Plan Milling Machine. Metal manufactures: (1) Aluminium, brass and copper wares. (2) Iron and Steel manufactures excluding containers. (3) Non-ferrous metal products. Textiles: (1) Cotton piece goods and cotton manufactures. (2) Cotton twist and yarn. (3) Flax manufactures. (4) Sisal ropes and twine. (5) Jute manufactures.

Vehicles: (1) Bicycles. (2) Motor Cars. Miscellaneous: (1) Indian films exposed. (2) Light engineering goods: centrifugal pumps, G.I. buckets, hurricane lanterns, sewing machines. (3) Plastic manufactures. (4) Shellac. (5) Mica. (6) Asbestos cement sheets. (7) Cement. (8) Hume pipes. (9) Builder's hardware. (10) Tyres and tubes. (11) Belting for machinery. (12) Paper. (13) Bituminous composition. (14) Agricultural implements. (15) Disinfectants.

Part III

Goods Available for Export From India to The Tibet Region of China

Food Products and Tobacco: (1) Confectionery. (2) Hydrogenated Oil. (3) Timned fruits and vegetables. (4) Cigarettes.

Raw materials and articles mainly unmanufactured Oils, Vegetable: (1) Castor oil. (2) Kardiseed oil. (3) Linseed oil (4) Mustard oil. (5) Nigerseed oil. (6) Rapeseed oil. Textiles-Apparel.

Miscellaneous—Gums other than gum arabic.

Articles mainly manufactured

Instruments, apparatus and appliances: (1) Accumulators. (2) Electric wires and cables. (3) Scientific instruments. (4) Transmission line equipment. (5) Wireless instruments.

Machinery—Control and transmission gear.

Metal manufactures: (1) Bolts and nuts. (2) Enamelware. (3) Wood Screws. Stationery including paper—Paper and stationery. **Vehicles:** (1) Trucks. (2) Carriages and carts. (3) Wheels and shafts for carts. **Miscellaneous:** (1) Candles. (2) Clocks. (3) Coral manufactured. (4) Matches. (5) Soaps and washing powders. (6) Toilet requisites. (7) Lard. (8) Pork. (9) Sugar. (10) Rain coats. (11) Rubber shoes. (12) Reinforcement steel bars. (13) Galvanised iron wire. (14) Barbed wire. (15) Steel plates and sheets. (16) Road Rollers. (17) Gasoline, Kerosene, Diesel and Engine Oils. (18) Galvanized iron sheets, plain and corrugated. (19) Leather and leather goods. (20) Safety razor blades. (21) Biscuits. (22) Rubber manufactures other than tyres and tubes. (23) Sheet glass and glasswares. (24) Sports goods. (25) Hard wood.

LETTERS

No. 1

Government of India Ministry of Commerce and Industry

New Delhi, the 14th October, 1954

Dear Mr. KUNG,

In the course of the discussions that have led to the conclusion of the Trade Agreement between the Government of the Republic of India and the Government of the People's Republic of China, it was agreed that the intentions of the two Governments regarding Article VI and the procedure for its implementation should be placed on record by an exchange of letters.

2. On the basis of equality and mutual benefit, both Governments desire to maintain and develop the existing customary trade between India and the Tibet Region of the People's Republic of China.

3. The Government of the Republic of India appreciate that the Tibet Region of the People's Republic of China may need certain commercial goods that cannot be obtained in India and are, therefore, willing to give reasonable facilities for the clearance of such goods through Calcutta for movement to the Tibet Region of the People's Republic of China, provided the goods are of Chinese origin.

4. It is agreed that the following broad lines of procedure may be adopted for the clearance and movement of the goods mentioned in the preceding paragraphs: (i) With a view to facilitating clearance and transport, the Government of the People's Republic of China will give advance intimation to the Government of India of such goods to be transported to the Tibet Region of the People's Republic of China, in order to ascertain with reference to the availability of such goods in India, whether clearance and movement facilities can be accorded. Matters pertaining to the transportation of such goods will be discussed and settled between the Chinese Embassy in New Delhi and the Government of India. (ii) The goods agreed to be cleared shall, on import, be entered at the Custom House in the Port of Calcutta.

(iii) Subject to the Indian Customs Regulations, and on a deposit being made as required by the Customs Authorities, the goods will be cleared under Customs seal for onward despatch to the Tibet Region of the People's Republic of China by the agreed routes. (iv) The goods will be produced with the Customs seals intact before the Land Customs Officer at the point of final exit and cleared for export to the Tibet Region of the People's Republic of China. (v) The Land Customs Officer will, if the goods are received with seals intact, clear the goods and grant a certificate to that effect. (vi) On presentation of such certificate to the Customs Authorities at the Port of Calcutta, the deposit shall be returned with such deductions for incidental charges as may be mutually agreed upon.

5. This letter and your confirmation will be treated by both Governments as forming part of the Agreement.

Yours sincerely,

H.V.R. IENGAR

His Excellency Mr. KUNG YUAN,

Vice Minister for Foreign Trade and Leader of the Chinese Trade Delegation, New Delhi.

No. 2

New Delhi, the 14th October, 1954

Shri IYENGAR,

I have today received with thanks your letter dated the 14th October, 1954 which reads as follows: (Here follows the text of letter No. 1) I agree to the contents stated in your aforesaid letter on behalf of the Central People's Government of the People's Republic of China. Your letter and this confirmation will be treated as forming part of the agreement.

Yours sincerely,

KUNG YUAN

Shri H.V.R. IYENGAR,

Secretary to the Government of India, Ministry of Commerce and Industry, New Delhi.

No. 3

GOVERNMENT OF INDIA MINISTRY OF COMMERCE AND INDUSTRY

New Delhi, the 14th October, 1954

Dear Mr. KUNG,

During the course of the negotiations which have led to the conclusion of the present Trade Agreement between India and China, both the Delegations recognised that the problems concerning inspection, surveys, shipping, insurance and travel by businessmen should be considered and solved in a practical manner so that the objectives of the Agreement are better achieved and trade relations between the two countries further strengthened. These problems relate to questions of detail rather than of principle and the two Delegations have accordingly agreed to defer the discussion on these matters to a later date. It is hoped that in these subsequent discussions our two Governments will be able to arrive at constructive solutions that will help to encourage and stimulate the smooth flow of trade between our two countries.

2. In the meanwhile, the trade between the two countries will continue to be conducted on such basis as may be agreed upon between the importers and exporters concerned.

3. This letter and your confirmation will be treated by both Governments as forming part of the Agreement.

Yours sincerely,

H.V.R. IENGAR

His Excellency Mr. KUNG YUAN, Vice Minister for Foreign Trade and Leader of the Chinese Trade Delegation, New Delhi.

No. 4.

New Delhi, the 14th October, 1954

Shri IENGAR,

I have today received with thanks your letter dated the 14th October, 1954, which reads as follows: (Here follows the text of letter No. 3) I agree to the contents stated in your aforesaid letter on behalf of the Central People's Government of the People's Republic of China.

Your letter and this confirmation will be treated as forming part of the Agreement.

Yours sincerely,
KUNG YUAN

Shri H.V.R. IENGAR,

Secretary to the Government of India, Ministry of Commerce and Industry, New Delhi.

EXCHANGE OF LETTERS, NEW DELHI, 25 MAY 1957

Embassy of The People's Republic of China in India

New Delhi, the 25th May, 1957.

Dear Mr. RANGANATHAN,

I have the honour to refer to the recent discussions regarding promotion of trade between the People's Republic of China and India when it was agreed that the trade relations between our two countries will continue to be regulated by the terms and conditions embodied in the Trade Agreement concluded on the 14th October, 1954 for a further period ending 31st December, 1958, subject to the substitution of Article VII of the old Agreement by the following Article:

"All commercial and non-commercial payments between the People's Republic of China and the Republic of India may be effected in Indian rupees. For the purpose of facilitating such payments, the People's Bank of China and/or other commercial banks in China will open one or more account(s) with one or more commercial bank(s) in India authorised to deal in foreign exchange. In addition, the People's Bank of China will open another account with the Reserve Bank of India. All payments between the two countries will be made through the account(s) maintained with the commercial bank(s). Payments to be made by residents of India to residents of the People's Republic of China will be effected by crediting Ova amounts of such payments to the above-mentioned account(s) with the commercial bank(s) in India. Payments to be made to residents of India by residents of the People's Republic of China will be effected by debiting the said account(s) with the commercial bank(s) in India. The account(s) with the commercial bank(s) in India will be replenished as and when necessary by one of the following methods, namely:

(i) by transfer of funds from another account(s) of the People's Bank of China or the commercial bank(s) in China with another commercial bank(s) in India, or

(ii) by transfer of funds from the account of the People's Bank of China with the Reserve Bank of India, or

(iii) by sale of sterling to the bank concerned.

The account of the People's Bank of China with the Reserve Bank of India will be replenished either by sale of sterling to the Reserve Bank of India or by transfer of funds from the account(s) of the People's Bank of China or the commercial bank(s) in China with the commercial bank(s) in India.

2. Article VII of this Agreement covers the following payments: (i) Payments for the commodities imported or exported under the present Agreement; (ii) Payments connected with commercial transactions and covering insurance, freight (in case of shipments of goods by the ships of either country), port charges, storage and forwarding expenses and bunkering; (iii) Payments for distribution of films, for incomes and expenses of cultural performances and other exhibitions; (iv) Payments of expenses on account of tours of delegations of commercial, cultural, social or official nature; (v) Payments for the maintenance of the Embassy, Consulates and Trade Agencies of the People's Republic of China in India and for the maintenance of the Embassy, Consulates and Trade Agencies of the Republic of India in China; (vi) Other non-commercial payments on which agreement is reached between the Reserve Bank of India and the People's Bank of China.

3. Any balance in the Rupee account maintained by the People's Bank of China with the Reserve Bank of India will be convertible on demand into sterling at the usual Banks selling rate for sterling as fixed from time to time by the Indian Exchange Banks' Association. The above-mentioned balance will also be convertible into sterling after the expiry of this Agreement.

4. Payments for Border Trade between the People's Republic of China and the Republic of India, however, will be settled according to the customary practices." The new Article VII will come into force with effect from the 1st July 1957. I shall be glad if you will please confirm that the above correctly sets out the understanding reached between us.

Yours sincerely,

Sd/- PAN T'zu-Li

Ambassador Extraordinary and Plenipotentiary of the People's Republic of China to India.

Shri S. RANGANATHAN, I.C.S.

Secretary to the Government of India,

Ministry of Commerce and Industry, New Delhi.

Government of India Ministry of Commerce and Industry

New Delhi the 25th May, 1957

Dear Mr. PAN Tzu-Li,

I write to acknowledge the receipt of your letter dated May 25, 1957, which reads as follows: (Not reproduced) I confirm that the foregoing correctly sets out the understanding reached between us.

Yours sincerely,

(Sd.) S. RANGANATHAN
Secretary to the Govt. of India

H.E. Mr. PAN TZU-LI,

Ambassador Extraordinary and Plenipotentiary of the People's Republic of China, New Delhi.

Government of India Ministry of Commerce and Industry

New Delhi, the 25th May, 1957

Dear Mr. TU YU-YUN,

In the course of discussions which we had recently regarding further development of trade between the People's Republic of China and India, it was agreed that the Government of the

People's Republic of China will encourage the State Trading Corporations of China to establish and strengthen contacts to the extent practicable with the State Trading Corporation of India in those commodities which are handled by the State Trading Corporation of India. I shall be grateful if you would kindly confirm that the foregoing correctly sets out the understanding reached between us.

Yours sincerely,

(Sd.) K.B. LALL
Joint Secretary to the
Government of India

Mr. TU YU-YUN,
Counsellor for Commercial Affairs,
Embassy of the People's
Republic of China, New Delhi

Embassy of The People's Republic of China in India

New Delhi, 25th May, 1957

Dear Mr. LALL,

I have the honour to acknowledge the receipt of your letter of today's date which reads as follows: (Not reproduced)

I confirm that the foregoing correctly sets out the understanding reached between us.

Yours sincerely,

(Sd.) Tu YU-YUN
Counsellor for Commercial Affairs,
Embassy of the People's
Republic of China in India

Shri K.B. LALL
Joint Secretary to the Government
of India, Ministry of Commerce and
Industry, New Delhi

TRADE AGREEMENT EXTENSION (1959) EXCHANGE OF LETTERS, 25 MAY 1959

Government of India Ministry of Commerce and Industry

New Delhi, May 25, 1959

Dear Mr. TU YU-YUN,

With reference to Article IX of the Trade Agreement between the Republic of India and the People's Republic of China concluded on the 14th October, 1954 and the recent discussions regarding the promotion of trade between the two countries, I have the honour to say that the two contracting parties have agreed that the present Trade Agreement as modified by the letters exchanged on the 25th May, 1957, shall remain valid up to the 31st December, 1959.

Yours sincerely,

(Sd.) K.B. LALL
Additional Secretary to the
Government of India

MR. TU YU-YUN
Counsellor for Commercial Affairs,
Embassy of the People's Republic of
China, New Delhi

Embassy of the People's Republic of China in India

New Delhi, May 25, 1959

Dear Mr. LALL,

With reference to Article IX of the Trade Agreement between the People's Republic of China and the Republic of India concluded on the 14th October, 1954 and the recent discussions regarding the promotion of trade between the two countries, I have the honour to say that the two contracting parties have agreed that the present Trade Agreement as modified by the letters exchanged on the 25th May, 1957, shall remain valid up to the 31st December 1959.

Yours sincerely,

(Sd.) Tu YU-YUN Counsellor
for Commercial Affairs

(Sd.) MR. KB LALL, I.C.S.
Additional Secretary to the Government
of India, Ministry of Commerce and
Industry, New Delhi

CHAPTER 3

Protocol between the Governments of India and China Regarding the Handing over of Postal, Telegraph and Public Telephone Services in the Tibet Region of China

Lhasa, 1 April 1955

In accordance with the provisions of sub-paras (2) and (3) of the notes exchanged between His Excellency Chang Han-Fu, Vice-Minister of Foreign Affairs of the People's Republic of China and His Excellency Nedyarn Raghavan, Ambassador Extraordinary and Plenipotentiary of the Republic of India accredited to China, on the occasion of the signing at Peking on 29 April 1954 of the agreement between the People's Republic of China and the Republic of India on trade and intercourse between the Tibet region of China and India, and the negotiations held subsequently between the Foreign Ministry of China and the Indian Embassy in China on the concrete measures to be taken for the handing over to the Government of China, by the Government of India, of the postal, telegraph and public telephone services with their equipment, operated by the Government of India in the Tibet region of China without compensation as a gesture of friendship and the twelve rest houses with their equipment of the Government of India in the Tibet region of China at a mutually agreed price. Mr. Yang Kungsu, Foreign Affairs Assistant to the Representative of the Government of the People's Republic of China in Tibet, had appointed Mr. Yin Fa-Tang and Mr. P.N. Menon, Consul-General of India, Lhasa, had appointed Mr. S.L. Chhibber to jointly proceed with the work of counting the above mentioned postal, telegraph and public telephone services with their equipment and the rest houses with their equipment and also to appraise the value of the equipment of the rest houses.

During the period from 10 December 1954 to 3 March 1955, the officials on both sides completed the counting and appraisal work and on 3 March 1955, signed at Gyantse, the general lists showing the details on the above mentioned and counted postal, telegraph and public telephone services with their equipment, and the rest houses with equipment, as well as the negotiated price of the equipment of these rest houses. The general lists are attached to this Protocol and form an integral part of it. The People's Republic of China and the Republic of India agree that, from the date of the signing of this Protocol by the representatives of both sides, the entire postal, telegraph and public telephone services with their equipment and the rest houses with their equipment formerly operated by the Government of India in the Tibetan region of China are handed over by the Government of India to the Government of China, and become the possessions of the Government of China. The People's Republic of China have appointed Mr. Yang Kungsu, Foreign Affairs Assistant to the Representative of the Government of the People's Republic of China in Tibet, and the Republic of India have appointed Mr. P.N. Menon, Consul-General of India, Lhasa, to sign this Protocol on behalf of their respective Governments, thus concluding both the handing over and taking over work.

DONE in duplicate, in Lhasa, on the 1st day of April 1955, in the Chinese and English languages, both texts being equally valid.

CHAPTER 4

Press Note on The New Arrangements Regarding India-Tibet Travel

New Delhi, 17 April 1955

In pursuance of the provisions of the Sino-Indian Agreement on the Tibetan region of China of 29 April 1954, it is proposed to establish a system of trans-border travel on certificates issued by the Ministry of External Affairs. The object of imposing this system of travel with certificate instead of passport is to maintain the customary pattern of trade between India and the Tibet region of China. In the case of pilgrims and customary trans-border traffic and petty trade, however, no certificates will be required.

Details of the new arrangements are:

1. Traders from India known to be customarily and specifically engaged in trade between the Tibet region of China and India, their wives and children who are dependent on them for livelihood and their attendants will be allowed entry for purposes of trade into the Tibet region of China, in accordance with custom, on the production of certificates. Porters and mule team drivers from India, who cross the border to perform necessary transportation services, shall also be required to have certificates. The Ministry of External Affairs are making arrangements to issue these certificates in places which are easily accessible. Full details of the issuing authorities will be published by the State Governments shortly. All check-posts along the border which lie on the routes used for customary border trade will issue certificates. Arrangements have also been made to station photographers at these check-posts so that photographs can be taken on-the-spot and supplied to individuals free of cost for affixing on the certificate.

2. Traders, who hold the certificates, can visit the following trade marts in Tibet: Yatung, Gyantse, Phari, Gartok, Taklakot, Gyanima-Ebargo, Gyanima-Chakra, Ramura, Dongbra, Poling, Nabra, Sangtse and Tashigong.

3. Pilgrims from India of Lamaist, Hindu and Buddhist faiths may visit Kailas and Manasarovar in the Tibet region of China in accordance with custom. Pilgrims customarily visiting Lhasa may continue to do so in accordance with custom. The pilgrims need not carry documents of certification but shall register at the border check-post, in the Tibet region of China and receive a permit for pilgrimage.

4. Traders and pilgrims are required to travel by the following passes and route:

I. Shipki La Pass

II. Mana Pass

III. Niti Pass

IV. Kungri Bingri Pass.

CHAPTER 5

Communist China's Role in Non-Communist Asia[1]

National Intelligence Estimate, USA, 3 December 1957

THE PROBLEM

To examine Communist China's activities in non-Communist Asia and the impact of these activities on the non-Communist countries of the area, and to estimate the future role and influence of Communist China in Asia during the next five years or so.

SUMMARY AND CONCLUSIONS

1. Communist China's already powerful impact on non-Communist Asia will probably increase, although only gradually, over the next few years, unless there is a serious crisis within China, a major change in the world situation, or a substantial increase in the strength of the factors which work against Peiping's aspirations.

2. Asia is impressed by the progress which the Chinese Communists have made in developing their economy and increasing their military power. Most Asian governments believe that the Communist regime is firmly in control of the country and growing in strength. The countries of the area, whether firmly anti-Communist or neutralist, take possible Chinese Communist reactions into consideration when making major policy decisions.

3. Against the background of power which Peiping is able to project, many Asian countries are susceptible to its varied appeals and pressures. Communist China will continue to pose

1. Non-Communist Asia as used in this estimate Includes: Japan, Korea. Nationalist China, Philippines, Vietnam, Laos, Cambodia, Malaya, Singapore, Indonesia, Thailand, Burma, India, Nepal, Pakistan, Ceylon. Hereinafter non-Communist Asia is referred to as Asia.

as the champion of peace and economic development and to identify itself with the wide-spread anti-Western prejudices which arose out of colonial experience. Many Asian leaders have an intellectual sympathy for Marxist economic concepts. Many believe also that in their underdeveloped countries there is no feasible alternative to state planning and financing of major economic development. In these circumstances, there is a tendency to be more tolerant of the Communist economic system even when there is recognition of and opposition to its excesses.

4. On the other hand, there are important factors which work against Peiping's aspirations. Many Asian leaders dislike Communism, fear Communist China and mistrust its intentions. The most important factor limiting the expansion of its influence is the presence of the US in Asia as an opposing force, supplying elements of strength which the free nations still lack. Another major factor will be the degree of success of non-Communist governments in achieving a level of economic, political, and social progress acceptable to their people.

5. For the most part, the present leaders of Asia value their hard-won independence and recognize the ultimate threat of indigenous and Chinese Communism. They are seeking—with varying degrees of skill and energy—to satisfy the needs and potential pressures for social and economic betterment without sacrificing the basic values of their own cultures. Although the various Asian countries will react differently to Communist China in accordance with their varying backgrounds and interests, those that are not firmly anti-Communist are more apt to continue on or to take the road to neutralism than the road to affiliation with Peiping. Among such countries there will probably be an increase in contacts with Peiping, which will enhance the prestige of Communist China.

6. Although Communist China's military strength will almost certainly increase, we believe that it will refrain from using military means to achieve its objectives in Asia so long as its leaders believe that this would result in effective US military counteraction. Rather they will seek to expand their power and influence in Asia, and to reduce that of the US, through

which confronted them. Furthermore, insurrectionary activities, external aggression, and Communist subversion have at one time or another disrupted the internal development of most of them. As a result, economic, political, and social progress has been far below their expectations.

13. Most Asian governments have tended to follow a paternalistic or authoritarian approach in their efforts to cope with these problems. Because private capital, domestic or foreign, is not available to build the basic economic structure (power, transportation, etc.) required for industrial development, they have concluded that government must provide planning, management, and funds. Many leaders have been strongly influenced by Marxist doctrine. Furthermore, they tend to associate capitalism with colonialism. These attitudes, together with the Asian traditions of authoritarian and communal organization of society, create a certain susceptibility to the efforts of Moscow and Peiping to increase their influence.

14. Communist economic achievements in China have impressed many Asian leaders; the economic problems and certain development techniques of Communist China appear to them to have greater relevance to the situations in their underdeveloped countries than do those of the West. In addition, there is a disposition among certain Asian intellectual elements to contrast unfavorably the immense difficulties being experienced in their own societies with the cohesion and sense of national purpose which in their view exist in Communist China.

15. However, the appeal of the Communist solution is tempered by opposition to the excesses inherent in the Communist system. Many Asian leaders believe that they can achieve economic progress by their own methods. Even where the appeal of democracy is not strong, the determination of the ruling groups to maintain their own positions is an important deterrent to the growth or internal Communist influence.

Anti-Colonialism and Nationalism

16. Nationalism in most of Asia bas drawn its force largely from a reaction to colonialism. Most of the present leaders of the new states of Asia were leaders of the struggle for independence.

Many of them attribute their country's present backwardness to Western exploitation and have bitter memories of discriminatory treatment during the colonial period. Generally speaking, their experiences have been with Western and not with Communist colonialism. This predisposes them to believe Communist explanations of imperialism. Antagonisms arising from race and color are mingled with the resentments that survive from the colonial period. Communist China, by stressing that it is an Asian country and by propagandizing its own experiences with Western exploitation, at times can capitalize on the colonialism and nationalism issues. Although these both remain important factors which can work to Communist China's advantage, there are indications that nationalism in Asia is becoming less motivated by virulent anti-colonialism and based more upon indigenous values and objectives. Such a change could increase the importance of nationalism as an obstacle to Communist China's direct influence in Asia.

The East-West Struggle and Neutralism

17. One of the important factors in Asia is the East-West struggle and the pressure it exerts on Asian states which would like to concentrate on their own problems. Although there is an undercurrent of apprehension regarding Communist China's real intentions, a desire to stand aside from the world's strife, while not universal, is widespread and in some countries is translated into a policy of neutralism. Most Asian states fear that war between the major powers would inevitably embroil them and jeopardize their hopes of progress if not destroy their independence. These neutralist sentiments are reinforced by sensitivity on the subject of nuclear war. In this setting, Peiping's tranquilizing call for "peace" is more appealing than US reminders that continued national independence requires alertness and sacrifice.

18. There are small but quite influential groups of Asians (particularly in intellectual circles) who are prone to make unfavorable comparisons between the Western and the Communist countries. Some of them consider that the West is crass, materialistic, and contemptuous of the aspirations of the Asian races, while they look upon the citizens of the Communist

countries as dedicated and self-sacrificing toilers for progress. Even in the more numerous groups that regard Western ideas of political democracy as superior to Communism, there are a considerable number who habitually judge Western actions by Western criteria, which they do not apply in their assessment of Communist behavior. The application of this double standard often gives to the Communists, and withholds from the West, the benefit of the doubt in the interpretation of events.

The Presence in Asia of Major Military Forces

19. Both the West and the Sino-Soviet Bloc have major military forces in the Asian area. This confrontation reinforces the Asian concern over the danger of war and its destructiveness. Furthemore, the fact that Communist China has the strongest Asian military force has led some states to seek to placate Peiping. At the same time, many Asians, including even some neutralists, recognize the value of strong us forces as a major deterrent to Communist aggression. Six Asian countries have entered into alliance with the US, and these countries, especially, are highly sensitive to indications of any change in US capability and intention to stand firm against Communist encroachment in Asia.

Sino-Soviet Alliance

20. Communist China's ability to exert influence in Asia is also affected by its relations with the USSR. Soviet economic assistance programs and diplomatic efforts in Asia, together with the visits of its top leaders, have supported the general Communist line and thus indirectly enhanced Communist China's position. Peiping has benefited from Soviet actions to the extent that they create the image of Communist "peaceful" intentions, as for example, Moscow's simple call for "ban the bomb"; but bas been harmed to the extent that Soviet aggressiveness, as in Hungary, disillusions Asian observers. On balance, we believe that Communist China's prestige in Asian eyes has been enhanced by its association with the USSR and by its recognized position within the Bloc.[2]

2. The Director of Intelligence and Research, Department of state, believes that most: Asian leaders dislike the Soviet political system and

Local Communist Movements in Asia

21. The existence of indigenous Communist parties or movements in Asian countries provides an important auxiliary channel for implementing of Chinese Communist policies. However, because of their real or assumed links with Peiping, these parties and movements have at times worked to the disadvantage of Communist China's current strategy of peace and coexistence, especially when they have resorted to political agitation or military action.

The Overseas Chinese

22. The large Overseas Chinese communities in many of the Southeast Asian countries represent both an asset and a liability to Peiping. In most of these countries, Overseas Chinese control much of the commercial activity and play an important role in financial and industrial fields. As a result, they exercise influence and power disproportionate to their numbers and provide points of contact for Chinese Communist trade and subversive activities. Peiping has met with considerable success in inducing the return of Overseas Chinese students in Southeast Asia to the mainland. Of the Overseas Chinese that have any feeling of involvement in the future of China, more probably tend to identify themselves with Communist China than with Taipei. However, a substantial majority, because of their p1imary concern with business activities and with maintaining good working relations with their host country, has sought to avoid entanglement in the political activities of both communist and Nationalist China.

---

are aware that the ultimate objectives of international Communism are inconsistent with their own objectives. This attitude is to some degree reflected In their thinking on Communist China, particularly when that country, as in the past year, has repeatedly expressed its support of the soviet Union. This reaction to communist China's close association with the Soviet Union is only partially balanced by other factors such as possible feeling of vicarious pride in Peiping's stature In the bloc. Accordingly, it is believed that the last sentence should read: "On balance, we believe that Peiping's self-Identification with the Soviet Union and its policies has probably tended to work to Peiping's detriment in the achievement of its Immediate objectives in non-Communist Asia."

23. Local antagonism to Overseas Chinese, due to their economic position and their insistence on maintaining their separate identity, poses some obstacles to the extension of Peiping's influence. In particular, many governments are concerned that increased Chinese Communist activity within their country will aggravate the problem posed by the existence of these unassimilated Chinese communities. The Overseas Chinese would become an important asset to Communist China only in case they became convinced that a successful Chinese Communist military invasion was imminent and that they had no alternative but to declare their allegiance to the homeland. In these circumstances, the Overseas Chinese would acquire importance as a "fifth column."

Non-Communist Strength and Influence in Asia

24. Although Western political control has virtually disappeared from Asia during the past decade, Western influence and commitments remain in the area and are important factors limiting the expansion of Communist China's influence. Western aid was essential to the countering of the Communist threat to Korea, Taiwan, Vietnam, Malaya, and the Philippines. Aid from the US and, to a lesser extent, from other Western countries, sustains a number of Asian states and seeks to improve their strength and stability so that present vulnerabilities in their societies will diminish. More Asian leaders are coming to feel that accepting US aid is not inconsistent with maintaining the independence of the recipient state, but in fact often gives it sufficient strength to take increasing, independent initiative in the conduct of its affairs. Furthermore, trade with the West is an important factor in sustaining the economies of most non-Communist Asian countries.

25. The Chinese Communists must also take into account the strength of non-Communist elements in the various countries. In South Korea, Taiwan, the Philippines, South Vietnam, and Japan, the governments and large portions of the population are vigorously anti-Communist. The governments of Thailand, Malaya, and Pakistan have also followed anti-Communist policies both externally and internally. South Korea and the Republic of China have large and relatively well-equipped

military forces. Even the neutralist governments of South and Southeast Asia, while prone to support certain Communist foreign policy positions, have sought, with the present exception of Indonesia, to weaken the position of native Communists.

26. The existence of Nationalist China has continued to hamper Peiping's efforts to extend its influence. Competition with the GRC for Overseas Chinese loyalties sharpens Communist China's dilemma of having to demonstrate its interest in the Overseas Chinese at the same time that it seeks to underplay this interest in its relations with the host governments. The fact that five Asian countries recognize Nationalist China and three additional countries have adopted the policy of recognizing neither Nationalist nor Communist China restricts Peiping's diplomatic activities.

27. Peiping's leadership aspirations are hampered by the present or potential influential roles which India and Japan are capable of playing. However, the aspirations of New Delhi and Tokyo appear to be defined in terms more limited than those of Peiping: i.e., India in terms of moral and political leadership rather than domination; Japan as a principal industrial and commercial power in Asia.

Exclusion from the UN

28. Communist China's exclusion from the UN has provided Peiping and Moscow with a significant propaganda point among those Asians who, like the Indians, believe strongly that Peiping should represent China in the UN and that only US intransigence prevents this. On balance, however, we believe Peiping's continued exclusion from the UN has worked to the disadvantage of Peiping's Asian ambitions. Although claiming to be a leading member of the Asian-African bloc, Communist China is forced to sit on the sidelines during discussions of important issues in the UN, which has become an increasingly important forum for the Asian states.

Chinese Communist Tactics in Asia

29. The Communist indigenous armed revolutions, which were initiated in the years just after World War II, have failed in Indonesia, Burma, Malaya, and the Philippines, and fell

short of success in Vietnam. Especially since the conclusion of hostilities in Indochina in 1954, Peiping, in line with the shift in international Communist tactics, has ceased to stress "national liberation movements" and has sought, by pursuing a generally non-violent line, to exploit Asian vulnerabilities and desires for neutrality and peace. To this end, it has developed a diverse tactical arsenal, including diplomacy, "people's diplomacy," propaganda, subversion, military pressures, and economic inducements.

30. There is little evidence concerning the division of responsibilities between Moscow and Peiping in directing and supporting Communist activities in Asia, or the balance which exists between external Communist direction and local Communist initiative. Soviet influence has appeared to be superior in most of the Asian Communist movements, with the exception of Malaya and Thailand, though there are indications which suggest that Peiping's influence within the Asian Communist parties is increasing. In any event, Moscow and Peiping appear in the main to be in close accord regarding the Communist campaign in Asia, whether their efforts involve the local Communist groups or are aimed more directly at the non-Communist countries.

Diplomacy

31. Peiping has placed considerable stress upon attempts to achieve formal diplomatic recognition as the sole government of China and has attempted to create an atmosphere of normalcy in its relations with the six non-Communist Asian countries that have recognized it.[3] It has placed considerable emphasis

3. Peiping is recognized by six non-Communist countries in the Asian area: Burma, Ceylon, India, Indonesia, Nepal, and Pakistan. Of these states, only Nepal has recognized Peiping since the initial flurry of recognitions in 1949-1950. The Republic of China 18 recognized by five countries of the area: Japan, Korea, Philippines, Thailand, and Vietnam. Laos and Malaya have been extended recognition by both Peiping and Taipei, but have diplomatic relations with neither. In addition, Peiping has an economic mission and Taipei a consulate in Cambodia, which officially recognizes neither the GRC nor the Peiping regime.

on the exchange of official visitors between states. In particular, the leaders of many South and Southeast Asian countries have traveled to Peiping and have been visited at least once in return by Premier Chou En-lai. Communist China has made political capital of its stated willingness to negotiate at any time with any state, the us included.

"People's Diplomacy"

32. Peiping has supplemented its conventional diplomacy by an extensive program of "people's diplomacy," designed both as an entering wedge for the establishment of full diplomatic relations and as a means of in creasing its influence in countries with which it already has official relations. To these ends, it has sponsored the exchange of delegations of all types: cultural, scientific, economic, religious, ethnic, educational, athletic, journalist, and civic.

33. Despite the many demands on it: stringent budget, Peiping bears most of the expenses of these exchanges. In 1956, according to Peiping, about 60 Chinese Communist groups visited Asian countries and over 150 groups, totaling perhaps 2,000 persons, came from non-Communist Asia to visit Communist China. On occasion these groups signed agreements relating to trade, labor, fisheries, and "friendship." Of the Asian countries, Japan has received the greatest attention. Approximately 1,200 Japanese visited Communist China in 1956, including such diverse representatives as coal miners, theatrical performers, former imperial army and navy officers, and members of the Japanese Diet.

34. Widespread sponsorship of front organizations in Asia is an important aspect of "people's diplomacy." "Chinese Friendship Societies" now exist in many Asian countries, as do "National Peace Councils" which take their directives from the Communist World Peace Council. Exploitation of religious groups and Asian students, including offers of scholarships and other inducements, is another facet of "people's diplomacy."

35. "People's diplomacy" has proved to be an effective instrument. Susceptible visitors often accept Peiping's claims, most notably in the field of economic development. Foreign

delegations are flattered by the availability of Mao Tse-tung, Chou En-lai, and other high officials, who grant an unusual number of time-consuming interviews and appear well briefed on the composition and interests of the group in question. Although some Asian visitors have voiced criticisms of the Peiping regime, many have publicly registered their favorable impressions of the regime's effective administration and economic progress. Even the visits of some confirmed anti-Communists have been exploited, either because they were impressed with what they saw in China, or were themselves persons whose very presence contributed to furthering Peiping's aims.

Propaganda

36. Closely allied with "people's diplomacy" is Communist China's propaganda effort throughout Asia. Peiping's propaganda broadcasts have doubled in volume since 1955, and are presently made in English, Spanish, Chinese, and a variety of other Asian languages. Chinese Communist literature and films are calculated in many countries of the area. Peiping often underwrites the costs of locally written publications. Visiting Chinese delegations and cultural or theatrical groups are part of the total propaganda effort.

37. Propaganda efforts to exploit and encourage Asian neutralism are centered largely on the "five principles" which were first proclaimed in their present form in a Chinese Communist-Indian agreement of 1954: "Mutual respect for each other's territorial integrity and sovereignty, mutual nonaggression, mutual noninterference in each other's internal affairs, equality and mutual benefit, and peaceful coexistence." These "five principles" have widespread appeal in Asian countries because they hold out a promise of peace and friendly relations. In recent years, Peiping's propaganda has refrained from criticism of the Asian neutrals or their domestic policies, and has sought to minimize apprehensions concerning Communist China's ultimate intentions in Asia.

Economic Inducements

38. Communist China has achieved considerable political gain from its relatively small foreign trade, and has made

effective propaganda use of the few grants it has extended.[4] More importantly, it has created a growing impression in many Asian countries that closer economic relations with Communist China would be profitable. At present Communist China is not capable of exporting large quantities of manufactured goods to the Asian markets nor does its economic policy call for the importation of large quantities of the products which most countries of Asia have available for export. However, it probably will increase its trade, and it will in any case continue to import such commodities as rubber, cotton, jute, and coconut oil.

39. Communist China has on several occasions been able to gain considerable political advantage from well-timed economic agreements, such as its rice for rubber deal with Ceylon in 1952. Moreover, Peiping has sought, through the negotiation of trade agreements, participation in trade fairs, and the despatching of trade missions to Asian countries, to create an impression of growing economic power and a benevolent attitude. Since 1954 it has concluded trade agreements with Burma, Ceylon, India, Indonesia, and Cambodia, expressing, in the main, a desire to expand trade of mutual benefit and exchanging "shopping lists" of the prominent exports of each country. A gradual increase in its maritime capabilities will facilitate Communist China's ability to derive political advantages from commercial activities.

40. Japan needs raw materials which Communist China could furnish and Is seeking to develop additional markets for its own exports. The Chinese Communist regime has attempted to capitalize on this situation by vague offers of grand scale economic collaboration. These offers are linked with political conditions and ate part of the Chinese Communist effort to neutralize Japan. In Peiping's series of unofficial trade agreements with private Japanese business groups, it has sought to weaken Japan's adherence to CHINCOM controls by offering such commodities as coal and iron ore, which Japan must import in large quantities, in exchange for restricted goods. However,

4. Communist China has recently extended economic aid grants to Cambodia (US $22,400,000 in goods), Nepal ($12,800,000 in goods and currency), and most recently Ceylon ($15,750,000, in lieu of continued preferential prices for rubber.)

most Japanese recognize the vital importance of trade with the US and would be reluctant to take steps which would jeopardize this trade.

Subversion

41. Peiping appears to be employing a wide variety of subversive tactics which range from covert operations, designed to assist local Communists to overturn governments, to support of overt front groups, designed merely to influence opinion in favor of local or Chinese Communist causes. Working through Overseas Chinese, Peiping's subversive efforts include economic pressures, the underwriting of front groups, penetration of schools and labor organizations, and the direction of espionage and clandestine operations. The Chinese Communists also provide funds and covert support to indigenous Communists and Communist sympathizers to help them build good will and mass voting strength for the Communist cause and to infiltrate government bureaucracies and armed forces. However, Peiping is not adverse to bypassing or undercutting the Asian Communist parties where other tactics promise to better advance Peiping's over-all objectives.

42. The Chinese Communists have used the Bank of China as an instrument to increase their influence, especially among Overseas Chinese. Peiping controls the branches in Hong Kong, Singapore, Kuala Lumpur, Penang, Surabaya, Djakarta, Calcutta, Bombay, Karachi, Rangoon, and Chittagong. These banks use their assets to finance pro-Communist political groups, front organizations, publications, and schools. They make low interest loans to those who favor Communist causes or are willing to follow the Communist line, and they use defaulted loans as a means of political blackmail. The Burmese government has become alarmed by the activities of the Rangoon branch of the Bank or China and has taken steps to reduce its effectiveness.

Military Pressures

43. Although now pursuing a "peaceful" line, Peiping has employed military pressure in pursuit of its goals. In addition to its pressures against the Offshore Islands, its military assistance to North Vietnam, and its intervention in Korea, Peiping has

made military incursions into poorly defined areas of its borders with Burma and the Indian sub-continent, and has continued to train and assist the North Korea and the North Vietnam armed forces. Furthermore, Peiping has probably given some monetary and training support to the armed rebellions in Malaya and Burma. However, the principal pressure in this field is the widespread recognition that communist China's growing military strength is already greater than all non-Communist Asian forces put together. The proximity of this military strength has served to reinforce neutralism in such countries as Burma and Laos and has led to a wish to avoid antagonizing Communist China even in some countries aligned with the West. Sensitivity to Communist China's military strength will remain high in Asia as Chinese Communist ground, air, and naval forces continue to obtain modern equipment and to improve in efficiency.

The Impact of Communist China on Asia

44. Communist China is now regarded throughout Asia as a major Asian power. Most Asian leaders probably believe that the Communist regime has established firm control over its 635 million people and that it will continue to rule the country for the foreseeable future. Furthermore, they appear to believe that Communist China has made substantial progress toward establishing a modem industrial economy and has developed the strongest Asian military establishment. The Chinese Communists have been able, by the tactics discussed above, to impress most Asians with the magnitude of their accomplishments and to play down the extent and nature of their sacrifices and internal difficulties.

45. Asian nations, particularly in South and Southeast Asia, look upon Communist China with a mixture of admiration for its accomplishments and fear of its size, power, and dynamism. Peiping has exploited colonial, nationalist, and imperialist issues at the international level, has emphasized the problems it shares with other underdeveloped Asian countries, and has asserted its willingness to help them. It has succeeded in obscuring its external objectives by directing Asian attention to the similarity between its own economic and social aspirations and those of

most Asian countries—to end poverty and illiteracy, to raise the standard of living, and to press forward with programs of economic development.

46. Furthermore, since the Indochina armistice, Communist China has posed, with considerable success, as a country which is seeking Its objectives by peaceful means. The fluctuating tensions arising over the Taiwan Strait appear to many Asian leaders to spring not so much from the truculence of Communist China as from its desire to regain control of its own territory. The peaceful appearance of the Chinese Communist has been enhanced by the many Communist inspired "peace" movements and calls for banning of nuclear weapons.

47. In all Asian states there is a fundamental desire to work out their national destinies without outside interference. This has placed certain limits on the expansion of Peiping's influence. Although the Asian states are, in varying degrees, susceptible to outside guidance and willing to accept foreign aid, none of them regard themselves as followers of any foreign leader. Asian or otherwise.

Impact of Communist China on Specific Countries

48. The impact of Communist China in Asia, as reflected in official governmental policies, varies widely from country to country. Furthermore, in most Asian countries there are groups—political, economic, and ethnic—whose reactions to Communist China differ from those of their governments. In some instances these groups have sufficient strength and their views of Communist China are at such variance with the official policies of their governments that, over the longer run or in periods of crisis, they might force a change in present official policies.

49. *The Republics of China, Korea, and Vietnam*: The GRC and the Korean government both view Communist China as an aggressor and a direct threat to their existence. They both feel that military action will ultimately be required to remove this threat. The GRC denies that the Peiping regime is stable or that it enjoys popular support. Taipei considers itself in direct competition with Peiping for the loyalties of the Overseas Chinese

and for international recognition as the legitimate government of China. Vietnam views Communist China chiefly in terms of Peiping's support of North Vietnam and consequently actively seeks to prevent any extension of Chinese Communist influence.

50. *Thailand, Philippines, and Pakistan*: Although all these countries are members of SEATO, their primary motives for lining up with the West differ.

(a) Thailand views Communist China as a potential military threat and is suspicious of the loyalty of its large Overseas Chinese minority. In the postwar period, in the Thai view, there has been safety and profit in alignment with the West. Although the Thai government has not altered its official policies, Communist China's growing economic and military might, its proximity to the Thai borders, and its current line of peaceful coexistence are beginning to have a significant impact in. Thailand. There is a growing desire for at least limited economic and cultural contacts with Communist China. There has been some increase in neutralist sentiment, and growing reluctance to follow foreign policies directly antagonistic to Communist China.

(b) The Philippines aligned itself with the West because of its historical association with the West and its close relations with the US. It views the Peiping regime as a somewhat remote threat and has no particular desire for contacts with Communist China.

(c) Pakistan's alignment with the West appears to have been motivated in the first instance by its desire to obtain weapons to counter the threat which it believes is posed by India, and only secondarily by the dangers of external Communist aggression. To the extent the latter is recognized, Pakistan is more apprehensive concerning possible Soviet action than Chinese Communist. It attributes its growing Communist problem in East Pakistan to Indian, rather than to Chinese, influences. Pakistan is impressed by Communist China's material accomplishments and, despite its membership in SEATO, maintains a friendly posture toward Peiping.

51. *Japan*: Japan tends to view the long-range Communist threat more in terms of the USSR than Communist China. Because of Japan's close and deeply-rooted cultural and other ties with the China mainland, most Japanese tend to regard the Peiping regime as more Chinese than Communist, and do not consider that the Chinese Communists pose a direct threat to Japan itself. Pressures for closer relations with Peiping, particularly for increased trade, are strong and are increasing. On the other hand, Japanese conservative leaders, though impressed by Communist China's material accomplishments, are beginning to show concern at the buildup of a rival industrial power in Asia; they are becoming particularly disturbed over the threat of Chinese Communist economic competition in South and Southeast Asia. While they have little faith in the durability of the Nationalist government on Taiwan, most responsible Japanese leaders believe that Communist control of the island would threaten Japan's security. Despite the attraction of the continent, the Japanese generally recognize the primary importance of their defense and economic ties with the US and the West; fear that these ties may be jeopardized inhibits them from seeking too close a relationship with the Chinese Communist regime.

52. *Laos and Cambodia*: Both these countries feel the impact of Communist China's proximity, although Laos tends to regard North Vietnam as a more immediate threat to its independence. The Royal Lao government is preoccupied with the Pathet Lao problem and will continue to view its relations with Communist China in terms of that problem. The Cambodian government has adopted a policy of nonalignment. Although it accepts aid from the US and does not want to lose the protection it enjoys as a result of the SEATO protocol, most of its leaders view Communist China with considerable awe and admiration and have encouraged numerous contacts, including trade and ald. However, they oppose Communism within Cambodia as a threat to their position, and they are fearful of any increased Chinese Communist influence in their country, especially among the Overseas Chinese.

53. *India, Ceylon, and Nepal*:

(a) India, the most important and influential of the unaligned Asian countries, takes a conciliatory attitude toward Communist China and plays up Peiping's professions or peaceful intent. India believes it is thus carrying out its self-assigned mission of reducing international tensions by mediating between the Bloc and the West. It hopes also to contain possible Communist Chinese expansionist aims by putting Peiping on record against aggression and interference in other countries' affairs. Indians feel an affinity for Communist China as a fellow Asian nation which has rid itself of foreign encroachment and which is now facing problems similar to those of India. Indian leaders were concerned by Chinese Communist activities in Nepal, in Tibet, and along the Burma border; many Indian leaders apparently believe that Communist China presents a possible long-range security threat to India. The Indian government has quietly been devoting considerable attention to improving India's strategic and political defenses in the northeast and to strengthening India's position in Nepal, Sikkim, and Bhutan. Indian leaders currently think of themselves as competing with Communist China in the field of economic development, and they emphasize New Delhi's efforts to progress economically by democratic means in contrast to Peiping's totalitarian methods.

(b) Ceylon's attitudes toward Communist China are based on a feeling of remoteness from any aggressive threat from Communist China and on the profitable trade relationship which has developed between the two countries. Ceylon bas shown a marked willingness to increase its cultural and economic ties with Communist China since the Bandaranaike government came to power in Ceylon in 1956.

(c) Nepal has been increasingly receptive to Communist China's stepped up overtures as a counterweight to Indian attempts to influence Nepali affairs. The trend was reversed when the Singh government came to power in July 1957 and adopted a policy of closer ties with India and tactful de-emphasis of the relationship with China. However, Singh was ousted in November, and continuing political instability may provide opportunities to Peiping to increase its influence there.

54. *Burma*: The Burmese government maintains an official position of neutrality. However, its outlook is affected by fear of Communist China's strength, proximity, and ultimate aims, and by a belief that it can best preserve its independence by not antagonizing Peiping. As Communist China's strength glows, the Burmese leaders tend to count more and more on the protection afforded by the US presence in Asia, but they do not admit this publicly. Burma's attitudes toward Communist China are clouded by the border dispute between the two countries, by its problems with Communist insurrectionists, by growing left-wing opposition, and by Overseas Chinese problems.

55. *Indonesia*: Indonesia's governmental leaders, particularly Sukarno and his immediate entourage, are greatly impressed by the economic achievements and the apparent unity and purpose in Communist China. A number of them view the Indonesian Communist Party (PKI) as an important and comparatively respectable nationalist group and have sought its support. Sukarno in particular desires to adapt certain features of Chinese Communism to Indonesian problems and to bring the PKI into the government. Although most Indonesian leaders feel then country is not immediately threatened by Chinese Communist aggression, there are political leaders, parties and groups who oppose Sukarno's views and who identify the PKI with international Communism. Moreover, there is some conce1n with Peiping's possible hold over the Overseas Chinese minority and with the activities of the Chinese Communist embassy among this group. If the PKI is successful in its efforts to gain power in Indonesia by parliamentary means, an added impetus would be given to Communist movements throughout Asia and the general prestige of Communist China would be enhanced, even though the PKI's success was achieved Without visible assistance from Peiping.

56. *Malaya*: The newly independent Malayan government views Communist China almost entirely in terms of its long struggle against the Communist insurrection and the problems created by a large, unassimilated Chinese population. It is especially fearful of the impact Communist China may have among Malaya's Overseas Chinese who have begun to compete politically on a more nearly equal basis with the slightly larger but economically backward Malay community. It desires to minimize contacts with communist China, except for a certain amount of trade conducted through Hong Kong, or any forms of Chinese Communist influence which would aggravate these problems. It is also fearful that Chinese Communist influence and infiltration in Singapore may threaten its own security.

57. *Singapore*: The Crown Colony of Singapore is approximately 85 percent Chinese. Consequently, both the UK and the present Singapore government are especially concerned with the Impact of Communist China and have taken strong measures to repress left-wing and Communist-front political, labor, and student organizations. However, significant pro-Peiping sentiment continues to exist in the Chinese population of Singapore and there will almost certainly be continuing opportunities for Chinese Communist subversion.

Future Trends

58. Assuming that there is no outbreak of war directly involving Communist China, the Chinese Communist regime probably will remain in firm control of the mainland of China, will continue to direct its resources and energies largely to internal problems, and will achieve some degree of progress in economic development. Its military capabilities will almost certainly increase as it improves the efficiency, arms and equipment of its ground forces, continues to develop its air force, and expands its naval and maritime capabilities. However, Communist China will probably refrain from overt military aggression so long as its leaders believe that this would result in effective US military counteraction against the mainland.

59. Under these conditions and assuming no drastic changes in US policy or in the intensity or character of the struggle

between the Communist and non-Communist worlds, we believe that over the next few years the already powerful impact of Communist China on Asia will continue to increase, although only gradually. The presence of the US in Asia will continue to be the major factor damping down the growth of Peiping's influence and obstructing Peiping's efforts to translate its growing prestige into specific action, such as diplomatic recognition or admission to the UN. There are many other factors which may counteract the impact of Communist China. One of particular importance would be the success of non-Communist governments in achieving a level of economic, political, and social progress acceptable to their people. In any event, we believe that there will be an increase in Peiping's cultural and economic relations with other Asian countries, which will enhance its prestige. With respect to the two most important countries of the area, India is unlikely to make any significant change in its policy toward Communist China as long as Nehru heads the government; Japan, although moving toward an increase of officially approved trade and cultural relations, is likely to stop short of any over-all rapprochement that would jeopardize its relations with the US. Nevertheless, we believe that five years hence the weight of Communist China on Asia and its ability to influence developments in the area will have increased somewhat.

60. Any modification of US policy which was interpreted in Asia as tending toward a significant softening of US constancy and firmness in opposing Communist China would enhance Peiping's prospects for expanding its influence. This would be particularly true if such modification resulted in a significant weakening of US military capabilities against Communist China. Likewise a substantial eduction in US support and assistance to Asian countries would probably be interpreted as a lessening of US interest in the destiny of the countries affected and would increase economic difficulties in these countries. This would, in varying degrees, enhance Communist China's prospects.

61. A significant change in the intensity of the East-West struggle could have important effects. If the Sino-Soviet Bloc dropped its general line of peace and coexistence in Asia and became bellicose and threatening, we believe that throughout

Asia there would be a general re-examination of national positions and of the relative power positions of the US and of the Sino-Soviet Bloc. There would probably be a clearer demarcation of Communist and non-Communist influence in Asia, although not necessarily along present lines. For example, Thailand especially is sensitive to trends in the relative strengths of the major powers in the Far East and might shift to neutralism if its leaders concluded a war of uncertain outcome was imminent. Burma, on the other hand, might seek increased ties with the West.

62. If Communist behavior is such that tensions in the Far East are substantially reduced, most Asian countries, except Nationalist China, Korea, and Vietnam, would probably cautiously relax their present suspicions of Peiping and move gradually toward broader contacts and normal diplomatic relations with Communist China. This, in time, would enlarge Peiping's ability to influence these countries.

63. Major developments within Communist China could also affect the impact of Communist China in Asia. A serious and prolonged crisis on the mainland would impede Peiping's efforts by undermining its pose as a progressive and dynamic state, while a marked improvement in conditions would, on the other hand, enhance Peiping's prestige. Moreover, serious economic and political difficulties in any of the Asian countries would increase its vulnerability to Peiping's blandishments, while an improvement in internal stability would have an opposite effect.

CHAPTER 6

Sino-Indian Relations

National Intelligence Estimate, USA, 17 May 1960

THE PROBLEM

To assess Sino-Indian relations and their international implications.

CONCLUSIONS

1. Sino-Indian border clashes have shattered the appearance of cordiality between the two states. Early agreement on the boundary dispute is unlikely. However, both sides are probably willing to live with the present stalemate for some time, although further border clashes may occur. In the event of a prolonged failure to re solve the dispute, the climate could alter significantly, particularly if Nehru leaves the scene before a settlement. Nevertheless, we are inclined to believe that an eventual settlement could be achieved probably involving Indian concessions in Ladakh in return for Chinese recognition of India's claims in the North East Frontier Agency (NEFA). However, even if the border issue is settled, it is unlikely that the friendly relations which existed in the past can be fully restored. (*Paras*, 5-81, 16-25)

2. Peiping's moves have sharply increased anti-Chinese sentiment in India. They have also tended to create in India a more sympathetic view of US policies, though India remains dedicated to the principle of nonalignment, and will also be influenced by interest in continued large scale Soviet aid and by some hope that the USSR will restrain Communist China. The position of the Indian Communist Party has been made more difficult, but it has not suffered a critical setback. (*Paras*, 11, 14-15, 27-28)

3. To date Communist China has outstripped India in economic growth. The present wide gap in growth rates is expected to narrow, but the absolute disparity between the economies will probably continue to widen. As a result China will be able to maintain—and probably increase—its military superiority over India. However, as long as India is making significant economic progress, most Asian countries will probably continue to derive encouragement from India's example. (*Paras*, 26, 34)

4. Communist China's growing strength and its aggressiveness have caused a more somber assessment of Chinese Communist motivations among Asian leaders. Even if the Sino-Indian border dispute is resolved through negotiations, the more apprehensive Asian view of Communist China that has recently developed probably will not be erased. Nevertheless, it is likely that Communist China's strength and dynamism and its ambitions for political hegemony will figure more prominently in Asia than will India's influence. (*Paras*, 33, 35)

DISCUSSION

I. DEVELOPMENT OF SINO-INDIAN RELATIONS

5. The Tibetan revolt and the border clashes which took place during 1959 precipitated a crisis in Sino-Indian relations and forced both countries to re-examine their policies toward each other.

6. Communist China's leaders have long regarded the Indian Government as a bourgeois regime with which there could be no permanent cooperation. However, they considered that India was not ripe for Communist revolution and sought to take advantage of India's policy of nonalignment and of its support for a larger role for Communist China in world affairs. Peiping regarded this policy as profitable since it demanded little of Communist China beyond lip service to peace, Sino-Indian friendship, and Asian solidarity.

7. India's attitude toward Communist China reflected the belief that good relations between the two were essential for the peace of Asia. Most Indian leaders initially regarded the Chinese Communists as more Asian than Communist in outlook, and welcomed their revolution as a major step in Asia's resurgence.

Nehru hoped that by befriending China, supporting its admission to the UN, and publishing assurances of Peiping's peaceful intent—as in the case of the *Panch Shila* (Five Principles of Peaceful Coexistence)—the likelihood of Chinese expansionism could be reduced and its ties to Moscow lessened. India also surrendered the special rights in Tibet which it had inherited from British India, and recognized Tibet as part of China.

8. Nevertheless, India bad somc suspicions of Chinese intentions, particularly after the occupation of Tibet in 1950-1951. Recognizing its military weakness vis-a-vis Communist China, India sought to protect itself by obtaining assurances of an autonomous status for Tibet and by negotiating new treaties with Nepal, Bhutan, and Sikkim aimed at insuring India's primacy in those areas. India's misgivings increased steadily after 1956 because of the hardening of Peiping's policy, as indicated by its support of the USSR in the crushing of the Hungarian revolution and the execution of Nagy, by Chinese attacks on Yugoslavia, by the abrupt termination of the brief "hundred flowers" period of liberalism, and by the imposition of the communes. Indian leaders were also disturbed by Peiping's continued publication of maps showing as part of China large areas claimed by India.

The Border Conflict

9. A border dispute was inherent in the absence of a jointly recognized boundary and the inability of either side to make a clear-cut case for its border claims.[1] However, until

1. The 110-mile Sikkim-Tibet border is the only part of the 2,400-mlle Sino-Indian frontier that has been demarcated. In the east, the dispute concerns the North East Frontier Agency (NEFA) in Assam State, an area of about 30,000 square miles inhabited by about 700,000 primitive tribesmen. India claims that the border in this area is the McMahon Line, which generally follows the Himalayan watershed. This line was drawn at the 1914 Simla Conference by representatives of the United Kingdom, Tibet, and China, but the Simla agreement was not ratified by the Chinese Government. China—both Communist and Nationalist—claims that the boundary is at the southern edge of the Himalayan foothills. Although Chinese maps show about 1,300 square miles in eastern Bhutan adjoining NEFA as Chinese, Chou En-lai stated in New Delhi In April 1960 that Peiping bad no claims on Bhutan.

1959 when the seriousness of Communist China's claims first became clear to India, the issue was largely quiescent and both countries attempted to keep it from public view. Neither India nor Communist China had felt much sense of urgency in settling the issue, since the territory was sparsely occupied, difficult of access, and only partially administered. Communist China occupied Sinkiang and Tibet in 1950-1951, and soon established military garrisons near the frontier and built roads to improve its position. India reacted by establishing some new frontier posts and constructing some new roads into the frontier lands, although it did little to strengthen its military forces in the border areas. In 1954, the Indian Government formed the North East Frontier Agency (NEFA) and placed it under direct central government control, in part for reasons of defense. In 1956-1957, the Chinese built a road across northeastern Ladakh. All of these moves brought some officials and troops of each country into regions claimed by the other and made an overt dispute almost inevitable.

10. The outbreak of the Tibetan revolt in early 1959 caused China to take rapid and ruthless action to put it down. Peiping, regarding Tibet as an internal Chinese problem and suspicious that the revolt was being supported by India, gave little thought to Indian sensibilities. Chinese accusations that the Indians had imperialist designs on Tibet increased in scope and intensity, particularly after the Dalai Lama was granted asylum in India. The number of Communist troops in the frontier area was expanded and the Himalayan passes occupied in an effort both to stop the outward flow of refugees and to prevent any inward

In the west the dispute centers on the 10,000 square mile Aksai Chin plateau In the Ladakh region of Kashmir State. This area, which lies between the Karakoram and Kunlun Ranges, is desolate and uninhabited. Both India and communist China base their claims on the "traditional" border which, however, has never been identified by treaty.

There are also several small disputed areas totaling several hundred square miles along the frontier between Ladakh and Nepal. The 1954 Sino-Indian agreement on Tibet specifies that certain passes will be open to travelers, but China claims this agreement has no bearing on the location of the border.

flow of arms and armed rebels. India, alarmed by increasing numbers of Chinese troops on its frontier, strengthened its units in the border areas, where they met the Chinese patrols. Border clashes were followed by the first formal presentation of Peiping's territorial claims and by an exchange of public accusations.

II. REPERCUSSIONS OF THE DISPUTE IN INDIA

11. Peiping's actions resulted in a sharp up surge of anti-Chinese sentiment in India. Most educated Indians were sharply disillusioned, and vigorous demands for a strong Indian stand were made in Parliament and the press. The failure of Nehru's policy of befriending Communist China caused a noticeable decline in his prestige, and public pressure encouraged him to harden his position against the Chinese. While he retains great prestige, he is unlikely again to enjoy the virtually unquestioned power to direct India's foreign policy.

12. The Chinese threat has enhanced the position of the Indian military forces. The entire Sino-Indian frontier has been placed under army control, and a retired Chief of Staff has been named Governor of Assam. Military leaders have been assured that resources will be provided for strengthening border defenses. Despite the increased authority accorded to the military, the government has made it clear that there will be no diminution of civilian control While there is likely to be some friction between the military and the government as long as Krishna Menon remains as Defense Minister, the military leaders have a basic respect for the principle of civilian control and are unlikely seriously to challenge it.

13. The deterioration of Sino-Indian relations will affect the goals—and possibly the progress-of the Indian economic effort. Indian leaders believe that success in meeting the long-term Chinese threat requires increased emphasis on industrialization—particularly heavy industry and defense production—in India's development program. Additional funds win almost certainly be expended for expansion and modernization of the Indian military forces[2] and for development of the border areas. While

2. An Increase of $73 million in defense expenditures is planning for the FY 1961 budget.

the amount of these increases probably will be small in relation to India's total expenditures, they will place additional burdens on the Indian economy.

14. The initial failure of the Communist Party of India (CPI) to support India's position in the border dispute not only intensified the antagonism of non-Communists toward the CPI but also sharpened dissensions within the party itself. The moderate faction of the CPI eventually pushed through a compromise "patriotic resolution, but factionalism will continue to weaken the party. In addition, the Indian Government, although unlikely to out-law the CPI, will almost certainly keep it under greater surveillance.

15. Nevertheless, communism in India probably has not suffered a critical setback. The prestige of the Soviet Union, which has maintained a neutral stand on the border dispute, remains high. The CPI itself cannot be written off. It is still the best organized and most capably led of the opposition groups. Recent local elections indicate that its popular base has probably not been seriously damaged. Finally, India's unsolved social and economic problems will continue to provide many potential supporters for the party.

III. THE FUTURE OF SINO-INDIAN RELATIONS

16. Although New Delhi has been shocked by the extent of Communist China's truculence, it apparently remains convinced of the desirability of maintaining amicable relations with Peiping. Nehru has stressed that India will rely on diplomatic methods to settle the border dispute. Although any further Chinese incursions will probably be forcibly resisted, Nehru will almost certainly continue to reject extremist demands that India use force to eject the Chinese from Indian-claimed territory.

17. Chinese communism is highly nationalistic, and the regime will not sacrifice what it considers important Chinese interests in order to improve relations with India. Nevertheless, Peiping probably believes that continuation of a militant policy toward India would force India toward closer relations with the West and further damage Communist China's prestige in Asia. In addition, China probably hopes that India will continue to

press for broader international acceptance of Communist China. Thus China will continue to seek negotiations over the border dispute and a general improvement in Sino-Indian relations.

The Border Negotiations

18. The Chou-Nehru talks of April 1960 apparently made no material progress, although discussions are to continue at a lower level. Considerations of national prestige on both sides will limit the bargaining freedom of both countries. In addition, there is strong public sentiment in India against any territorial concessions. Nehru's position will be further complicated by the recent decision of the Indian Supreme Court that New Delhi cannot transfer Indian territory to another country without a constitutional amendment. Thus we believe that an early settlement is unlikely.

19. Despite the failure of the recent negotiations we believe that each side wishes to damp down the dispute. Hence we believe that both sides will be willing to live with the present undefined condition of stalemate for some time.

20. In the event of a prolonged failure to resolve the dispute, the climate could alter significantly. Further border clashes may occur, and the firmness of New Delhi's position could become an issue in the 1962 Indian general election. If Nehru leaves the political scene before the dispute is settled, a successor Indian government would probably take a basically harder line. Nor can it be assumed that Peiping will maintain indefinitely a conciliatory posture in the face of a continued adamant stand by India on its claims.

21. Nevertheless, each country has strong reasons to desire a resolution, and we are inclined to believe that an eventual settlement could be achieved. The general outline of such a settlement has already been foreshadowed. Communist China almost certainly will not yield control of the strategically important trans-Ladakh road, which provides the only feasible link from Xinjiang to western Tibet. Northeastern Ladakh lies beyond India's natural defense boundary, a fact admitted by Indian military leaders. Hence India will probably be willing eventually to concede Chinese control of this area.

22. In return, India will insist on the abandonment of Chinese claims on the area of the NEFA, which India regards as vital to its defense. The Chinese have already that they are prepared, as part of a general settlement recognizing their claims in Ladakh, to accept a border which substantially follows the McMahon Line. Once agreement has been reached on Ladakh and NEFA, agreement on the smaller areas—if not already reached—probably would follow.

23. A border agreement would not solve India's frontier problems. The actual demarcation would take a number of years in view of the rugged terrain involved, and there would be many disputes over details. Moreover, China will probably attempt to subvert the border peoples, most of whom are culturally and ethnically closer to the Tibetans than to the Indians. Yet India probably will be able to limit Chinese subversion and maintain control of its border areas.

Nepal, Bhutan, and Sikkim

24. Chinese Interest in Sikkim and Bhutan appears to be peripheral, and Peiping will probably avoid directly challenging India's primacy in them. On the other hand, the Chinese are likely to continue active competition with India for influence in Nepal, and the tendency of Nepal to try to play off one side against the other will probably continue to cause problems in Sino-Indian relations.[3]

Border Issues

25. Even if a border agreement is achieved, it is unlikely that the friendly relations which existed in the past can be fully restored. Peiping undoubtedly calculates that it is less able to exploit its relations with India to its own advantage. India recognizes more clearly that the two countries have divergent interests, but will probably continue to support Peiping on various matters, for example the UN seat. However, neither country will forget the disputes over the Tibetan issue and the border. Moreover, as time passes, India will probably become increasingly aware of the long-term problem it faces in

3. See NIE 65-59, "The Outlook for Nepal, Bhutan, and Sikkim," dated 24 November 1959.

Communist China's growing economic and military power and its political ambitions.

26. Communist China has outstripped India in economic growth to date. China's gross national product increased about twice as rapidly as that of India during their first five-year plans, and the difference in growth rates has been even greater in the past several years. Communist China probably will be unable to maintain its recent very high rate of growth, however, and India's rate of growth is likely to increase somewhat. Thus the wide gap between Chinese and Indian growth rates is expected to narrow. Nevertheless, the absolute disparity between the two economies will probably continue to widen, and Communist China will increasingly overshadow India in tennis of industrial output and general economic self-sufficiency. As a result China will be able to maintain—and probably increase—its military superiority over India and probably will also be able to play a more influential role in the economic life of other Asian countries.

IV. REPERCUSSIONS ELSEWHERE

Indian Relations with the West and with the USSR

27. Chinese aggressiveness has tended to create among Indian leaders a more sympathetic view of US opposition to Communist China. There is probably also some greater appreciation of the value of a strong Western—particularly US—position in Asia to counterbalance China. India also remains acutely conscious of its need for Western economic aid. However. Nehru has no intention of altering India's basic policy of non-alignment, and the bulk of Indian opinion apparently still shares his attachment to this policy.

28. India's willingness to cooperate more closely with the West will also be limited by a hope that the USSR will restrain Communist China, although Indian leaders are aware that there are limits on Soviet ability and willingness to influence Peiping. The neutral position adopted by the Soviet Union on the border dispute indicates that the USSR has been perturbed by the crudeness if not the substance of China's actions. The USSR is likely to continue to urge the two countries to seek a negotiated

settlement of the issue. In addition, the extent of India's willingness to cooperate with the West will also be limited by a reluctance to jeopardize continued Soviet economic aid.

Indian Relations with Pakistan

29. The deterioration of Sino-Indian relations has increased Indian interest in improving relations with Pakistan. President Ayub's concern over the growth of Soviet influence in Afghanistan has had a corresponding effect in Pakistan. During recent months, most of the border disputes between India and Pakistan have been resolved, and some progress has been made toward settling longstanding financial disputes. In addition, the problem of dividing the waters of the Indus River system appears to be moving toward a solution. On the other hand, no settlement of the important Kashmir issue is in sight.'[4] The continuation of this dispute, combined with Nehru's continuing adherence to nonalignment, make it likely that Nehru will continue to reject Ayub's call for a joint defense agreement. India has, however, moved one division from the Pakistani to the Communist Chinese border, and there is likely to be further deployment of troops away from the Indian-Pakistani border if outside pressures on the subcontinent grow.

Impact on other Asian Countries

30. Developments in India and China and the relationships between these two giants of Asia are bound to affect their Asian neighbors. This is particularly true in Southeast. Asia, which historically has been a meeting place of Chinese and Indian influences.

31. Among the uncommitted nations of Asia, India's prestige has been high as a result of its prominent role in the UN, its strong stand against imperialism and colonialism, its efforts to promote world peace, and Nehru's international stature. However, those Asian nations aligned with the west have considered Indian foreign policy dangerously weak.

---

4. Indeed the Kashmir quarrel may be complicated by Pakistan's insistence that India has no right to yield to Communist China any territory in Ladakh, which is part of Kashmir.

32. These pro-Western countries view Communist China's growing strength with profound alarm. On the other hand, the uncommitted nations have taken some vicarious pride in China's development as a symbol of Asian importance in world affairs. They have been both attracted and repelled by the Chinese Communist revolution and by the rapid growth of Chinese economic and military power. Following India's lead, they have sought comfort in China's professions of peaceful intent and respect for its neighbors' independence as set down in the *Panch Shila* and reiterated in the Bandung principles.

33. Communist China's ruthless suppression of the revolt in Tibet and its aggressive actions on the Indian border have stimulated more somber assessments of China's underlying motivations. Although there are varying views of the immediacy of the threat, all the Asian countries are aware of China's subversive potential and are sensitive to growing Chinese strength and truculence. Fear of China has led some uncommitted nations to make accommodations in their policies in order to avoid irritating Peiping. This tendency has not been so strong, however, as to cause these nations to yield on matters which they considered to be of vital importance to them. (A recent illustration is Indonesia's firmness in restricting the activities of overseas Chinese merchants despite Peiping's protests.) Even if the Sino-Indian border dispute is resolved through negotiations, the more apprehensive Asian view of Communist China that has developed during the past two years probably will not be erased.

34. As long as India makes significant economic progress, most Asian countries are likely to derive encouragement from Indian ability to maintain economic growth without sacrificing traditional values. Nevertheless, many younger Asians are impatient for rapid national progress and are searching for economic growth, if coupled with an image of rapid Chinese advances, might greatly aid Communist subversive efforts. The Asian countries will, however, be more influenced by their ability to move forward under economic organizations of their own devising than by impressions concerning the relative progress of Communist China as compared to India.

35. Many factors other than the nature of Sino-Indian relations and the relative strength of the two countries will affect Asian trends in the coming years. Nevertheless, it is likely that Communist China's strength and dynamism and its ambitions for political hegemony will figure more prominently in Asia than will India's influence.

Chapter 7

Short-Term Outlook and Implications for the Sino-Indian Conflict

National Intelligence Estimate, USA, 9 November 1962

SUMMARY AND CONCLUSIONS

With China's recent attacks on India's northern border, the Sino-Indian quarrel has become a serious military struggle. While fighting is likely to continue, we believe the conflict will remain essentially confined to the disputed border areas at least for the near future. The conflict is already causing a change in India's foreign and domestic attitudes favorable to the West, and the USSR's prestige in India has diminished. Nevertheless, India is unlikely to abandon nonalignment as such, and will continue to look to both East and West for assistance in its vast economic development program. Pakistan sees any military strengthening of India as a threat to its security and would react strongly against a major Western program to modernize and re-equip the Indian military establishment.

THE ESTIMATE

I. Development of The Crisis

1. Ever since the first clash between Indian and Chinese forces in 1958, India has been devoting considerable efforts to strengthening its position along the entire border. Roads and trails in the Himalayas have been improved and expanded, air transport capacity increased, and growing numbers of Indian troops stationed at key locations on the border. Increasingly confident of its ability to deal with the situation, India, in the spring of 1962, set out to establish new forward posts in Ladakh behind Chinese outposts, though in Indian-claimed territory. While these provoked strong Chinese protests, Peiping's actions

in the area were restrained. By mid-summer, however, Indian leaders became extremely concerned that they had overextended themselves, and Nehru openly spoke about renewed discussions with the Chinese on the border dispute. The outcry in India against this course was so strong, however, that he was in effect forced to abandon any practical steps toward negotiations.

2. Despite their concern about possible clashes in Ladakh, Indian leaders felt relatively safe in strengthening India's position in the North East Frontier Agency (NEFA). In the discussions on the border dispute held between India and Communist China during 1960, Peiping had made it reasonably clear that it was prepared to respect—though not recognize—the McMahon Line.[1] Indeed, China had even indicated its willingness to abandon its claims in NEFA if New Delhi would relinquish its claims in Ladakh. To strengthen its position in NEFA, India sent troops slightly north of the location of the McMahon Line as shown on all but the latest Indian maps. The Indians claimed that the true location of the line-which in general follows the Himalayan watershed—was in fact north of the position on earlier maps. They also asserted with more vigor their determination to expel the Chinese from Indian territory.

3. Peiping resisted these deployments of Indian troops, and clashes of increasing severity occurred. Commencing on 20 October, the Chinese initiated large-scale attacks against Indian positions in NEFA and occupied substantial territory. In addition, virtually all of India's advance outposts in the Ladakh region of Kashmir have been overrun. Heavy fighting resulted in total Indian casualties of about 5,000, about half of whom are killed and missing. Chinese propaganda has lashed out at Nehru and Krishna Menon in terms usually reserved for US and Chinese Nationalist leaders. Despite the military reverses it has suffered, New Delhi has rejected the terms of China's cease-fire offer by demanding that Chinese troops must withdraw to their September positions before any talks are possible. The Chinese, for their part, have refused any cease-fire requiring them to evacuate the posts they have seized in Ladakh.

1 The McMahon Line was the result of a British, Chinese and Tibetan convention in 1914, ratified by the UK and Tibet, but not by China.

II. Dimensions of the Conflict

4. In the immediate border areas of dispute, Communist China had a distinct military advantage over India.[2] Chinese units held the initiative and were better trained and equipped with more suitable weapons. In both NEFA and Ladakh they were positioned in bases on the Tibetan and Sinkiang plateaus with only a short ascent necessary to penetrate the outer Indian positions, since Chinese roads in Tibet approach to within a few miles of their initial attack positions. Conversely, India's original approaches to the border were over much more rugged terrain relying on a rudimentary road and trail system. Supply to a large proportion of Indian forces, particularly in the NEFA area, was limited to air drop or porter carry of several days. However, as the Chinese advance and the Indians retreat, Peiping's advantage lessens. The Indians have fallen back to positions that can be supplied by jeep trails or roads while the Chinese must traverse rugged terrain and rely on trails for resupply.

5. While Peiping has announced that, Chinese forces will no longer respect the "illegal McMahon Line," Communist China's ultimate intentions in the conflict are uncertain. In Ladakh, a primary Chinese intention is to protect the very important Tibet-Sinkiang road which they have built across the disputed territory. The Chinese advances have pushed the Indians out of virtually all Chinese-claimed areas up to the natural barrier of the main Karakoram Range. Further deep penetrations would involve the Chinese in supply and terrain problems almost as difficult as those that face the Indians. In NEFA, the numbers of troops in combat are far larger than in Ladakh. The Chinese have taken the important area around Tawang and made advances in the Walong area, on two of the key approaches to the Assam plains. The Chinese may aim to occupy further areas of NEFA in order to strengthen their military position and perhaps to use as a bargaining counter for use in any future negotiations.

6. While still desirous of limiting the conflict, the Indians are heavily committed to reversing the tide of battle and eventually ousting the Chinese from Indian-claimed territory. Present

2. See Military Annex.

Indian strategy is to hold the Chinese advance through the winter while preparing for a counter offensive in the spring. To this end the Indians are building up their forces along the entire frontier. However, strains are becoming increasingly evident on the transport net serving north-eastern India, and there will continue to be supply problems at the front. If the Chinese advance continues, India's civilian leaders may feel compelled to reverse their decision against carrying out air attacks on Chinese positions and supply lines. However, New Delhi will be reluctant to do so because of the danger of further escalation and because of fear that the Chinese would bomb Indian cities in retaliation.

III. The Outlook

7. In an attempt to portray a "reasonable" attitude, the Chinese have called for an end to the current conflict and have proposed that both sides withdraw 20 kilometers from the line of control as of 1 November 1959. As this would represent an Indian concession to the extensive Chinese claims in Ladakh, it is unlikely that the two sides will reach agreement in the near future. Unless a political settlement is reached, fighting will almost certainly continue in both Ladakh and NEFA, as both sides jockey for position. While the Indians probably will try to regain some of their lost territory, they are unlikely to make much progress in the face of superior Chinese manpower and position. In particular, the Chinese are almost certainly determined to hold the Tawang area, in view of its political as well as its strategic importance. If the Chinese renew their attacks before or during the winter they will make some gains, but we believe the conflict will remain confined to the areas of present fighting.

8. The conflict may Involve much larger numbers of troops next spring. The Indians will probably not attempt to advance beyond their own territorial claims. However, more powerful Chinese attacks are possible, especially in the event of a strong Indian effort to recover lost territory, and fighting could well spread further in NEFA and perhaps even to new areas of Ladakh. Any major expansion of the conflict might involve the territories of Bhutan and perhaps even of Sikkim.

9. The principal limiting factor is logistics. Especially if the Chinese should attempt to move beyond their present territorial claims in NEFA, it seems unlikely that their transport system could support a force capable of withstanding the Indian counter-attacks which could be brought against it. It would require massive and lengthy preparations, including major road-building in both Tibet and NEFA, stockpiling of supplies, etc., for the Chinese to initiate a serious invasion of India. Hence, whatever may be the long-run Chinese aspirations to dominate India, we believe it unlikely that Peiping will undertake an expansion of the present conflict beyond NEFA or attempt further significant advances in Ladakh.

IV. The Indian Position

10. The Sino-Indian conflict has had a dramatic effect on Indian attitudes. The setbacks at the hands of Peiping, combined with Moscow's stand, have prompted Prime Minister Nehru publicly to admit that India has been "living in an artificial atmosphere of our own creation" ...and has been "out of touch with reality." In making the decision to request military aid from the West, the Indian Government discarded a precept which had long been one of the cornerstones of its non-alignment policy. While this does not mean the abandonment of non-alignment as such, it evidences a change favorable to the West in India's posture. In particular, it will strengthen the awareness in India of the part that a strong US position in Asia plays in the containment of Communist China.

11. Within India, the pro-Western elements in the Congress Party have been strengthened, and moderate pro-Westernism is likely for some time at least to be an asset for an Indian politician. The influence on policy of the generally pro-Western Indian military will probably grow. Krishna Menon is probably finished as a major political force in Indian affairs, although he probably will continue to have some influence with Nehru. The moderate nationalist majority of the Communist Party of India has adopted a position that is in conflict not only with Peiping but with Moscow's position as well. The majority support of the Nehru government's position has infuriated the extremists in the party, and a formal party split could well result.

12. The Indian effort to gear up for the difficult and costly task of expelling the Chinese is also likely to have adverse effects on India's economic development effort. Despite Nehru's brave words about India's determination to carry out the ambitious Third Five-Year Plan, the necessity of financing the war effort will force some cutbacks. If the Indians continue their heavy emphasis on long-range investment projects, the whole economy is likely to falter. However, giving priority to imports of raw materials and spare parts in order to utilize presently available excess industrial capacity would probably limit the adverse consequences to the economy. An increase of the Indian Army from 550,000 to 800,000 men—as has been suggested—would require extensive external military aid. In addition, it would also seriously hamper the economic development effort, even assuming economic assistance from both the Soviet Bloc and the West at presently projected levels.

V. The Pakistani Reaction

13. Pakistan's reaction to the West's support of India has been a bitter one. The Pakistanis regard Western willingness-eagerness, in their eyes—to supply military equipment to India as seriously detrimental to Pakistan's interests. They also see it as negating the advantage of their alliance with the US. They are convinced that India will not negotiate "realistically" on Kashmir under normal conditions, and they believe that India's present difficult position offers What may be the only real hope to secure an acceptable settlement there. Additionally, Pakistan sees any military strengthening of India as a threat to its security. Pakistan has become increasingly concerned about India's intransigent attitude toward its neighbors during the past year or so-particularly since the Goa episode. In these circumstances, Pakistan has been unwilling to give India any public assurances. India for its part, despite the Chinese threat, has failed to redeploy substantial numbers of its own troops from the Pakistan border.

14. The eventual Pakistani reaction will depend on the magnitude and type of the aid the West extends to India. A modest program of infantry weapons and transport aircraft, for example, would probably engender chiefly widespread

grumbling. On the other hand, a massive program to re-equip the Indian military establishment with modem weapons, unless balanced by comparable aid to Pakistan and accompanied by Western pressure on India to achieve a Kashmir settlement, would impose grave strains on US-Pakistan relations. For example, Ayub would be unwilling to agree to any expansion of special US facilities in Pakistan, and might demand the elimination of some of them.

VI. The Soviet Problem

15. The expansion of the Sino-Indian conflict has presented the USSR with a troublesome choice. One of the basic tenets of post-Stalin foreign policy has been friendship with the neutral nations. India played a key role in this policy, as demonstrated by Moscow's previous willingness to incur Chinese wrath by remaining publicly neutral in the Sino-Indian dispute and even supplying military transport aircraft for use against China. Whether by design or not, Peiping's enlargement of the fighting, especially coming at the time of US-soviet confrontation over Cuba, has forced Moscow, for the time being at least, reluctantly to support "fraternal China" over "friendly India." The immediate Soviet objective is probably the achievement of the earliest possible resolution of the conflict.

16. India's reaction to the Soviet stance has been one of acute disillusionment—particularly on the part of the more pro-Soviet elements. As a result, Soviet influence in India has diminished sharply and any future attempt by Moscow to rebuild its positively will be dogged by the Indian memory of Soviet support of China in India's hour of need. Nevertheless, India's leaders will continue to wish to maintain their posture of nonalignment. They will continue to hope for Soviet Bloc economic aid and for support on such questions as Kashmir.

ANNEX A—MILITARY

Current Military Situation

1. Along India's northern border lies China's Tibet Military Region with a total troop strength of about 103,000. These forces are organized into 3 infantry divisions, 9 independent

infantry regiments, an artillery regiment, a cavalry regiment, and 5 border defense regiments.

Ladakh

2. By deploying one infantry regiment, a cavalry regiment, and border defense forces against elements of one Indian brigade, the Chinese succeeded in reducing Indian Army outposts and curing uncontested control of all their claimed Ladakh territory. Although the Indians have evacuated additional outposts and fighting continues in the Chushul area, Chinese forces generally have remained within the confines of Chinese territorial claims. It is roughly estimated that 7,000 Chinese init1ally opposed a like number of Indian troops. Reinforcements have now brought the numbers to about 10,000 on each side.

Sikkim-Bhutan Area

3. Following reports that the Chinese were effecting a military buildup in the Chumbi Valley between Sikkim and Bhutan, the Indian Army positioned two infantry divisions in Sikkim and adjacent India. The Chinese reinforcement possibly involved at least one regiment of the infantry division based at Shigatse, south central Tibet.

North East Frontier Agency

4. In the North East Frontier Agency (NEFA) the Chinese launched three separate offensives employing a total of approximately six infantry regiments. In the Tawang area up to three infantry regiments with supporting artillery assaulted Indian defenses manned by an infantry brigade. The attack penetrated approximately 11 miles inside the border to a point five miles east to Towang. At present one Indian infantry division is deployed in defensive positions in the Se La Pass area.

5. In the Longju-Asafila area, one regiment overran platoon-size Indian border posts. This attack has progressed only a short distance inside the NEFA and has been blocked by possibly one Indian brigade.

6. In the extreme eastern part of the NEFA—the Rima area—two Chinese infantry regiments crossed the border and advanced 15 miles to threaten Walong. This Communist advance

has been checked by an Indian infantry brigade in the vicinity of the town. In the NEFA area, Indian Army strength numbers some 35,000 with about 15,000 troops committed to forward area defense against more than 20,000 Chinese forces.

Reinforcement Capabilities

7. Excluding border defense regiments, which probably have been held back along the Sino-Nepal-Indian border and assigned primarily security and secondarily reserve "infantry" roles, uncommitted and immediately available Chinese forces in central and eastern Tibet consist of the equivalent of two infantry divisions, three infantry regiments, and elements of an artillery regiment.

8. Indian Army brigade and division reinforcements have been moved into Ladakh, northern Uttar Pradesh, and the NEFA; other units have been alerted for possible movement. As far as can be determined Indian forces facing the Pakistani border have not been weakened.

9. It is estimated that the Indians could reinforce the single infantry division presently committed in Ladakh with possibly two additional infantry divisions. The two infantry divisions defending in the NEFA could be reinforced by an additional three divisions. These reinforcements would require the decision to redeploy units now positioned along the Indo-Pakistani borders, and would virtually deplete India's strategic reserve force.

10. Meanwhile, a total of 10 infantry and 2 artillery divisions, located in the Sinkiang, Lanchou, Chengtu, and Kunming Military Regions, are available for possible movement into Tibet. Although reinforcements for the northern Ladakh area could move on either the north-west rail-highway route through Sinkiang or the motor road across Tibet via Lhasa, it is believed that logistic considerations would force the utilization of the Sinkiang route. Deployments into Tibet can be truck transported into Lhasa from Lanchou in north-west China and along the east-west highway from Yaan in western Szechwan Province. It is estimated that the interregional transfer of 4 infantry divisions—2 divisions from north-west China and 2 divisions from southwest China—would require approximately

24 to 30 days to close in the Lhasa area. The redeployment of 1 infantry division either from Lhasa to the Towang area or from Changtu in eastern Tibet to the Rima area would require 5 days; from Lhasa westward 1 division would require about 17 days to reach Ladakh.

11. Assuming that cargo requirements would pre-empt civil air transport aircraft, military troop carriers operating at maximum range (550 nautical miles—n.m.) could provide an initial lift capacity (80 percent aircraft availability) of about 2,000 troops. If civil aviation were pressed into service, this lift capacity could be increased to 3,000 troops. It should be noted that when transport aircraft occupy western China airfields, their forward utilization will effect a corresponding reduction in airbase facilities available to combat aircraft.

12. Parachute-trained troops from China's three airborne divisions could be employed in battalion-size operations against bridges, airfields, or key terrain features, but only at lower elevations.

13. It is believed that altitude restrictions limit the use of airborne troop carriers to the southern route west of the Chengtu and Kunming airbase complexes into the NEFA and from southern Sinkiang into Ladakh.

Air Operations

14. The Chinese Communists are not likely to introduce air in support of their current ground operations unless Indian forces, augmented by substantial Western military aid, pose a major threat to their positions. If introduced, the Chinese will use tactical air primarily in support of ground forces with strikes probably restricted to Indian positions in the Ladakh, the NEFA, and upper Brahmaputra River valley areas of India.

15. Those Chinese airfields with runways of 6,000 feet or more within range of the disputed areas are in two groups. The first group contains 3 airfields in the region north of Nepal, Bhutan, and the NEFA. They are Tingri Dzong with a 12,000 foot temporary runway at 15,000 feet altitude, Lhasa with a 13,000 foot permanent runway at 14,000 feet altitude, and Nagchhu Dzong with a 12,000 foot temporary runway at

15,000 feet altitude. The other group contains two airfields in the region north of Jammu and Kashmir. These are Pull with a 10,000 foot natural surfaced runway at 10,000 feet altitude and Soche with an 8,000 foot natural surfaced runway at 4,400 feet altitude. On the basis of 45 jet day fighters per airfield, 225 aircraft could be accommodated.

16. A total of 400 combined MIG-15 and MIG-11 jet day fighter interceptors, however, could be deployed to all of the Chinese air bases closest to the threatened areas of India to provide air cover to tactical strikes as well as air defense. Approximately 100 IL-28 jet light bombers and 120 TU-2 piston attack bombers could also be deployed to adjacent air bases for use in close support missions.

17. For tactical strikes, the TU-2 would be the most dependable aircraft. Carrying a normal 3,300 pound bomb load, these aircraft could operate from even those bases at altitudes up to 15,000 feet. The combat radius of the TU-2 in such strikes would be approximately 400 n.m. The slower speeds of this aircraft, including takeoff speed, would enhance its viability; first, in terms of minimizing the hazards from dust, rocks, and other debris because of the inferior surfacing of Chinese runways north of India; secondly, due to the reduced danger of tire blowouts in comparison with jet operations from airfields at 10,000-15,000 feet altitudes; and thirdly, because of the increased maneuver ability in flying at minimum altitudes between mountain peaks where weather permits.

18. Logistics, and particularly POL, however, would be the most serious limiting factor on such operations. Available POL storage facilities would limit combat operations to not more than 10 days and in view of the remoteness of the area and the lack of transportation facilities, resupply would be very difficult. Therefore, the key to sustained air operations in support of Chinese Communist ground operations 1n the Indian border area would be the extent of logistic support which could be provided, particularly POL.

19. The Indian Air Force is roughly one-quarter the size of the Chinese Communist Air Forces. It has operating advantages,

however, which partially compensate for its inferior numerical strength. There are an adequate number of forward airfields available, and logistic and operating conditions would be more favorable than at the few, more isolated, extremely high elevation Chinese airfields previously cited. The Indians are likely to initiate air operations against the Chinese only if future Red advances prove significant. In this event, Indian strikes probably would be restricted to Chinese positions and supply lines in Indian claimed territory in the hope that Chinese retaliation could be contained. If the Chinese were able to resolve their extremely difficult logistics problems, they could overpower the Indians in a sustained effort involving large segments of both air forces. However, such operations are not expected. So few aircraft probably would be employed during a given period that the Indians, especially if they were to receive substantial outside assistance, could hold their own for a much longer time than a comparison of overall strength would indicate.

TACTICAL AIR ORDER OF BATTLE
(in selected categories)

	India	Communist China[a]
Fighter (jet)	315	2,000
Attack Bomber/Fighter Bomber	260 (jet)	120 (piston)
Light Bomber (jet)	60[b]	330
Medium Bomber (piston)		10

[a] Includes naval aircraft.

[b] Plus 20 piston.

Logistics

20. Regional supply bases in southern Sinkiang and in central Tibet are supplied from general depots located at Lanchou and Cherlgtu. A small air transport effort supplements overland haulage. Lhasa bases receive their supplies by truck over two main supply routes, which are sufficient to satisfy the combat needs of up to 10 infantry divisions (standard) at Lhasa. However, variable capacities of roads radiating from Lhasa affect tonnages that can be delivered to the border areas.

21. Chinese combat units in Ladakh are logistically supported from both the Sinkiang and Lhasa bases. The two supply routes

leading Into the Ladakh area are probably capable of handling the combat requirements of from 4½ infantry divisions (standard) to 6½ Infantry divisions (light). Heavier fighting would reduce this capability to 1½ or 2 divisions. Supplies diverted from the Lhasa-Ladakh supply route support one Infantry division in the Chumbi valley.

22. Supplies of all classes can be truck transported up to the Bum La and Longju areas along the northern NEFA border. Here the Chinese can deliver the combat requirements of 2 infantry divisions (standard) or 3 infantry divisions (light). From the border southward into the Towang area Chinese logistic capabilities, stretched across rugged, mountainous terrain ·devoid of an adequate road system, are reduced considerably and their forces in the area are estimated to be operating on minimum supply requirements. By expanding the existing trail system into jeep tracks and later to roads of three-ton capacity the area's logistical capability could be increased proportionably.

23. In the Rima area of the NEFA present road capacities are capable of handling the tonnage requirements for 1 standard or 1½ lightly equipped infantry divisions. Forward of the border, however, road capacities reduce this capability to 20-mile advance by one infantry regiment.

24. Thus, it appears that the current Chinese offensives in the NEFA have approached estimated logistical support limits. Deeper penetrations, heavier fighting, or the introduction of additional ground forces, would not only require the Chinese to initiate an extensive road building program to increase tonnage capacities, but also force them to resort to aerial resupply operations to supplement their overland efforts.

25. Indian approaches into the areas of conflict also traverse especially difficult terrain, utilizing a road and trail system which is rudimentary despite recent Indian improvements. Many of the Indian forces, particularly in the NEFA, can be supplied only by porterage or air-drops. In addition, Indian supply routes suffer from the fact that rain and snowfall are much heavier than on the Chinese-held plateaus. This logistical disadvantage, however, has been lessened somewhat by the shortening of supply lines

occasioned by Indian withdrawals. While improvements in India's air transport capacity have received high priority, recovery rates for air-drops to units in Ladakh arid the NEFA during the recent campaigns have not exceeded 20 percent.

The Military Outlook

26. The current Indian Army buildup in Ladakh and the NEFA will continue. However, a general Indian offensive against Chinese-held positions will require a much greater concentration of forces equipped with more automatic and heavy support weapons. If units presently facing the Pakistani borders were released for action in the threatened areas, the Indian Army could muster sufficient forces to press forward and possibly force Chinese withdrawals. This buildup, requiring several months to complete, could reach its zenith upon the advent of the next favorable period for military operations-after the spring thaws (March) and before the arrival of the monsoon (July). At the same time, the Chinese will continue to improve their military posture. Roads will be built, supply points restocked, and defensive positions strengthened. Chinese Communist Army reinforcements of up to four infantry divisions with supporting artillery and possibly some tanks could be introduced into the Tibet Military Region without overtaxing logistic support capabilities. Reinforcements could be held in staging areas for rapid deployment to the frontier areas. This would maintain troop flexibility and prevent undue strain on forward supply routes.

27. By early next summer when the Indian Army could be prepared to launch its offensive, the Chinese Communists could have sufficient forces in place to resist and successfully hold or to counter-attack at will. If the Chinese decide to remain on the defensive, the border dispute could develop into a prolonged stalemate, with expenditures in both men and materiel economically costly to both sides. If the Chinese should elect to counter-attack, it is believed that they could penetrate deeper into Ladakh or NEFA, but it would require massive and lengthy preparations, including major road-building in both Tibet and NEFA, stockpiling of supplies, etc., for the Chinese to initiate a serious invasion of India.

CHAPTER 8

Communist China and Asia

National Intelligence Estimate, USA, 6 March 1969

THE PROBLEM

To survey recent Chinese foreign policy and alternate lines of development in the near term; to define the nature of the Chinese threat in Asia, and to estimate Chinese intentions in the area; and to estimate the longer term outlook for Chinese foreign policy.

CONCLUSIONS

A. The Chinese Communist regime has fallen far short of its aspirations for a position of dominance in East and Southeast Asia and for the leadership of the world revolution. Neither its efforts at conventional diplomacy nor at supporting revolutionary struggles have been pursued consistently or with a regard to objective realities. Mao's ideological pretensions have earned China the enmity of the USSR, and his bizarre domestic programs have cost China greatly in prestige and respect elsewhere in the world. Yet China's location and size, and the traditional apprehensions of its neighbors, ensure for it a major impact upon Asia regardless of the policy it follows.

B. As long as Mao is the dominant figure, major changes in China's international posture do not appear likely. Mao will remain an insurmountable obstacle to any accommodation with the USSR, and there is little alternative to continuing hostility toward the US. A failure by the Vietnamese Communists to achieve their aims might require some shift in tactics, hut the Chinese would almost certainly not launch an overt attack, nor would they be likely to open a major new front of conflict.

C. Nevertheless, Chinese aspirations for political dominance in Asia will persist. Almost certainly Mao and his immediate successors will not expect to achieve this by military conquest, although force and violence figure strongly in Mao's doctrines. The Chinese may hope that the possession of a strategic capability will give China greater freedom to support "people's war" or, more remotely, to engage in conventional war in Asia by diminishing the possibility of nuclear attack on China. Whatever Chinese hopes, however, the actual possession of nuclear weapons will not necessarily make China more willing to risk a direct clash with the US; indeed, it is more likely to have a sobering effect.

D. Whatever modifications in Chinese policy flow from its advance into the nuclear age, the principal threat from China will for many years be in the realm of subversion and revolutionary activity—mainly in Southeast Asia. In South Vietnam and Laos, Peking must take account of Hanoi's direct interests. China's policy toward Cambodia will be largely conditioned by Sihanouk's attitude. If he moves very far toward accommodation with the US, Peking's pressures against him—now minimal—would be increased. The Chinese may see Thailand as a more lucrative target for a Chinese-sponsored "people's war." Peking is already providing some training and support, but even the Chinese must realize that the Thai insurgency faces a long, difficult fight. The Chinese have a more clear-cut choice in Burma, and whether they significantly increase the insurgency or restore more normal diplomatic relations could be an indicator of trends in Peking's foreign policy.

E. The rest of Southeast Asia is less important in Peking's immediate scheme because the Chinese lack direct access and current prospects for insurgency in these areas are minimal. Peking seeks to weaken and embarrass India, but not to confront it directly so long as there is no threat to Tibet.

F. It is in the area of conventional diplomacy, which suffered severely in the Cultural Revolution, that Peking could most easily achieve significant changes. Restoration of normal diplomacy would facilitate a trend toward recognition of Peking, and this would in turn put pressure on other countries, particularly Japan, which does not want to be left behind in opening relations with the mainland. Taipei would undoubtedly suffer diplomatic losses in this process.

G. The departure of Mao could, in time, bring significant change in China's relations with the outside world. There could be contention and struggle for leadership that would freeze major policies during a long interregnum. But on balance, we believe Mao's departure will generate a strong movement toward modifying his doctrines.

H. A less ideological approach would not necessarily make China easier to deal or live with in Asia. Pursuit of its basic nationalist and traditional goals could sustain tensions in the area, and a China that was beginning to realize some of its potential in the economic and advanced weapons fields could become a far more formidable force in Asia than is Maoist China.

DISCUSSION

I. Introduction

1. During 20 years of rule, the Chinese Communists have not come close to realizing China's aspirations for leadership or domination in Asia. There are many reasons for this. China has of course had to operate from an economic base inadequate to support the full range of its pretensions. Maoist preoccupation with making China the leader of the world revolution has often led to policies and actions harmful to other more traditional or conventional Chinese goals in Asia. The tension and inconsistencies in the basic Chinese approach to foreign policy have been magnified by frequent shifts in actual tactics and strategy. In consequence, Peking has failed to pursue any single course with consistency and maximum effect over a prolonged period.

2. In the flush of victory in 1949, Peking joined the USSR in proclaiming Asia ripe for revolution and called for "people's war" against all existing governments in the area. But China was not ready to offer much practical assistance to this end, local communist parties lacked the strength for revolution, and the principal result was to alienate the leaders and supporters

of the newly independent Asian governments who considered themselves anti-imperialist and deserving of Peking's support, not its enmity.

3. The Korean war forced China to concentrate on more immediate security concerns, and in its aftermath Peking shifted to the line of peaceful coexistence abroad while concentrating on construction at home. But this line, which had considerable promise of winning friends, diplomatic recognition, and broad commercial opportunities for China, gradually gave way to a more belligerent and revolutionary line. By the late 1950's, the dispute with the USSR began to take shape and has since consumed a good deal of China's energies and attention. During the early 1960's, China suffered a great loss of prestige as the absurdities, administrative confusion, and economic chaos of the Great Leap became evident to the world.

4. By 1964, however, China seemed to be back on an even keel and growing in strength and influence. A working balance between support for revolutionary goals and improving China's international position seemed to exist in Chinese foreign policy. China was closely aligned with North Vietnam and North Korea, commanded respect among numerous communist parties, and had established an "axis" with Indonesia. The revolutions in Vietnam and Laos were progressing. Maneuvering was underway for a new Afro-Asian conference, which the Chinese hoped to turn against the USSR Several non-communist states were considering recognition, and France actually took this step. Chou En-lai embarked on an extensive tour of Africa. In October 1964, Mao's archenemy Khrushchev fell and the Chinese exploded their first atomic device.

5. But once again a combination of circumstances intervened to produce major shifts in the Chinese posture in foreign affairs. Suddenly, in 1965, the war in Vietnam became much more than another war of liberation. With the US intervention, Mao's theories on the validity of guerrilla war were being subjected to extreme test, and China itself felt the risk of direct conflict with the US. The problem was a delicate one: how to assure success in the Vietnam war without provoking an American attack on North Vietnam and ultimately China.

6. The entire question of how to confront the US was apparently the subject of a debate during 1965, a debate which was greatly complicated by changes in the USSR, where the new leadership was bent on rebuilding its position with Asian Communists, especially in Hanoi. The Soviet proposal for "united action" to support Hanoi, however, was regarded by Mao as a trap which would hamstring Chinese freedom of action and undermine Peking's claim to be the center of a new revolutionary movement. Most important, Mao saw that any accommodation with Moscow would contribute to the erosion of morale and ideological purity which he apparently feared was already spreading rapidly throughout the Chinese party and society.

7. In the rest of the world, the Chinese found that they had, overestimated the revolutionary enthusiasm of their friends. Chou En-lai's African tour was cut short, after embarrassing reaction to his vivid descriptions of Africa's ripeness for revolution. With the collapse in 1965 of the "Bandung II" Conference in Algiers, China was rebuffed in its effort to form an anti-Soviet and anti-US bloc of Afro-Asians. The recognition by France was not followed by a rush of other countries. And the alliance with Sukarno collapsed in a massive bloodbath for the Indonesian Communists and a wave of violent repression of the overseas Chinese community there.

8. China reacted to these circumstances, not by muting its revolutionary propaganda, but by calling for an acceleration of the worldwide revolutionary movement. Supposedly, the various Insurgencies, activists, parties, and front groups would step up their efforts in order to divert US resources and wear down the US will. At the same time, the USSR and its clients would be excluded from the new phase of intensified revolutionary activity, and China would remain the center of the movement.

9. The net effect of this line was to create an even wider gap between Chinese ideological prescriptions and objective reality. In dealing with major problems of national security, especially those involving a threat of confrontation with the US, China was forced to remain cautious and prudent. As the domestic

crisis of the Cultural Revolution deepened, Peking became more and more rigid and doctrinaire, insensitive to the voice of its friends, utterly hostile and inflexible towards its enemies, and increasingly oblivious to the deterioration of its international position.

10. Even so, the Chinese leaders might have been content with their position had it not been for new developments in 1968. The onset of negotiations over Vietnam was tantamount to a repudiation of the Chinese by Hanoi, seemed to vindicate the position of the USSR, and pointed to growing Soviet influence. And the USSR engaged in a substantial military buildup in the Far East which was clearly directed against China. The Chinese have not reacted by a similar buildup of their own along the Soviet frontier, and they probably do not expect an open Soviet attack. But they are no doubt concerned about Soviet efforts to influence internal developments in China in one way or another. All this was brought into sharper focus by the invasion of Czechoslovakia and the subsequent promulgation of the "Brezhnev doctrine."

11. In sum, by the end of 1968, the revolutionary line bad failed in its principal objectives. It was becoming increasingly clear that a settlement in Vietnam was not likely to validate Mao's strategy of "people's war." The influence of the USSR in the region had not been contained but had in fact grown, both in the communist capitals of Pyongyang and Hanoi, and in South and Southeast Asia. China had failed completely to achieve a "broad united front" against the imperialist US and the revisionist USSR. Instead it found itself "encircled," as Chou En-lai acknowledged, and isolated on most key policy issues.

12. Yet Peking's lack of progress toward its revolutionary objectives has by no means completely vitiated its influence in Asia. China's location, size, and history, buttressed by the traditional apprehensions of its neighbors, ensure for it a major impact upon Asia regardless of the policy it follows. Awareness of China's existence and potential for making trouble affects the current policies of every country in the area.

II. Immediate Prospects

13. In the near term, there does not appear to be much chance for a major change in China's international posture. As long as Mao is the dominant figure of the regime and the source of ideological guidance, Chinese policy will probably be confined within fairly narrow limits. He is likely to remain an insurmountable obstacle to any accommodation or modus vivendi with the USSR. Indeed, Chinese enmity for the Soviet Union has recently reached a level at latest equal to that against the US; China now has two "number one enemies." With age, Mao has become less flexible and even more obsessed with revolutionary goals. There is not likely to be any slackening in his commitment to the notion that China is the center for inspiring the world revolution and that its principal allies are not to be found in the established Communist regimes and parties, but in the guerrilla movements that have accepted "Mao's thought" and intend to persist in protracted struggle. In this sense, there is little alternative lo continuing hostility toward the US.

14. Yet within this fairly rigid strategic framework, there are signs of some greater flexibility in tactics. These signs are often contradictory and confusing, but they could be significant if domestic affairs are entering a new phase. The growing concern that the US and USSR are pursuing parallel, anti-Chinese policies may be a factor dictating Chinese moves to complicate or disrupt what they see as a tacit alliance. What such moves might be is not at all clear, and in the end they may be of no great significance. As long as Maoist ideology is dominant, however, the road to Moscow is blocked. Ironically, the Chinese may be coming to feel that they have more room for maneuver vis-a-vis the US than the USSR, though of course the Taiwan question will continue to obstruct Sino-US relations.

15. Whether shifts in Chinese tactics do occur could depend, of course, on developments in Vietnam. The Chinese already perceive that the war in Vietnam is likely to end in a negotiated settlement. They have taken some steps to mute their opposition to negotiations. And at some point in this process, they are likely to re-emphasize their broad political interest in the area, seeking

to make it clear that no lasting settlement can be achieved without Peking's approval.

16. Of course, it is possible that the Chinese will choose not to adjust to developments in Indochina, but rather seek to disrupt them. However, a failure by the Vietnamese Communists to achieve their aims would probably not lead to extreme reactions by the Chinese. Almost certainly the Chinese are not going to launch an overt attack in Vietnam or seize some territory elsewhere, nor are they likely to open a major new front of conflict, using their own resources. At the other extreme, there is little likelihood that the Chinese will suddenly become quiescent because of the outcome in Vietnam. They are going to remain active in support of those movements that they believe are loyal to Maoist concepts and have some potential for effective development.

17. In any case, China's foreign policies are likely to be influenced to a significant degree by the internal crisis. Even if the extremes of the Cultural Revolution are already past, it is possible that a new phase of coercive social programs and disruptive economic initiatives may prove as debilitating as the political purge. If, on the other hand, a more moderate line in internal policies prevails, then order may also be gradually restored, and the Foreign Ministry professionals may gain greater influence over policy. But as long as Mao lives and rules in Peking, there will be an inherent instability in China. Foreign policy in a general sense will be subordinate to and reflect the internal line. Accordingly, Peking .will be more likely to respond to outside events than to launch major new initiatives of its own.

III. The Chinese Threat in Asia

18. All these considerations do not mean that China will be a negligible factor in Asia or in international politics. Chinese goals, in Asia at least, are fairly clear. Almost all Chinese—whether in Peking or on Taiwan—would agree that China's rightful position is one of political dominance on the Asian mainland, and ultimately throughout East and Southeast Asia. Such aspirations have deep historical roots. In this sense, China poses a threat to Asia and to those outside powers which seek to

play an important role in Asian affairs. The question is how the Chinese intend to accomplish their objectives.

A. *Military Power*

19. Almost certainly the Chinese do not expect to achieve a dominant position by military conquest, even though force and violence figure strongly in Maoist philosophy and Chinese Communist practice. In the cases where the Chinese have resorted to military means—in Korea and India—this was, in their view, defensive to protect the security of their borders. Indeed, a principal objective of China, like most states, is to insure its security against unfriendly powers ranged along its frontiers. Where the Chinese see an immediate threat to their security, they will be prepared to use force, even preemptively. But neither Mao nor his immediate successors are likely to believe that the Chinese revolution can be exported by the People's Liberation Army, or that armed conquest in the style of Imperial China is a safe or profitable course.

20. All this, of course, applies primarily to China as a conventional military power, but its acquisition of nuclear weapons will not necessarily increase its aggressiveness. The Chinese may hope that the possession of a strategic capability will give China greater freedom to support "people's war" or, more remotely, to engage in conventional war in Asia by diminishing the possibility of nuclear attack on China. The Chinese certainly hoped to gain such freedom in the Taiwan Strait crisis of 1958 by exploiting the Sino-Soviet alliance to deter the US. Moscow's refusal in that instance to back China with nuclear threats was probably a major factor in convincing Peking that it must have its own nuclear weapons.

21. Whatever may have been Chinese hopes in the past, however, the actual possession of nuclear weapons is likely to have a sobering effect. China has no hope of achieving parity with either the US or the USSR in nuclear weapons in the foreseeable future.[1] Despite its propaganda concerning China's

1. The Intelligence Community currently estimates that the earliest possible initial operational capability for a Chinese intercontinental ballistic missile is 6-12 launchers in 1972, and that if the Chinese

ability to withstand nuclear attack, Peking will almost certainly come to realize, if it does not already, that either the US or the USSR possesses more than sufficient nuclear weapons to devastate China.

22. In these circumstances, China is likely to remain cautious in areas of possible direct confrontation with the US or the USSR, calculating that its own possession of nuclear weapons may increase, rather than lessen, the chances of a preemptive nuclear strike against it. For some time, China is likely to value its nuclear capability primarily as a Great Power status symbol and for its political effects. In sum, when China actually becomes a nuclear power during the next decade, it will probably be subjected to the same constraints and complications of policy as the other nuclear powers.

23. We cannot predict the ultimate effect of Chinese acquisition of nuclear weapons on the rest of Asia. At a minimum, China will gain greater prestige and respect; translated into political gains, this will probably mean that more countries will seek some relationship with Peking at Taiwan's expense, and that some will explore the possibility of accommodation, if Chinese policy is sufficiently flexible to permit such accommodations. However, few countries are likely to respond favorably to China's desire to monopolize nuclear power in Asia and to provide "protection" for the area against all outside powers. Indeed, the Chinese attitude may increase pressures in some Asian countries to develop their own nuclear capabilities or to cling more closely to other nuclear powers.

B. *People's War*

24. Whatever modifications in Chinese policy flow from its advance into the nuclear age, the principal threat from China will, for many years, be in the realm of subversion and revolutionary activity. Such activity will be conducted mainly in Southeast Asia where it relates directly to Peking's security interests in denying the US or other unfriendly powers positions

---

achieve that date, they might have between 10 and 25 launchers in 1975. A modest program for deployment of medium-range ballistic missiles will also probably he underway in the next few years.

close to China's borders. It also serves to satisfy the more general interest of China in establishing its own dominance in the area and in the world revolutionary movement.

25. *Vietnam and Laos.* To these ends, Peking supports and assists the Communists in Vietnam and Laos. For the present, at least, Peking has to take account of North Vietnam's direct interests in both South Vietnam and Laos. Peking could try to circumvent the North Vietnamese and open competing lines to the National Liberation Front and to the Pathet Lao. But its chances of gaining significant influence are poor and the cost in relations with Hanoi potentially so great that such a maneuver is unlikely. Though sharp disagreement could develop over tactics in Laos, in general Hanoi and Peking almost certainly share the same immediate goal: communist control of Laos, with Hanoi in the dominant role.

26. *Thailand.* As a close ally of the US and as a US strategic base, Thailand is a key object of Chinese policy in Southeast Asia and will probably receive increased emphasis after the war in Vietnam is settled. In this respect, Thailand is the most obvious target for "people's war." The political leadership of the Thai insurgency is now lodged in Peking, and the Chinese are providing some training and arms. Moreover, the Chinese have assumed a heavy propaganda commitment; recently they have announced the formation of a Thai "People's Army" supreme command and publicized the new manifesto of the Thai Communist Party.

27. The Chinese will almost certainly continue to support the Thai insurgents. Yet they must realize that the insurgency faces a long, difficult fight; it has made little progress in gaining the allegiance of ethnic Thais. And Thailand possesses many strengths. Thus, it is possible that at some point the Chinese might want to reconsider their support, if in doing so they could induce Bangkok to draw away from its alliance with the US.

28. *Burma.* A period of cordial Sino-Burmese relations was broken by Peking in the midst of the Cultural Revolution nearly two years ago. Since then the Chinese have openly supported the Burmese Communist movement and publicly endorsed the

formation of a united front with the ethnic insurgents. During much of 1968, the insurgency did increase along the Sino-Burmese border. There is, on the other hand, some evidence that the Chinese may want to restore more normal relations. Neutralist Burma would, of course, be receptive to such a move, especially if accompanied by a letup in the insurgency. Thus the Chinese have a fairly clear-cut choice between increasing the insurgency in northern Burma and restoring more normal government-to-government relations. How they decide could provide some indication concerning the extent of their commitment to the policy of insurgency in general.

29. *Cambodia*. Relations with Phnom Penh have fluctuated in recent years, partly because of Sihanouk's belief that Peking is sponsoring an insurgency, which he styles the Khmer Rouge. But the Chinese have been willing to tolerate a number of insults and taunts from Sihanouk and to furnish him rums, mainly because of the importance of Cambodia to the prosecution of the Vietnam war. The Chinese also value the fact that Cambodia is ostensibly neutral and frequently anti-American. Finally, in the long term Cambodia could be of potential significance in developing an insurgency in Thailand, with Cambodian territory possibly serving some of the same purposes it has served in the Vietnam war.

30. Thus, a major change in relations will probably depend less on Peking than on Sihanouk. He has long believed that China will become the dominant force in the Far East, and he sees value in trying to use the Chinese as a counterweight to his traditional enemies, the Vietnamese and the Thais. In these circumstances, Peking will probably continue to have considerable influence in Phnom Penh. Nevertheless, if Sihanouk feels that the tide is setting against the Communists in Vietnam, he is capable of becoming more cooperative with the US. Should he attempt to move very far in this direction, however, neither Hanoi nor Peking would be reluctant to step up political pressures against him and to increase support to dissident groups in Cambodia.

31. *Other Areas*. Insurgencies in the rest of Southeast Asia are much less important in the Chinese scheme, mainly because the Chinese have no direct access and the insurgents' prospects

are currently minimal. The attempt of the Maoist oriented Indonesian Communists to develop an insurgency in East Java last summer resulted not only in failure but in the death of key leaders. Peking occasionally publicizes the exploits of the Malayan Communist Party, which in turn pays homage to Mao. Peking, of course, has a considerable potential asset in the large ethnic Chinese population in Malaysia, but the Communist movement's over-identification with the Chinese hampers its avowed policy of forming a broadly based movement with the Malays. Peking has little influence in the Huk movement in the Philippines, though China periodically publicizes the exploits of Filipino insurgents.

32. *India.* In the late 1950's, China came to regard India as a competitor for leadership in Asia, especially because India seemed to benefit from the support of both the USSR and US. Thus Chinese policy has been framed to harass and intimidate India and demonstrate that it was generally incapable of taking the role of a lending Asian power. Since the border war of 1962, the Chinese have maintained some level of tension and threat along the Indian frontier; their military aid to Pakistan serves the same general purpose.

33. If China chose to, it could probably cause considerable trouble by supporting dissidents along the Indian frontier, especially in the northeast. The Chinese eagerly publicized the Naxalbari uprisings in Darjeeling, as the beginning of a Mao-inspired peasant upheaval. In Eastern India, the Chinese have propagandized and apparent have provided limited arms and training to Naga and Mizo tribesmen. Pekings aim seems to be to embarrass and worry New Delhi without becoming deeply involved, and we do not foresee much change In this attitude.

C. *Politics and Diplomacy*

34. In general, China's relations with the non-communist world have suffered in consequence of the Cultural Revolution. Its extreme xenophobia and hysteria impinged on Chinese diplomatic relations. Foreign diplomats in Peking were abused and humiliated; Chinese embassy staffs abroad were reduced and ambassadors withdrawn. Even now, the functioning of

the Ministry of Foreign Affairs remains disrupted by political campaigns and factional disputes.

35. Nevertheless, it is in the area of normal political relations and conventional diplomacy that the Chinese probably have the greatest room for change. Without much effort, the Chinese could resume normal diplomatic activity in Europe, Africa, and the Middle East. Moreover, there appears to be a new movement towards diplomatic recognition of China. Though the Chinese have exhibited no eagerness for such recognition, there is no doubt they would regard it as a gain, especially if such a trend adds to pressures in Japan and elsewhere for closer relations with China.

36. The next two years should present the Chinese with new opportunities for exerting some influence on Japanese politics. The tensions associated with the Okinawa question and the US-Japanese Security Treaty all lend themselves to exploitation by Peking. China could make a serious overture to restore more normal commercial relations and could encourage the visits of influential Japanese politicians. To have a significant impact in Japan, however, Chinese maneuvers would require a more skilled and flexible diplomacy than Peking has been willing to adopt thus far.

37. Eventually, a return to more normal diplomacy does seem likely. The flow of visitors to China has begun to increase, relations with the foreign embassies in Peking have been cased, some new economic agreements have been concluded in recent months, and rumormonger that the Foreign Minister or Chou En-lai may visit abroad. Some reports have indicated that Chinese ambassadors are to return to their posts this spring. However, both China's internal politics and the reaction of Chinese lenders to foreign events could serve to delay moves to restore greater normalcy to Chinese diplomacy. Peking's abrupt postponement of the 20 February session of the Warsaw Talks—rationalized by references to the case of defecting Chinese diplomat Liao Ho-shu—suggests that Peking is as yet undecided about its foreign policy posture.

D. *China's Vital Interests: Korea and Taiwan*

38. In North Koren, the Chinese have seen their influence diminish significantly, largely because of their own rude arrogance and partly because of the consequences of the USSR's renewed cultivation of Pyongyang and Kim II-sung. Such a deterioration, however, is not likely to be a permanent state of affair. Developments in Korea arc of major importance to China, especially if illusions there continue and the danger of hostilitics grows. Eventually, we expect the Chinese to repair their position and attempt to gain some influence over the Korean leadership. Probably, however, China will not pursue a policy intended to increase the risks of war. Its behavior during the past year, particularly in the Pueblo crisis, suggests that the Chinese are not about to pledge themselves unreservedly to Kim II-sung's adventurism.

39. Taiwan, of course, is a central clement in Chinese foreign policy. US support for the GRC is a monumental obstacle to any Chinese reconsideration of its relations with the US. Peking will almost certainly not abandon its claim to Taiwan, and this position appears to rule out acceptance of a two-China solution. Yet there is not much Peking can do to gain possession of Taiwan as long as it is reluctant to engage in a military confrontation with the US. There is the possibility of pressure on the offshore islands (Chinmen and Matsu). Such a move might appeal to Peking as a test of US intentions in the post-Vietnam period, especially if it could be used to aggravate relations between Washington and Taipei.

IV. The Post-Mao Perspective

40. In some respects it is fruitless speculate on the longer term development of Chinese foreign policy. The prospect of Mao's departure overshadows all other considerations. In many respects, the situation is analogous to that of the USSR in the early 1950's, when the death of Stalin unlocked Soviet foreign policy and led to a series of significant new departures. Naturally, this question is uppermost in China's case also. Will Mao's departure open a new era of significant change in China's relations with the outside world?

41. We believe that Mao's departure will generate a strong movement toward modifying his doctrines and jettisoning his disruptive programs. In foreign affairs, new leadership will ultimately seek to focus more effectively on national interests understood in terms of n more realistic world view. Even if Maoist rhetoric should temporarily survive, we believe the trend will be toward moderating the Maoist line in favor of more practical diplomacy. Some modus vivendi with the USSR is possible, though anything approaching n renewal of the old alliance is most unlikely. Moreover, we would not exclude n return to the tactics of peaceful coexistence as part of an effort to undermine the US position in Asia.

42. But such a process is not inevitable and it would not in any case have to be steady and uninterrupted. If there is contention and struggle for the leadership, major policies could be frozen for a long-term interregnum. The timing of Mao's departure and the identity of the principal survivors could be important to policy. Finally, there is the response of outside powers. It would make a great difference whether a new leadership had plausible alternatives or whether it believed that its enemies were seeking to exploit China's weaknesses and uncertainties. Thus, the transition from Mao and his generation many last many years before real changes evolve. Meanwhile, support to subversive movements, if not to active insurgencies, is likely to play a continuing role in China's external policy.

43. In any case, a less ideological approach would not necessarily make China easier to deal or live with in Asia. Pursuit of its basic nationalist and traditional goals could sustain tensions in the area, and a China that was beginning to realize some of its potential in the economic and advanced weapons Gelds could become a for more Formidable force in Asia than is Maoist China.

CHAPTER 9

Agreement on the Maintenance of Peace and Tranquility along the Line of Actual Control in the India-China Border Areas

Beijing, 7 September 1993

The Government of the Republic of India and the Government of the People's Republic of China (hereinafter referred to as the two sides), have entered into the present Agreement in accordance with the Five Principles of mutual respect for sovereignty and territorial integrity, mutual non-aggression, non-interference in each other's internal affairs, equality and mutual benefit and peaceful coexistence and with a view to maintaining peace and tranquility in areas along the line of actual control in the India-China border areas.

1. The two sides are of the view that the India-China boundary question shall be resolved through peaceful and friendly consultations. Neither side shall use or threaten to use force against the other by any means. Pending an ultimate solution to the boundary question between the two countries, the two sides shall strictly respect and observe the line of actual control between the two sides. No activities of either side shall overstep the line of actual control. In case personnel of one side cross the line of actual control, upon being cautioned by the other side, they shall immediately pull back to their own side of the line of actual control. When necessary, the two sides shall jointly check and determine the segments of the line of actual control where they have different views as to its alignment.

2. Each side will keep its military forces in the areas along the line of actual control to a minimum level compatible with the friendly and good neighbourly relations between the two countries. The two sides agree to reduce their military forces along

the line of actual control in conformity with the requirements of the principle of mutual and equal security to ceilings to be mutually agreed. The extent, depth, timing, and nature of reduction of military forces along the line of actual control shall be determined through mutual consultations between the two countries. The reduction of military forces shall be carried out by stages in mutually agreed geographical locations sector-wise within the areas along the line of actual control.

3. Both sides shall work out through consultations effective confidence building measures in the areas along the line of actual control. Neither side will undertake specified levels of military exercises in mutually identified zones. Each side shall give the other prior notification of military exercises of specified levels near the line of actual control permitted under this Agreement.

4. In case of contingencies or other problems arising in the areas along the line of actual control, the two sides shall deal with them through meetings and friendly consultations between border personnel of the two countries. The form of such meetings and channels of communications between the border personnel shall be mutually agreed upon by the two sides.

5. The two sides agree to take adequate measures to ensure that air intrusions across the line of actual control do not take place and shall undertake mutual consultations should intrusions occur. Both sides shall also consult on possible restrictions on air exercises in areas to be mutually agreed near the line of actual control.

6. The two sides agree that references to the line of actual control in this Agreement do not prejudice their respective positions on the boundary question.

7. The two sides shall agree through consultations on the form, method, scale and content of effective verification measures and supervision required for the reduction of military forces and the maintenance of peace and tranquillity in the areas along the line of actual control under this Agreement.

8. Each side of the India-China Joint Working Group on the boundary question shall appoint diplomatic and military experts to formulate, through mutual consultations, implementation

measures for the present Agreement. The experts shall advise the Joint Working Group on the resolution of differences between the two sides on the alignment of the line of actual control and address issues relating to redeployment with a view to reduction of military forces in the areas along the line of actual control. The experts shall also assist the Joint Working Group in supervision of the implementation of the Agreement, and settlement of differences that may arise in that process, based on the principle of good faith and mutual confidence.

9. The present Agreement shall come into effect as of the date of signature and is subject to amendment and addition by agreement of the two sides.

Signed in duplicate at Beijing on the Seventh day of September 1993 in the Hindi, Chinese and English languages, all three texts having equal validity.

(Sd.) R.L. Bhatia
Minister of State for External Affairs
Republic of India

(Sd.) Tang Jiaxuan
Vice-Foreign Minister
People's Republic of China

सत्यमेव जयते

CHAPTER 10

Memorandum between the Government of the Republic of India and the Government of the People's Republic of China on Expanding Border Trade

Beijing, 23 June 2003

The Government of the Republic of India and the Government of the People's Republic of China (hereinafter referred to as the two sides),

With a view to promoting the development of friendly relations between the two countries and two people's,

Pursuant to the Memorandum between the Government of the Republic of India and the Government of the People's Republic of China on the Resumption of Border Trade signed on 13 December 1991, and Protocol on Entry and Exit Procedures for Border Trade signed on 1 July 1992,

Desirous of opening another pass on the India-China border and setting up an additional point on each side for border trade,

Have agreed as follows:

Article I

The Indian side agrees to designate Changgu of Sikkim state as the venue for border trade market; the Chinese side agrees to designate Renqinggang of the Tibet Autonomous Region as the venue for border trade market.

Article II

The two sides agree to use Nathula as the pass for entry and exit of persons, means of transport and commodities engaged in border trade. Each side shall establish checkpoints at appropriate locations to monitor and manage their entry and exit through the Nathula Pass.

Article III

All the provisions of the Memorandum on the Resumption of Border Trade signed between the two Governments on 13 December 1991 and the Protocol on Entry and Exit Procedures for Border Trade signed between the two Governments on 1 July 1992 under the Memorandum shall also be applicable to the border trade through the Nathula Pass.

Article IV

This Memorandum may be amended or supplemented by agreement in writing between the two sides.

Article V

This Memorandum shall come into force as from the date of its signature and shall be valid during the validity of the Memorandum on Resumption of Border Trade signed between the two Governments in New Delhi on 13 December 1991.

Done in Beijing on 23 June 2003 in two originals each in the Hindi, Chinese and English languages, the three texts being equally authentic.

1. Memorandum of Understanding on Cooperation between the Ministry of Law and Justice of the Government of the Republic of India and the Supreme People's Prosecution Service of the People's Republic of China.

(Sd.) Shri Yashwant Sinha	(Sd.) Mr. Jia Chunwang
External Affairs Minister	Procurator General on the Chinese side
For the Government	For the Government
of the Republic of India	of the People's Republic of China

The MoU envisages facilitating closer cooperation in the judicial field between India and China, through the exchange of information, experience in legal matters, including drafting of laws and Implementation of legal provisions, exchange of experience and best practices, mutual support for training public procurators and auxiliary judicial personnel, and cooperation in other legal and judicial matters of interest to both countries. The MoU also provides for setting up of expert working groups, facilitation of direct contacts, conduct of joint seminars and exchange of experts to meet the objective of cooperation in the judicial field. Seminars and conferences on issues of mutual interest will also be organized.

2. Executive Programme on Educational Cooperation and Exchange between the Ministry of Human Resource Development, Government of the Republic of India and Ministry of Education, the People's Republic of China.

(Sd.) Shri Yashwant Sinha	(Sd.) Mr. Zhou Ji
External Affairs Minister of	Minister for Education
India	of the PRC on the Chinese side

Under this executive programme, both sides aim to consolidate and strengthen mutual cooperation in the field of education through sharing of experiences between the educational administrators and through the study of education systems and innovative education programmes in each country. The two sides agree to exchange views and conduct discussion on mutual recognition of academic degrees. They will also cooperate in such areas as the development of curricula for primary and secondary school education, exchange of teaching materials, teaching methodologies as well as the feasibility of conducting joint research in various modes of pre-research and in-service teachers' training and will examine the possibility of jointly establishing a Demonstration Centre for Teacher Training. They will also take measures to encourage higher education institutions from their respective countries to establish direct exchange and cooperation through exchange of lecturers, scholars, books, research materials and audio-visual aids, holding of joint seminars/symposia etc. They have noted the importance of student exchange programmes in various areas including IT and have provided for 25 post-graduate scholarships to be offered annually by both countries. They have also agreed to exchange two language teachers in Hindi and Chinese respectively. This programme will be valid from

June 2003 to 2006 and will be extended for another three years if both sides so agree.

3. Protocol of Phytosanitary Requirements for Exporting Mangoes from India to China between the Ministry of Agriculture of the Republic of India and General Administration of Quality Supervision, Inspection and Quarantine of the People's Republic of China.

(Sd.) Shri Yashwant Sinha
External Affairs Minister

(Sd.) Mr. Li Changjiang
Head of AQSIQ on the Chinese side

Under the India-China bilateral WTO accession agreement of February 2000, both sides agreed to sign a Sanitary and Phyto-Sanitary (SPS) protocol to facilitate exports of Indian fresh fruits and vegetables to China. An umbrella MoU on the application of Phyto-Sanitary Measures was signed during the visit of Premier Zhu Rongji in January 2002. India proposed 17 categories of fruit and vegetables (including mangoes, guavas, grapes, papayas, melons, gherkins, cucumbers, beans, aubergines, capsicums, gourds etc.) for coverage under this MoU. The Chinese side decided to deal with each item separately. The first item taken up for consideration under this procedure was the mango. After completion of a Pest Risk Analysis and detailed negotiations, agreement has now been reached on procedures relating to inspection, certification,packaging and labelling of all consignments of mangoes to be exported to China from India. Now that we have a basic understanding of the relevant procedures, it is hoped that agreement on similar protocols for all the other identified fruits and vegetables can be concluded expeditiously.

4. Memorandum of Understanding on Simplifying Visa Procedures between the Government of the Republic of India and the Government of the People's Republic of China.

(Sd.) Shri Kanwal Sibal
Foreign Secretary, on the Indian side

(Sd.) Mr. Wang Yi
Vice Foreign Minister of the
PRC on the Chinese side

This MoU lays down mutually agreed procedures for the issue of visas in various categories (business, employment, tourism, students, conferences and other short-term academic and cultural exchanges etc.) for private passport holders and on the Chinese side, also for holders of "ordinary passports for public affairs" who are mainly employees of state owned enterprises. This MoU provides clarity on the kind of documentation required for various visas and on the duration and validity of visas issued for different purposes. This will help streamline the process of obtaining visas for businessmen, tourists, students, academics and other experts travelling to each other's countries and will serve to promote people-to-people interaction.

5. Memorandum of Understanding for Enhanced Cooperation in the field of Renewable Energy between the Ministry of Non-Conventional Energy Sources, Government of the Republic of India and the Ministry of Water Resources, Government of People's Republic of China.

(Sd.) Shri Kanwal Sibal Foreign Secretary, on the Indian side	(Sd.) Mr. Wang Yi Vice Foreign Minister of the PRC on the Chinese side

This MoU seeks to establish cooperation in the field of small hydro-power, wind power and other areas of renewable energy through joint research and development activities, exchange of technical expertise and information networking. The ultimate objective is to commercialise the result of such cooperation, create business opportunities and facilitate sustainable market development in an environmentally responsible manner. Areas of cooperation will be defined by mutual consent in accordance with the interest of experience of the scientific, technological and industrial institutions and personnel of the two countries and the facilities available. The MoU provides for exchange of scientific and technological problems, formulation and implementation of joint research and development and demonstration projects on application of renewable energy technologies for augmenting energy availability in a cost-effective manner, training of personnel and setting up of technical demonstration projects in areas of renewable energy.

6. Memorandum of Understanding for Cooperation in the field of Ocean Science and Technology between Department of

Ocean Development, Government of the Republic of India and State Oceanic Administration, People's Republic of China.

(Sd.) Shri Kanwal Sibal Foreign Secretary, on the Indian side	(Sd.) Mr. Wang Yi Vice Foreign Minister of the PRC on the Chinese side

This MoU aims at promoting development and cooperation in areas such as integrated coastal zone management, sea-based resources exploration and exploitation technology, polar science, ocean energy, gas hydrate exploration and exploitation technology, marine resources assessment, seaweed production and processing, satellite oceanography and other fields of marine science of mutual interest to both sides. Such cooperation would be developed through the exchange of scientists, research workers, specialists and scholars; exchange of marine data and information; organization of bilateral symposium, training courses and seminars; joint identification of marine problems, projects and planning and their formulation and implementation; exchange of experience and know-how gained through development and activities in marine science and technology; mutual supply of equipment; utilization of facilities for R&D and other such mutually agreed means of cooperation.

7. Memorandum of Understanding between the Department of Science and Technology of the Republic of India and the National Science Foundation of China.

(Sd.) Shri Shivshankar Menon, Ambassador of India	(Sd.) Mr. Wang Yi, Vice Foreign Minister on the Chinese side

This MoU provides for maintenance and development of cooperative research activities in the field of natural sciences within the framework of the Agreement on Cooperation in Science and Technology between the Government of India and the Government of the People's Republic of China signed on 22 December 1988 in Beijing. The objective will be to ensure that the cooperation will bring real benefits to the development of science and technology in both countries. Collaborative activities will be undertaken in the fields of natural sciences with emphasis on Physical Sciences, Mathematical Sciences,

Chemical Sciences and Biological Sciences. It recognizes that as a first step, a practical means of initiating collaboration between scientists of the two countries is provided by holding meetings of equal numbers of researchers (to be known as N+N meetings) from each side alternatively in India and China. Other forms of collaboration, including individual outgoing and incoming visits by leading scientists and joint research in areas on subjects identified as a priority by scientists of both sides will be based on the relationship built by N+N meetings, or on other established relationships. Priority areas for cooperation will be identified as also a framework of cooperation for each selected area (key institutions, key persons, forms of cooperation, financing etc.). The MoU also provides for periodic reviews of on-going programmes and for the exchange of information.

8. Memorandum of Understanding between the Government of the Republic of India and the Government of the People's Republic of China on the Reciprocal Establishment of Cultural Centres in their Capitals.

(Sd.) Shri Kanwal Sibal,
Foreign Secretary on the Indian side

(Sd.) Mme Meng Xiaosi, Vice Minister of
Culture on the Chinese side

This MoU reflects the agreements reached in principle by both sides to establish independent cultural centres in each other's capital cities. Relevant details such as location, staffing patterns, broad consensus on activities to be undertaken by the centres and so on will be worked out through mutual negotiations in the near future.

9. Executive Programme of Cultural Exchanges between the Government of the Republic of India and the Government of the People's Republic of China for the years 2003-2005.

(Sd.) Shri Kanwal Sibal
Foreign Secretary on the Indian side

(Sd.) Mme Meng Xiaosi
Vice Minister of Culture on the
Chinese side

The Executive Programme of Cultural Exchanges (CEP) provides for exchange of cultural troupes, art exhibitions, and cultural festivals, cooperation in the fields of archaeology and library science, cooperation between the National Museum, national Gallery of Modern Art, National Library, Sangeet Natak Academy and their respective Chinese counterparts etc. It also provides for interaction in the fields of youth affairs and sports, social sciences and mass media, including exchange of radio and TV programmes and training of personnel in radio, TV and films. This is a programme valid for the period June 2003-2005. There is, however, a provision which states that after June 2005, this agreement will remain operative till such time as a new CEP is negotiated and formalized.

CHAPTER 11

Declaration on Principles for Relations and Comprehensive Cooperation between the Republic of India and the People's Republic of China

Beijing, 23 June 2003

At the invitation of Premier of the State Council of the People's Republic of China H.E. Wen Jiabao, Prime Minister of the Republic of India H.E. Atal Bihari Vajpayee paid an official visit to the People's Republic of China from 22 to 27 June 2003.

During this visit, Premier Wen Jiabao held talks with Prime Minister Vajpayee. Their Excellencies President Hu Jintao of the People's Republic of China, Chairman Jiang Zemin of the Central Military Commission, Chairman Wu Bangguo of the Standing Committee of the National People's Congress and Vice President Zeng Qinghong of the People's Republic of China held separate meetings with Prime Minister Vajpayee. The talks and meetings were held in a sincere and friendly atmosphere.

Leaders from both countries noted with satisfaction the progress made over recent years in bilateral relations. This is conducive not only to their respective development, but also to regional stability and prosperity. The two sides recalled the historical depth of their friendly contacts. India and China are the two largest developing countries of the world with centuries-old civilization, unique history and similar objectives. Both noted that the sustained economic and social development in the two countries, representing one third of humanity is vital for ensuring peace, stability and prosperity not only in Asia but also in the whole world.

The two sides agreed that India and China have a mutual desire for good neighborly relations and have broad common interests. They agreed to fully utilize the substantial potential and opportunities for deepening mutually beneficial cooperation.

Friendship and cooperation between the two countries meets the need to:

1. promote the socio-economic development and prosperity of both India and China;
2. maintain peace and stability regionally and globally;
3. strengthen multipolarity at the international level; and
4. enhance the positive factors of globalization.

Both sides affirmed that they would abide by the following principles, promote a long-term constructive and cooperative partnership and, on this basis, build a qualitatively new relationship:

1. Both sides are committed to developing their long-term constructive and cooperative partnership on the basis of the principles of Panchsheel, mutual respect and sensitivity for each other's concerns and equality;
2. As two major developing countries, India and China have a broad mutual interest in the maintenance of peace, stability and prosperity in Asia and the world, and a mutual desire in developing wider and closer cooperation and understanding in regional and international affairs;
3. The common interests of the two sides outweigh their differences. The two countries are not a threat to each other. Neither side shall use or threaten to use force against the other; and
4. Both sides agree to qualitatively enhancing the bilateral relationship at all levels and in all areas while addressing differences through peaceful means in a fair, reasonable and mutually acceptable manner. The differences should not be allowed to affect the overall development of bilateral relations.

Both sides agreed to hold regular high-level exchanges between the two countries. This will greatly enhance mutual understanding and expand bilateral relations. With a view to deepening their coordination and dialogues on bilateral, regional and international issues, both sides agreed on the need for annual meetings between Foreign Ministers of the two countries. They also agreed that personnel exchanges and friendly contacts between ministries, parliaments and political parties of the two countries should be further enhanced.

The two sides welcomed the positive momentum of bilateral trade and economic cooperation in recent years and shared the belief that continued expansion and intensification of India-China economic cooperation is essential for strengthening bilateral relations.

Both sides shared the view that existing complementarities between their two economies provide an important foundation and offer broad prospects for further enhancing their economic relations. In order to promote trade and economic cooperation, both sides will take necessary measures consistent with their national laws and rules and international obligations to remove impediments to bilateral trade and investment. They reaffirmed the importance of the ministerial meeting of the Joint Economic Group (JEG) and agreed to hold the next (seventh) JEG meeting within the year.

The two sides will set up a compact Joint Study Group (JSG) composed of officials and economists to examine the potential complementarities between the two countries in expanded trade and economic cooperation. The JSG would also draw up a programme for the development of India-China trade and economic cooperation for the next five years, aimed at encouraging greater cooperation between the business communities of both sides. The Group should present a study report and recommendations to the two Governments on measures for comprehensive trade and economic cooperation by the end of June 2004.

The two countries will launch a financial dialogue and cooperation mechanism to strengthen their dialogue and coordination in this sector.

The two sides agreed to enhance cooperation at the World Trade Organization, which is not only to mutual benefit but also in the broader interest of developing countries. The two sides will hold dialogues on a regular basis in this regard.

Historical and cultural links between India and China will be strengthened, inter-alia, through the promotion of exchanges in culture, education, science and technology, media, youth and people-to-people relations. They agreed to set up Cultural Centers in each other's capitals and facilitate their establishment.

Both sides will work towards the enhancement of direct air and shipping links, tourism, exchange hydrological data in flood season on common rivers as agreed, cooperation in agriculture, dairy, food processing, health and other sectors.

They agreed on the need to broaden and deepen defence exchanges between the two countries, which will help enhance and deepen the mutual understanding and trust between the two armed forces. They confirmed that the exchange of visits by their Defence Ministers and of military officials at various levels should be strengthened.

The two sides exchanged views on the India-China boundary question and expounded their respective positions. They reiterated their readiness to seek a fair, reasonable and mutually acceptable solution through consultations on an equal footing. The two sides agreed that pending an ultimate solution, they should work together to maintain peace and tranquility in the border areas, and reiterated their commitment to continue implementation of the agreements signed for this purpose, including the clarification of the Line of Actual Control.

The two sides agreed to each appoint a Special Representative to explore from the political perspective of the overall bilateral relationship the framework of a boundary settlement.

The Indian side recognizes that the Tibet Autonomous Region is part of the territory of the People's Republic of China and reiterates that it does not allow Tibetans to engage in anti-China political activities in India. The Chinese side expresses its appreciation for the Indian position and reiterates that it is firmly opposed to any attempt and action aimed at splitting China and bringing about "independence of Tibet".

The Indian side recalled that India was among the first countries to recognize that there is one China and its one China policy remains unaltered. The Chinese side expressed its appreciation of the Indian position.

India and China recognized the primacy of maintaining international peace. This is a prerequisite for the socio-economic development of all developing countries, including India and China. The world is marked by diversity. Every country has the right to choose its own political system and path to development. As two major developing countries, India and China acknowledged the importance of their respective roles in the shaping of a new international political and economic order. The international community must help the developing countries to eliminate poverty and narrow the gap between the North and the South through dialogue and cooperation so as to achieve common prosperity.

The two sides acknowledged the vital importance of the role of the United Nations in world peace, stability and development. They are determined to continue their efforts in strengthening the UN system. They reaffirmed their readiness to work together to promote reform of the UN. In reform of the UN Security Council, priority should be given to enhancing representation of the developing countries.

Both sides stood for continued multilateral arms control and disarmament process, undiminished and equal security for all at progressively lower levels of armament and for multilateral negotiations aimed at nuclear disarmament and elimination of nuclear weapons. They are firmly opposed to introduction of weapons in outer space, use or threat of force against space-based objects and support cooperation in development of space technology for peaceful purposes.

The two sides recognised the threat posed by terrorism to them and to global peace and security. They resolutely condemned terrorism in any form. The struggle between the international community and global terrorism is a comprehensive and sustained one, with the ultimate objective of eradication of terrorism in all regions. This requires strengthening the global legal framework against terrorism. Both sides shall also promote cooperation on counter-terrorism through their bilateral dialogue mechanism.

India and China face special and similar challenges in their efforts to protect the environment while simultaneously forging ahead with rapid social and economic development of their countries. In this context, the two sides agreed to work together in a practical manner to cooperate on preserving the environment and ensuring sustainable development and to coordinate positions on climate change, biodiversity and other issues in relevant multilateral fora.

The two sides supported multilateral cooperation in Asia, believing that such cooperation promotes mutually beneficial exchanges, economic growth as well as greater cohesion among Asian countries. The two sides viewed positively each other's participation in regional and sub-regional multilateral cooperation processes in Asia.

The two sides stated that the improvement and development of India-China relations is not targeted at any third country and does not affect either country's existing friendly relations and cooperation with other countries.

The two sides agreed that the official visit of the Prime Minister of India to the People's Republic of China has been a success, has contributed to enhancing mutual understanding and trust between the Governments, leaders and peoples of the two countries, and marks a new step forward in strengthening the all-round cooperation between India and China in the new century.

Prime Minister Vajpayee invited Premier Wen Jiabao to visit India at a mutually convenient time and conveyed to President Hu Jintao an invitation from President Abdul Kalam to visit India. The Chinese side accepted the invitations with appreciation. The dates of the visits will be settled through diplomatic channels. On behalf of the Government and the people of India,

H.E. Prime Minister Atal Bihari Vajpayee thanked the Government and the people of China for the warm welcome received by him and his delegation.

Signed in Beijing on 23 June 2003 in the Hindi, Chinese and English languages.

(Sd.) Atal Bihari Vajpayee
Prime Minister
The Republic of India

(Sd.) Wen Jiabao
Premier of the State Council
The People's Republic of China

CHAPTER 12

Synopses of Agreements/MOUs/Memoranda—Visit of Chinese Premier Wen Jiabao to India

New Delhi, 11 April 2005

1. Agreement on the Political Parameters and Guiding Principles for the Settlement of the India-China Boundary Question

(Sd.) Shri MK Narayanan
National Security Advisor

(Sd.) Mr. Dai Bingguo
Chinese Special Representative

(The full text of the Agreement is available on the MEA website www.mea.gov.in)

2. Protocol on Modalities for the Implementation of CBMs in the Military Field Along the Line of Actual Control in the India-China Border Areas

(Sd.) Shri Shyam Saran
Foreign Secretary

(Sd.) Mr. Wu Dawei
Vice Foreign Minister of China

This Protocol lays down modalities for the implementation of several measures contained in the Agreement of 1996 on Military CBMs along the LAC in the India-China Border Areas. The salient features of the Protocol include:

I. Details on avoiding the holding of large-scale military exercises in close proximity of the LAC as per the 1996 Agreement and in case an exercise is being conducted, to provide relevant information to the other side;

II. Dealing with air intrusions as per the provisions of 1996 Agreement;

III. Procedure to be followed by both sides in the eventuality of their border personnel coming in face-to-face contact as a result of differences in the alignment of LAC or any other reason;

IV. Holding of additional meetings at the existing three border personnel meeting points, namely, Spanggur, Nathu La and Bumla to celebrate National Day or Army Day of each side;

V. Extension of the mechanism of border meeting points to Kibithu-Damai in the Eastern Sector and the Lipulekh Pass in the Middle Sector;

VI. Exchanges between the relevant Military Regions of China and Army Commands of India;

VII. Exchanges between institutions of training, sports and culture of the two armed forces; and

VIII. Action to be taken by either side in case the personnel of one side cross over to the other side due to force majeure, such as natural disasters, as also action to be taken to prevent trans-border spread of infectious diseases.

(The full text of the Protocol is available on the MEA website www.mea.gov.in)

3. Report of the India-China Joint Study Group on Comprehensive Trade and Economic Cooperation

(Presented to the Prime Minister of India and the Premier of China by the Commerce and Industries Minister of India and the Commerce Minister of China.)

The Report of the Joint Study Group is the outcome of deliberations in the JSG over a period of one year, during which the JSG held four meetings alternately in China and India. The Report was finalised and signed by the two Co-Chairmen, Dr. Rakesh Mohan, Secretary (Economic Affairs) and Mr. An Min, Vice Minister, Ministry of Commerce, during the last meeting held in New Delhi from March 21-23, 2005.

The JSG Report consists of seven Chapters dealing with the Context of India-China Economic Cooperation, India-China Trade in Goods, India-China Trade in Services, Investments, India-China Economic Cooperation, India-China Regional Trading Arrangement and Recommendations for the Development of India-China Trade & Economic Cooperation.

The JSG in its Report has identified a series of measures related to trade in goods, trade in services, investments and other areas of economic cooperation, and recommended their expeditious implementation to remove impediments and facilitate enhanced economic engagement between India and China. The Ministerial-level India-China Joint Economic Group (JEG) will consider these recommendations and coordinate their implementation. The JSG has also recommended an India-China Regional Trading Arrangement, comprising of trade in goods and services, investments, identified understandings for trade and investment promotion and facilitation, and measures for promotion of economic cooperation in identified sectors. The JSG has recommended to the governments the appointment of a Joint Task Force to study in detail the feasibility of, and the benefits that may derive from, the India-China Regional Trading Arrangement and give recommendations regarding its content.

(The full text of the JSG report is available on the MEA website www.mea.gov.in.)

4. Agreement on Mutual Administrative Assistance and Co-Operation in Customs Matters between India and China

(Sd.) Shri Natwar Singh External Affairs Minister	(Sd.) Mr. Li Zhaoxing Chinese Foreign Minister

This agreement aims to further co-operation between the Customs Administrations of the two countries in matters related to the application and enforcement of the Customs Laws. The agreement enables provision of administrative assistance for the proper application of customs law and for the prevention, investigation and combating of Customs offences and lays down that either Customs Administration shall, in making enquiries on behalf of the other Customs Administration, act as if they were being made on its own account.

The agreement will allow the Customs Administrations to share information and intelligence relating to new Customs law enforcement techniques, new trends, means or methods of committing Customs offences and the movement of persons or goods known to have, or suspected of having contravened the Customs law of the other side. The agreement also provides for special surveillance over goods either in transport or in storage notified by the Requesting Administration as giving rise to suspected illicit traffic towards the customs territory of the Requesting Administration.

The agreement envisages exchange of customs officers or experts when mutually beneficial for advancing the understanding of each other's customs techniques. It also suggests the exchange of information relating to a number of areas including usage of interdiction and detection equipment, customs legislation and procedure, technical cooperation with third countries and simplification and harmonization of customs procedure.

5. Memorandum of Understanding on Civil Aviation between India and China

(Sd.) Shri Ajay Prasad
Secretary, Ministry of Civil Aviation

(Sd.) Mr. Yang Yuanyuan
Director, General Administration of Civil Aviation

The MOU provides for major liberalisation of air links between India and China with multiple designation of carriers and an 'Open Skies' policy for cargo, an increase in capacity entitlements, more points of call and an increase in the number of intermediary and beyond points. According to the Memorandum, the designated airlines of both parties are entitled to have unlimited third, fourth and fifth freedom traffic rights with unlimited capacity entitlement for dedicated cargo services. The designated airlines of both parties may co-terminalize any two points in its own territory and/or any two points in the territory of the other party without any cabotage rights with the exception for airlines designated by India to combine Beijing and Shanghai, Beijing and Guangzhou, Shanghai and Guangzhou.

The designated airlines of each party have the following capacity entitlement for combination services:

14 weekly frequencies as of 2005 IATA summer season

28 weekly frequencies as of 2005 IATA winter season

42 weekly frequencies as of 2006 IATA summer season

The Memorandum also provides for simplification of the Visa procedures for operating and cabin crew, employment of foreign pilots by designated airlines of either party, use of dry leased aircraft for both combination services and cargo services.

It lays down the guidelines for issues such as code-sharing arrangement, co-terminalization and the weekly frequency of flights.

6. Protocol of Phytosanitary Requirements for the Export of Grape From India to China between the Ministry of Agriculture of India and the General Administration of Quality Supervision, Inspection and Quarantine of China

(Sd.) Smt. Radha Singh
Secretary, Ministry of Agriculture

(Sd.) Mr. Li Changjiang
Director General Administration of Quality Supervision Inspection and Quarantine (AQSIQ) on the Chinese side

The MOU aims to facilitate the export of grapes from India to China by putting in a place a regulatory mechanism on Sanitary and Phytosanitary standards and laying out in detail the procedural aspect, including certification and labeling requirements. The document specifies Dalian, Tianjin, Beijing, Shanghai, Qingdao, Nanjing as entry ports for grape from India to China.

7. Protocol of Phytosanitary Requirements for Exporting Bitter Gourds from India to China between the Ministry of Agriculture of India and the General Administration of Quality Supervision, Inspection and Quarantine of China

(Sd.) Smt. Radha Singh
Secretary, Ministry of Agriculture

(Sd.) Mr. Li Changjiang
Director General Administration of Quality Supervision Inspection and Quarantine (AQSIQ) on the Chinese side

The MOU aims to facilitate the export of bitter gourd from India to China by putting in a place a regulatory mechanism on Sanitary and Phytosanitary standards and laying out in detail the procedural aspect, including certification and labeling requirements.

8. Memorandum of Understanding on Cooperation between the Indian Council of World Affairs, India and the Chinese People's Institute of Foreign Affairs, China

(Sd.) Shri Shyam Saran
Foreign Secretary

(Sd.) Mr. Wu Dawei
Vice Foreign Minister of China

The MOU intends to enhance mutual understanding and friendship by promoting the development of friendly institutional relations.

The MOU envisages, inter alia, mutual exchange of visits, participation in conferences, seminars and symposia, co-sponsoring of bilateral symposiums on issues of common interest, exchange of publications and other forms of cooperation agreed upon by both parties through consultations

Memorandum of Understanding on the Launch of the India-China Financial Dialogue.

(Sd.) Dr. Rakesh Mohan	(Sd.) Mr. Wu Dawei
Secretary, Department of Economic Affairs	Vice Foreign Minister of China

This MOU is aimed at promoting mutual understanding and practical cooperation between the two sides in the financial sector.

The Dialogue will enable the two sides to exchange views on domestic and international macro-economic situations, national fiscal and monetary policies, financial reforms and regional or global developments of mutual interest in the financial sector and facilitate the development of develop bilateral cooperation between their banking sectors, budget and taxation authorities, financial regulatory agencies and capital markets.

The Dialogue seeks to enhance commercial and economic exchanges between the two countries and increase mutually beneficial bilateral cooperation and coordination in the International Monetary Fund, the World Bank, the Asian Development Bank and other International financial and development institutions.

9. Memorandum of Understanding between the Ministries of Water Resources of India and China upon Provision of Hydrological Information of the Sutlej/Langqen Zangbo River in Flood Season by China to India

(Sd.) Shri J. Hari Narayan	(Sd.) Mr. Wu Dawei
Secretary, Ministry of Water Resources	Vice Foreign Minister of China

The MOU envisages provision of hydrological information in respect of the Sutlej/Langqen Zangbo River in flood season for flood control and disaster mitigation in downstream areas. The arrangement entails building of a hydrological station by the Chinese side on the Sutlej/Langqen Zangbo River before the flood season of year 2006 and provision of hydrological information to the Indian side beginning the flood season of year 2006. The Chinese side will bear the cost for setting up of the hydrological station and the Indian side will bear the cost for provision of the hydrological information and the operation of the hydrological station. The detailed implementation plan for exact modalities will be further discussed and finalised between the two sides. According to the MOU, the Chinese side will provide information on any abnormal rise/fall in the water level/discharge and other information, which may lead to sudden floods on the basis of existing monitoring and data collection facilities on real time basis. Both sides will continue to discuss the possibility of providing hydrological information during flood season by China to India in respect of two more rivers—Parlung Zangbo and Lohit/Zayu Qu.

10. Protocol on India China Film Cooperation Commission

(Sd.) Shri Navin Chawla Secretary, Ministry of Information and Broadcasting	(Sd.) Mr. Wu Dawei Vice Foreign Minister of China

The Protocol envisages the constitution of the India-China Film Cooperation Commission to strengthen cooperation and promote bilateral exchanges between India and China in the Entertainment Sector, with special focus on films, both feature and documentary and animation.

It will also consider issues such as increasing the import of each others original films, exchanging of information and technical know how in the sphere of film-making and allied sectors, providing location and studio facilities for shooting of films by one country in the other's territory and extending marketing and distribution facilities of each country's films in the other country.

The Commission has also been tasked with exploring avenues of bilateral co-operation in developing animation and facilitate their diffusion, conducting Film Weeks in the presence of the other party's delegation regularly and reciprocally in the two nations and organize movie professionals of the two nations to participate in international film markets, seminars and film festivals in India and China. The Protocol also envisages concrete implementation of the Sino-Indian co-production agreement. It lays out the composition of the India-China Film Commission and outlines its administrative and financial aspects.

11. Memorandum on the Construction of an Indian Style Buddhist Temple on the Western Side of The White Horse Temple In Luoyang, China

(Sd.) Shri Nalin Surie Ambassador of India	(Sd.) Mr. Wu Dawei Vice Foreign Minister of China

This Memorandum seeks to carry forward India-China Buddhist cultural links, with India and China jointly constructing an Indian style Buddhist temple in the International Garden of the Luoyang White Horse Temple. The Memorandum envisages that India would provide the Buddha Idol and other accompanying materials for the Temple. The Indian side will also be responsible for providing the main architectural design of the Temple project, its blue print, materials used for the Temple and the landscape planning. The Chinese side will provide 2,666.67 square meters of land for constructing the Temple. It will also be responsible for advising and offering suggestions for the construction of the Temple, obtaining the support and approval of Chinese Government, Henan Provincial Government and the local administration and to handle all relevant procedures and formalities. The Chinese side will also facilitate the visits of experts and architects of the Indian side to visit the project site to supervise and inspect the quality of the work.

CHAPTER 13

Joint Statement of the Republic of India and the People's Republic of China

New Delhi, 11 April 2005

1. H.E. Mr. Wen Jiabao, Premier of the State Council of the People's Republic of China, is currently paying a state visit to the Republic of India from 9 to 12 April 2005 at the invitation of H.E. Dr. Manmohan Singh, Prime Minister of the Republic of India.

During the visit, Premier Wen Jiabao held talks with Prime Minister Dr. Manmohan Singh, called on President Dr. A.P.J. Abdul Kalam and Vice President Shri Bhairon Singh Shekhawat, and met with Chairperson, United Progressive Alliance Smt. Sonia Gandhi. External Affairs Minister Shri K. Natwar Singh and Leader of Opposition, Lok Sabha Shri L.K. Advani will call on him. Premier Wen paid a visit to Bangalore and will deliver a speech at the Indian Institute of Technology in New Delhi.

Leaders of the two countries had an in-depth exchange of views in a sincere, friendly and constructive atmosphere and reached broad consensus on bilateral relations and international and regional issues of common concern.

2. The two sides reviewed the friendly contacts and progress in their bilateral relations in recent years and agreed that India-China relations have entered a new stage of comprehensive development. Both sides noted with satisfaction that with the frequent exchange of visits between leaders of the two countries, the process of building trust and understanding has gained momentum. Rapid growth of trade and economic cooperation has been coupled with the expansion of exchanges and cooperation in other fields. The two sides have made incremental

progress in addressing outstanding issues. The two sides have also maintained good communication and collaboration in international and regional affairs. Both sides agreed that India and China have made satisfying progress in developing their long-term constructive and cooperative partnership.

The two sides recalled the Declaration on Principles for Relations and Comprehensive Cooperation between the two Prime Ministers on 23 June 2003 and reiterated that the Declaration provided a shared vision of bilateral relations and an agreed framework for cooperation.

3. In the light of the development of their bilateral relations, in order to promote good neighbourliness, friendship and mutually beneficial cooperation and taking into account the profound changes in the regional and international situation, the two sides agreed that India-China relations have now acquired a global and strategic character. The leaders of the two countries have, therefore, agreed to establish an India-China Strategic and Cooperative Partnership for Peace and Prosperity.

Such a partnership is based on the principles of Panchsheel, mutual respect and sensitivity for each other's concerns and aspirations, and equality; provides a sound framework for an all-round and comprehensive development of bilateral relations based on mutual and equal security, development and prosperity of the two peoples; and contributes to jointly addressing global challenges and threats. It reflects the readiness of the two sides to resolve outstanding differences in a proactive manner without letting them come in the way of the continued development of bilateral relations.

4. The two sides agreed that high-level exchanges between the governments, parliaments and political parties of the two countries play an important role in expanding overall bilateral cooperation. They conveyed their determination to maintain and strengthen the momentum of such exchanges in future and agreed to hold regular meetings between the leaders of the two countries. In this context, the two sides also reiterated their intention to promote regular ministerial-level exchanges and make full use of the India-China strategic dialogue and other bilateral dialogue mechanisms.

5. The year of 2005 marks the 55th anniversary of the establishment of diplomatic relations between India and China. To mark the occasion, the two countries will organize a series of commemorative activities. It was noted that "Cultural Festival of China" was currently underway in India and that a corresponding "Cultural Festival of India" would be organized in China later in the year. The two sides would also organize other cultural activities to further promote mutual awareness and deepen the friendship between the two peoples. The two sides declared 2006 as the "year of India-China friendship".

Both sides expressed satisfaction with strengthened exchanges in the area of culture, and affirmed that mutual understanding and cultural exchanges would facilitate development of cooperation in other areas as well. In order to reinforce traditional cultural links, an agreement was concluded for the construction of an Indian-style Buddhist temple at Luoyang in Henan Province of China.

6. The two sides stressed that an all-round expansion of India-China economic cooperation, including trade and investment, constitutes an important dimension of a stronger India-China relationship. The two countries agreed to make joint efforts to increase the bilateral trade volume to US$ 20 billion or higher by 2008. The two sides welcomed the report of the Joint Study Group (JSG) that was set up to examine the potential complementarities between the two countries in expanded trade and economic cooperation. The JSG in its Report has identified a series of measures related to trade in goods, trade in services, investments and other areas of economic cooperation, and recommended their expeditious implementation to remove impediments and facilitate enhanced economic engagement between India and China. The two Prime Ministers tasked the Ministerial-level India-China Joint Economic Group (JEG) to consider these recommendations and coordinate their implementation. For this purpose, the two sides will make their best endeavour to hold the next meeting of the JEG within the next six months. The JSG has also recommended an India-China Regional Trading Arrangement, comprising of trade in goods and services, investments, identified understandings for

trade and investment promotion and facilitation, and measures for promotion of economic cooperation in identified sectors. The Prime Ministers agreed to appoint a Joint Task Force to study in detail the feasibility of, and the benefits that may derive from, the India-China Regional Trading Arrangement and give recommendations regarding its content.

Both sides noted that the Agreement on the Establishment of a Financial Dialogue Mechanism would further facilitate the dynamic and diversifying economic cooperation between the two sides. They will continue consultations on concluding the Bilateral Investment Promotion and Protection Agreement.

The two sides noted with satisfaction that the two countries have signed the SPS Protocols for the export of grapes and bitter gourd from India to China. The two sides also agreed to constitute a Joint Working Group to implement expeditiously the MOU on Application of SPS between the Chinese General Administration of Quality Supervision, Inspection and Quarantine and the Indian Ministry of Agriculture.

China positively evaluates market access for Indian rice to the Chinese market and will launch as early as possible the risk analysis procedure of the Indian rice in accordance with relevant Chinese laws and regulations.

7. The two sides agreed to further promote the cooperation in the spheres of education, science and technology, healthcare, information, tourism, youth exchange, agriculture, dairy development, sports and other fields on the basis of mutual benefit and reciprocity. The two sides decided to establish an India-China Steering Committee on Scientific and Technological Cooperation chaired by their Ministers for Science and Technology, and start consultations on an agreement on mutual recognition of academic certificates and degrees between India and China. The two sides announced the launching of regular youth exchange activities. China will invite 100 Indian youth to China within the year of 2005 and hold an exhibition this year on advanced and applicable technologies in India.

8. The two sides recognized the importance of strengthening mutual connectivity and agreed to jointly work towards further

enhancement of direct air and shipping links, tourism and people-to-people contacts. It was noted with satisfaction that an MOU on major liberalisation of civil aviation links between India and China was concluded during the visit.

9. The two sides will continue to cooperate in exchanging flood-season hydrological data of the trans-border rivers as agreed between them.

In response to concerns expressed by the Indian side, the Chinese side agreed to take measures for controlled release of accumulated water of the landslide dam on the river Parechu, as soon as conditions permit. It was noted with satisfaction that an agreement concerning the provision of hydrological data on Sutlej/Langqen Zangbo was concluded during the visit and that the two sides had also agreed to continue bilateral discussions to finalize at an early date similar arrangements for the Parlung Zangbo and Lohit/Zayu Qu Rivers.

The two sides agreed to cooperate in the field of energy security and conservation, including, among others, encouraging relevant departments and units of the two countries to engage in the survey and exploration of petroleum and natural gas resources in third countries.

10. The two sides noted the useful exchanges and interaction in the military field and decided to further promote such exchanges and interaction. They agreed that broadening and deepening of defense exchanges between the two countries was of vital importance in enhancing mutual trust and understanding between the two armed forces, and to ensuring a peaceful environment in which they could pursue their respective national development objectives. The two sides decided to further strengthen effective contacts and exchanges in this field.

11. During the visit, the two sides exchanged views on the India-China boundary question and reiterated their readiness to seek a fair, reasonable and mutually acceptable solution, through equal and friendly consultations and proceeding from the overall interests of bilateral relations. They expressed satisfaction over the progress made in the discussions between the Special Representatives of the two countries and welcomed

the conclusion of the Agreement on the Political Parameters and Guiding Principles for the Settlement of the Boundary Question. Both sides are convinced that an early settlement of the boundary question will advance the basic interests of the two countries and should therefore be pursued as a strategic objective. They expressed their commitment to the mechanism of Special Representatives for seeking a political settlement of the boundary question in the context of their long-term interests and the overall bilateral relationship.

Pending a final resolution, the two sides will continue to make joint efforts to maintain peace and tranquility in the border areas in accordance with the Agreements of 1993 and 1996. Both sides agreed that while continuing the discussions between the Special Representatives, it is also important that the Joint Working Group (JWG) continues its work to seek an early clarification and confirmation of the Line of Actual Control (LAC). Progress made so far on the clarification of the LAC in the India-China border areas was noted. It was agreed to complete the process of exchanging maps indicating their respective perceptions of the entire alignment of the LAC on the basis of already agreed parameters, with the objective of arriving at a common understanding of the alignment, as soon as possible.

The two sides expressed satisfaction at the progress achieved in the implementation of the Agreements of 1993 and 1996 and agreed to fully implement them expeditiously. Towards that end, they concluded a Protocol on Modalities for the Implementation of Confidence Building Measures in the Military Field along the Line of Actual Control in the India-China Border Areas.

12. The Indian side reiterated that it recognized the Tibet Autonomous Region as part of the territory of the People's Republic of China and that it did not allow Tibetans to engage in anti-China political activities in India.

The Indian side recalled that India was among the first countries to recognize that there is one China and its one China policy remains unaltered. The Indian side stated it would continue to abide by its one China policy.

The Chinese side expressed its appreciation for the Indian positions.

13. Both sides reviewed with satisfaction the implementation of the memorandum on the border trade through the Nathula Pass between the Tibet Autonomous Region of the People's Republic of China and the Sikkim State of the Republic of India.

14. The two sides noted with satisfaction that through friendly consultations an agreement in principle had been reached between the two countries to solve the long-pending issue of property originally belonging to Indian Consulate General in Shanghai with the Chinese side agreeing to provide a plot of land in lieu of the premises of the original Consulate General of India.

15. As two large developing countries, both India and China were aware of each other's important role in the process of promoting the establishment of a new international political and economic order. Both sides share common interests in the maintenance of peace, stability and prosperity in Asia and the world at large, and share the desire to develop closer and more extensive understanding and cooperation in regional and international affairs.

The two sides are supportive of democratization of international relations and multilateralism, stand for the establishment of a new international political and economic order that is fair, rational, equal and mutually beneficial, and promote North-South Dialogue and South-South Cooperation. The two sides believe that the international community should eliminate poverty, narrow the gap between North and South, and achieve common prosperity through dialogue and cooperation.

16. The two sides reiterated the importance of the United Nations in global peace, stability and common development and expressed their determination to continue their efforts, together with the international community, in strengthening the UN system to develop a sound multilateral basis to address global issues. Both India and China agree that reform of the United Nations should be comprehensive and multi-faceted and should put emphasis on an increase in the representation of developing

countries. The Indian side reiterated its aspirations for permanent membership of the UN Security Council. The Chinese side also reiterated that India is an important developing country and is having an increasingly important influence in the international arena. China attaches great importance to the status of India in international affairs. It understands and supports India's aspirations to play an active role in the UN and international affairs. The two sides reaffirmed their readiness to conduct close consultations and cooperation in the process of UN reforms.

17. The two sides, aware of the threats posed by terrorism to the peace and security of the two countries and the whole world, resolutely condemn terrorism in any form. The struggle between the international community and global terrorism is a comprehensive and sustained one, with the ultimate objective of eradication of terrorism in all regions. This requires strengthening the global legal framework against terrorism. Both sides noted the positive outcome of the meetings held so far of their bilateral dialogue mechanism on counter-terrorism and agreed to further strengthen and consolidate their discussions and cooperation. It was agreed to hold the next meeting of the dialogue mechanism on counter-terrorism later this year.

18. Both sides agreed to conduct regular exchange of views on major international and regional issues, strengthen cooperation in the WTO and other international multilateral organizations, and to continue the consultations on other issues of common concern. They agreed to work together to preserve stability and growth in the global economy and reduce disparities between developed and developing countries. They supported an open, fair, equitable and transparent rule-based multilateral trade system and resolved to safeguard the legitimate rights and interests of the developing countries.

19. Aware of their linked destinies as neighbours and the two largest countries of Asia, both sides agreed that they would, together, contribute to the establishment of an atmosphere of mutual understanding, trust and cooperation in Asia and the world at large, and facilitate efforts to strengthen multilateral coordination mechanisms on security and cooperation.

20. During the visit, the two sides signed and/or released the following documents.

I. Agreement on Political Parameters and Guiding Principles for the Settlement of the India-China Boundary Question

II. Report of India-China Joint Study Group on Comprehensive Trade and Economic Cooperation

III. Protocol on Modalities for the Implementation of CBMs in the Military Field Along the Line of Actual Control in the India-China Border Areas

IV. Agreement on Mutual Administrative Assistance and Cooperation in Customs Matters

V. MOU on the Launch of the India-China Financial Dialogue

VI. MOU on Civil Aviation

VII. Protocol of Phytosanitary Requirement for Exporting Grapes from India to China

VIII. Protocol of Phytosanitary Requirement for Exporting Bitter Gourds from India to China

IX. MOU on Provision of Hydrological Information of the Sutlej/Langqen Zangbo River in Flood Season by China to India.

X. Protocol on India-China Film Cooperation Commission

XI. MOU on Cooperation between the Indian Council of World Affairs and the Chinese People's Institute of Foreign Affairs

XII. Memorandum on the Construction of an Indian-style Buddhist Temple on the Western side of the White Horse Temple in Luoyang, China

21. The two sides believed that Premier Wen Jiabao's highly successful State visit to the Republic of India marked a new level of India-China relationship and opened a new chapter in the friendly relations and cooperation between the two countries.

Premier Wen Jiabao, on behalf of the Chinese Government and people, expressed his appreciation to the Government and the people of India for their warm hospitality, and invited Prime Minister Manmohan Singh to visit China at a mutually convenient time. Prime Minister Manmohan Singh appreciated the invitation and accepted it with pleasure. The Indian side also reiterated the invitation to President Hu Jintao to visit India. The exact time of the visit will be decided through diplomatic channels.

Prime Minister of the Republic of India

Premier of the State Council of the People's Republic of China

CHAPTER 14

Protocol between the Government of the Republic of India and the Government of the People's Republic of China on Modalities for the Implementation of Confidence Building Measures in the Military Field Along the Line of Actual Control in the India-China Border Areas

New Delhi, 11 April 2005

The Government of the Republic of India and the Government of the People's Republic of China (hereinafter referred to as the two sides),

Recalling that both sides are committed to developing their long-term constructive and cooperative partnership on the basis of the Five Principles of Peaceful Co-existence, mutual respect and sensitivity for each other's concerns and aspirations, and equality,

Reaffirming that the two sides seek a fair, reasonable and mutually acceptable settlement of the boundary question,

Reaffirming their commitment that, pending an ultimate solution to the boundary question, both sides shall strictly respect and observe the Line of Actual Control in the India-China border areas,

Noting the utility of confidence building measures already in place along the Line of Actual Control in the India-China border areas,

Recognising that the maintenance of peace and tranquillity along the Line of Actual Control in the India-China border areas accords with the fundamental interests of the two sides, and will facilitate the process of early clarification and confirmation of the alignment of the Line of Actual Control,

Convinced of the need for agreed modalities for the implementation of confidence building measures between the two sides in the military field along the Line of Actual Control in the India-China border areas, and

Recalling further the relevant provisions of the Agreement on the Maintenance of Peace and Tranquillity along the Line of Actual Control in the India-China Border Areas signed in September 1993 and Agreement on Confidence Building Measures in the Military Field along the Line of Actual Control in the India-China Border Areas signed between the two sides in November 1996,

Have agreed on the modalities as follows:

Article I

In accordance with Article II of the Agreement on Confidence Building Measures in the Military Field along the Line of Actual Control in the India-China Border Areas signed between the two sides in November 1996, the two sides should strictly respect and observe the Line of Actual Control and work together to maintain peace and tranquillity in the border areas.

Article II

In accordance with Article IV of the Agreement on Confidence Building Measures in the Military Field along the Line of Actual Control in the India-China Border Areas signed between the two sides in November 1996,

1. Both sides shall avoid holding large-scale military exercises involving more than one Division (approximately 15,000 troops) in close proximity to the Line of Actual Control. However, if such exercises are to be conducted, the strategic direction of the main force involved shall not be towards the other side.

2. If either side conducts a military exercise involving more than one Brigade Group (approximately 5,000 troops) in close proximity to the Line of Actual Control, it shall not be targeted against the other side. The side undertaking the exercise shall give, through Flag Meetings, the other side prior intimation

15 days in advance of the exercise with regard to type, level, planned duration and area of exercise as well as the number and type of units or formations participating in the exercise.

3. Each side shall be entitled to obtain timely clarification within 15 days from the side undertaking the exercise in respect of data specified in paragraph (2) above of the present article, through Flag Meetings. Each side shall give prior intimation of changes in the timing of any scheduled exercise 15 days in advance, through Flag Meetings.

Article III

In accordance with Article V of the Agreement on Confidence Building Measures in the Military Field along the Line of Actual Control in the India-China Border Areas signed between the two sides in November 1996,

1. In the event of an alleged air intrusion of its controlled airspace by the military aircraft of the other side, either side may seek a Flag Meeting within 48 hours of the alleged air intrusion in order to seek a clarification. The investigation shall be completed by the other side and its results communicated through a Flag Meeting within a period of four weeks.

2. If a military aircraft of either side is required to fly across the Line of Actual Control or to overfly the airspace of the other side, prior permission shall be sought from the other side according to procedures and formats to be mutually agreed upon.

3. If a military or civilian aircraft of either side is required to fly across the Line of Actual Control or to land on the other side of the Line of Actual Control in an emergency situation, the two sides will ensure flight safety in such situations by adhering to procedures to be mutually agreed upon.

Article IV

In accordance with Article VI of the Agreement on Confidence Building Measures in the Military Field along the Line of Actual Control in the India-China Border Areas signed between the two sides in November 1996, if the border personnel of the two sides come to a face-to-face situation due to differences on the alignment of the Line of Actual Control or any other reason, they shall exercise self-restraint and take all necessary steps to avoid an escalation of the situation. To this end, they shall follow the procedures as given below:

1. Both sides shall cease their activities in the area, not advance any further, and simultaneously return to their bases.

2. Both sides shall then inform their respective Headquarters and, if necessary, enter into immediate consultations through border meetings or diplomatic channels so as to prevent an escalation of the situation.

3. Throughout the face-to-face situation, neither side shall use force or threaten to use force against the other.

4. Both sides shall treat each other with courtesy and refrain from any provocative actions. Neither side shall put up marks or signs on the spots.

Article V

In accordance with Article VII of the Agreement on Confidence Building Measures in the Military Field along the Line of Actual Control in India-China Border Areas signed between the two sides in November 1996,

1. Both sides shall hold two additional border meetings each year at Spanggur Gap in the Western Sector, Nathu La Pass in the Sikkim Sector and Bum La in the Eastern Sector respectively in celebration of the National Day or Army Day of either side. Specific arrangements shall be decided through consultation between the border forces of the two sides.

2. Both sides agree in principle to expand the mechanism of border meeting points to include Kibithu-Damai in the Eastern Sector and Lipulekh Pass/Qiang La in the Middle Sector. The precise locations of these border meeting points will be decided through mutual consultations.

3. Both sides shall conduct exchanges between the relevant Military Regions of China and Army Commands of India. Specific arrangements shall be decided upon through mutual consultations between the relevant agencies under the Ministries of Defence of the two sides.

4. Both sides shall strengthen exchanges between institutions of training of the two armed forces, and conduct exchanges between institutions of sports and culture of the two armed forces. Specific arrangements shall be decided upon through mutual consultations between the relevant agencies under the Ministries of Defence of the two sides.

Article VI

In accordance with Article VIII of the Agreement on Confidence Building Measures in the Military Field along the Line of Actual Control in the India-China Border Areas signed between the two sides in November 1996,

1. In case the personnel of one side in the border areas cross over to the other side due to force majeure such as natural disasters:

I. The side having discovered it should promptly contact and notify the other side;

II. The personnel crossing over to the other side should, in the light of the prevailing circumstances, take measures to return to their own side or proceed to places designated by the other side en route to return to their own side;

III. The receiving side will provide all possible assistance to the personnel from the other side and ensure their earliest possible return; and

IV. At the request of the side affected by the natural disaster, the other side may consider all possible measures to help alleviate the situation.

2. In order to prevent infectious diseases in specific areas on either side in the border areas from spreading to the other side:

Both sides should share relevant information promptly through border meetings or diplomatic channels;

I. Each side should take measures to prevent the spread of diseases from spilling onto the other side; and

II. At the request of the side suffering from spread of infectious diseases, the other side may consider all possible measures to help alleviate the situation.

Article VII

The Protocol shall enter into force on the date of signature of this Protocol and will automatically be rendered invalid if the Agreement on Confidence Building Measures in the Military Field along the Line of Actual Control in the India-China Border Areas signed between the two sides in November 1996 ceases to be in force. Subject to agreement after mutual consultations between the two sides, the Protocol may be amended and supplemented at any time.

Done in duplicate in New Delhi on April 11, 2005 in the Hindi, Chinese and English languages, all three texts being equally authentic. In case of any divergence, the English text shall prevail.

For the Government of the Republic of India

For the Government of the People's Republic of China

Agreement between the Government of the Republic of India and the Government of the People's Republic of China on the Political Parameters and Guiding Principles for the Settlement of the India-China Boundary Question

New Delhi, 11 April 2005

The Government of the Republic of India and the Government of the People's Republic of China (hereinafter referred to as the two sides),

Believing that it serves the fundamental interests of the peoples of India and China to foster a long-term constructive and cooperative partnership on the basis of the Five Principles of Peaceful Co-existence, mutual respect and sensitivity for each other's concerns and aspirations, and equality,

Desirous of qualitatively upgrading the bilateral relationship at all levels and in all areas while addressing differences through peaceful means in a fair, reasonable and mutually acceptable manner,

Reiterating their commitment to abide by and implement the Agreement on the Maintenance of Peace and Tranquillity along the Line of Actual Control in the India-China Border Areas, signed on 7 September 1993, and the Agreement on Confidence Building Measures in the Military Field along the Line of Actual Control in the India-China Border Areas, signed on 29 November 1996,

Reaffirming the Declaration on Principles for Relations and Comprehensive Cooperation between India and China, signed on 23 June 2003,

Recalling that the two sides have appointed Special Representatives to explore the framework of settlement of the India-China boundary question and the two Special Representatives have been engaged in consultations in a friendly, cooperative and constructive atmosphere,

Noting that the two sides are seeking a political settlement of the boundary question in the context of their overall and long-term interests,

Convinced that an early settlement of the boundary question will advance the basic interests of the two countries and should therefore be pursued as a strategic objective,

Have agreed on the following political parameters and guiding principles for a boundary settlement:

Article I

The differences on the boundary question should not be allowed to affect the overall development of bilateral relations. The two sides will resolve the boundary question through peaceful and friendly consultations. Neither side shall use or threaten to use force against the other by any means. The final solution of the boundary question will significantly promote good neighbourly and friendly relations between India and China.

Article II

The two sides should, in accordance with the Five Principles of Peaceful Coexistence, seek a fair, reasonable and mutually acceptable solution to the boundary question through consultations on an equal footing, proceeding from the political perspective of overall bilateral relations.

Article III

Both sides should, in the spirit of mutual respect and mutual understanding, make meaningful and mutually acceptable adjustments to their respective positions on the boundary question, so as to arrive at a package settlement to the boundary question. The boundary settlement must be final, covering all sectors of the India-China boundary.

Article IV

The two sides will give due consideration to each other's strategic and reasonable interests, and the principle of mutual and equal security.

Article V

The two sides will take into account, inter alia, historical evidence, national sentiments, practical difficulties and reasonable concerns and sensitivities of both sides, and the actual state of border areas.

Article VI

The boundary should be along well-defined and easily identifiable natural geographical features to be mutually agreed upon between the two sides.

Article VII

In reaching a boundary settlement, the two sides shall safeguard due interests of their settled populations in the border areas.

Article VIII

Within the agreed framework of the final boundary settlement, the delineation of the boundary will be carried out utilising means such as modern cartographic and surveying practices and joint surveys.

Article IX

Pending an ultimate settlement of the boundary question, the two sides should strictly respect and observe the line of actual control and work together to maintain peace and tranquillity in the border areas. The India-China Joint Working Group and the India-China Diplomatic and Military Expert Group shall continue their work under the Agreements of 7 September 1993 and 29 November 1996, including the clarification of the line of actual control and the implementation of confidence building measures.

Article X

The Special Representatives on the boundary question shall continue their consultations in an earnest manner with the objective of arriving at an agreed framework for a boundary settlement, which will provide the basis for the delineation and demarcation of the India-China boundary to be subsequently undertaken by civil and military officials and surveyors of the two sides.

Article XI

This Agreement shall come into force as of the date of signature and is subject to amendment and addition by mutual agreement in writing between the two sides.

Signed in duplicate in New Delhi on 11 April, 2005, in the Hindi, Chinese and English languages, all three texts being equally authentic. In case of divergence, the English text shall prevail.

For the Government of the Republic of India

For the Government of the People's Republic of China

CHAPTER 16

Joint Communiqué on the Results of the Informal Trilateral Meeting of the Foreign Ministers of India, Russia and China

Vladivostok, 2 June 2005

The fourth informal trilateral meeting between the Foreign Ministers of the Russian Federation, the Republic of India and the People's Republic of China was held in Vladivostok on June 2, 2005.

The Ministers confirmed that India, Russia and China shared a common approach to key global developments in the 21st century and favoured the democratization of international relations aimed at building a just world order based on the observance of international law, equity, mutual respect, cooperation and progress towards multipolarity. The Ministers further underlined that UN, as the most universal international organisation, should play the central role in realizing this goal. They agreed on the objective requirement for comprehensive reforms of UN, including of UNSC, so that the Organization becomes more reflective of contemporary global realities and more effective in discharging its functions.

The Ministers declared the intention of India, Russia and China to cooperate in trilateral format in combating new threats and challenges. They stressed that terrorism in all its forms and manifestations and irrespective of its origins and motivations posed one of the most serious threats to international peace and security. They agreed that it should be combated in a consistent, sustained and comprehensive manner without any double standards. They underscored the need for coordinated action between the law enforcement authorities of the three countries to act against illegal drug-trafficking and other manifestations of trans-border crimes.

The Ministers discussed prospects for economic cooperation in the trilateral format. They acknowledged the considerable potential for mutually beneficial cooperation between Russia, India and China in such spheres as transport, agriculture, energy and high technologies. They agreed that relevant experts and officials from the three sides could meet to examine concrete possibilities in these and other sectors and make specific recommendations. Stressing the important role of direct business to business contacts, they supported the proposal of a trilateral business meeting hosted by India before the end of March 2006.

The Ministers recalled the considerable efforts made by the three countries in alleviating the suffering of the victims of the recent Tsunami. In this connection, they noted the need for coordination of trilateral efforts in their joint fight against natural disasters and their consequences in the Asia Pacific Region.

The Ministers expressed satisfaction at the dynamic development of bilateral relations between India and Russia, Russia and China, India and China. This opens up possibilities for India, Russia and China to raise their trilateral cooperation to a qualitatively new level.

The Ministers expressed shared confidence that their meeting in Vladivostok would provide a new impetus to the trilateral dialogue in all spheres of mutual interest. They confirmed that strengthening of partnership in the trilateral format met the long-term national interests of India, Russia and China. They were convinced that development of mutually beneficial cooperation between the three countries in practical terms would make considerable contribution to the strengthening of peace and stability not only in Asia but also globally.

Chapter 17

Joint Declaration of the Heads of State and/or Government of Brazil, China, India, Mexico and South Africa Participating in the G8 Gleneagles Summit

Gleneagles, 7 July 2005

Introduction

1. We, the Heads of State and/or Government of Brazil, China, India, Mexico and South Africa thank Prime Minister Tony Blair for the invitation to participate at the G8 Gleneagles Summit.

2. At the historical juncture of the UN 60th anniversary and other important upcoming events this year, including the process of UN reforms aimed at providing a greater voice to developing countries in UN decision-making, the Gleneagles Summit is an opportunity to give stronger impetus to these processes and to send a positive message on international cooperation. This should be achieved through the promotion of multilateralism, the enhancement of North-South cooperation, as well as through a renewed commitment to sustainable development and the harnessing of the benefits of globalization for all.

3. We reaffirm the role of South-South cooperation in the context of multilateralism, and the need to strengthen it. We are fully committed to close coordination and cooperation to meet the challenges arising from globalization, and to promote the common interest of developing countries by striving to more effectively bring together our priorities and international engagement strategies. We recall the outcome of the Second South Summit held in Doha in June 2005, which recognised the importance of initiatives such as the "Action against Hunger

and Poverty", and the proposal for the Southern Development Fund.

Global Economic Issues

4. More stability and certainty in the world economy are paramount, together with an international context that provides developing countries with better and more equitable opportunities. Developing countries usually bear the brunt of crises and macroeconomic imbalances in the major economies that are in a position to spur conditions for global economic growth and development.

5. The persistence of hunger and poverty, even when the means to eliminate them are available, is a major obstacle to sustainable development.

6. The mobilization of international support for raising additional financial resources for development and the fight against hunger and poverty, through the effective implementation of the agreements and commitments reached by the international community in the "Consensus of Monterrey" agreed at the Conference on Financing for Development of the United Nations, is a necessary condition to reach the targets and objectives established in the "Millennium Declaration". Thus, we should preserve the coherence, the association, the will, and the sense of shared responsibility that are the common elements and principles that have to be adopted by every member of the international community if we are to see successful results.

7. The Millennium Development Goals cannot be timely and fully implemented with the current levels of ODA, which remain focused on short-term projects and vary according to the budgetary and policy priorities of donor countries. Therefore, donor countries should fulfil their commitments and reach the target of at least 0.7% of their GDP's allocated to ODA. This would greatly assist the funding of national and regional initiatives to combat poverty and hunger.

8. We welcome the decision adopted by the G-8 Finance Ministers to promote further debt relief for a number of the Least Developed Countries.

9. The removal of trade barriers to products and services of interest to developing countries is essential for development, the fight against poverty and the protection of the environment. The Doha Development Agenda explicitly places the development dimension at the heart of current trade negotiations. However, more progress is needed to implement this collective commitment. There is a need to redress the development deficit which became more acute as a result of the Uruguay Round agreements.

10. The international community needs to send a clear and positive signal to the Doha round of trade negotiations that the success of the 6th Ministerial Meeting of the WTO, to be held in Hong Kong, China, in December 2005, is essential. In this connection, a fundamental requirement is to achieve substantive progress, by the end of July 2005, regarding agricultural negotiations, access to non-agricultural markets, services, trade facilitation and rules. Trade-distorting domestic support for agriculture in developed countries must be substantially reduced and all forms of export subsidies must be eliminated by a date to be agreed.

11. All members of the international community should work together for the reform of the current international economic system to make it stronger and supportive of development, including through reforming the Bretton Woods Institutions and assuring greater say to developing countries.

Climate Change

12. Climate change has, and for the foreseeable future will continue to have, a profound impact on the development prospects of our societies. The United Nations Framework Convention on Climate Change (UNFCCC) and its Kyoto Protocol establish a regime that adequately addresses the economic, social and environmental aspects of sustainable development.

13. The international regime represented by the UNFCCC and its Kyoto Protocol rests on the differentiation of obligations among Parties, according to the principle of common but differentiated responsibilities of States. Developed countries should therefore take the lead in international action to combat climate change by fully implementing their obligations of

reducing emissions and of providing additional financing and the transfer of cleaner, low-emission and cost-effective technologies to developing countries.

14. In line with the principle of common but differentiated responsibilities, the UNFCCC and the Kyoto Protocol do not provide for any quantitative targets for emission reductions for developing countries but still require these countries to implement appropriate policies and measures to address climate change, taking into account their specific circumstances and with the support of developed countries.

15. The Clean Development Mechanism (CDM) incorporated in the Kyoto Protocol provides an important and innovative framework for the participation of developing countries in international efforts to address climate change. In addition, our countries have already carried out mitigation and adaptation efforts that precede and complement those related to the CDM.

16. The Gleneagles Summit should recognise that the Convention establishes economic and social development and poverty eradication as the first and overriding priorities of developing countries. As such, there is an urgent need for the development and financing of policies, measures and mechanisms to adapt to the inevitable adverse effects of climate change that are being borne mainly by the poor.

17. Changes in the unsustainable production and consumption patterns in the industrialized countries must be implemented. Energy efficiency and renewable energy sources, such as solar, wind and hydro-electrical power, and bio-fuels such as ethanol and biodiesel, offer opportunities that deserve careful consideration.

18. We urge the G-8 leaders and the international community to devise innovative mechanisms for the transfer of technology and to provide new and additional financial resources to developing countries under the UNFCCC and its Kyoto Protocol. For this purpose, we propose a new paradigm for international cooperation, focused on the achievement of concrete and properly assessed results, taking fully into account the perspective and

needs of developing countries. Such a paradigm must ensure that technologies with a positive impact on climate change are both accessible and affordable to developing countries and will require a concerted effort to address questions related to intellectual property rights. Additional financial resources, apart from those already available through ODA, should be directed to developing countries to enable them to access critical technologies. Collaborative research for new technologies, involving both developed and developing countries, also needs to be encouraged.

CHAPTER 18

Joint Statement by the G8 Leaders, the Leaders of Brazil, China, India, Mexico and South Africa and the Heads of the International Organisations Present in Gleneagles on Terrorist Attacks on London

Gleneagles, 7 July 2005

1. We condemn utterly these barbaric attacks. We send our profound condolences to the victims and their families. All of our countries have suffered from the impact of terrorism. Those responsible have no respect for human life. We are united in our resolve to confront and defeat this terrorism that is not an attack on one nation, but on all nations and on civilised people everywhere.

2. We will not allow violence to change our societies or our values. Nor will we allow it to stop the work of this Summit. We will continue our deliberations in the interests of a better world. Here at this Summit, the world's leaders are striving to combat world poverty and save and improve human life. The perpetrators of today's attacks are intent on destroying human life.

3. The terrorists will not succeed.

4. Today's bombings will not weaken in any way our resolve to uphold the most deeply held principles of our societies and to defeat those who would impose their fanaticism and extremism on all of us. We shall prevail. They shall not.

CHAPTER 19

सत्यमेव जयते

Vision Statement of Australia, China, India, the Republic of Korea and the United States of America for a New Asia-Pacific Partnership on Clean Development and Climate

Vientiane, 28 July 2005

Development and poverty eradication are urgent and overriding goals internationally. The World Summit on Sustainable Development made clear the need for increased access to affordable, reliable and cleaner energy and the international community agreed in the Delhi Declaration on Climate Change and Sustainable Development on the importance of the development agenda in considering any climate change approach.

We each have different natural resource endowments and sustainable development and energy strategies, but we are already working together and will continue to work to achieve common goals. By building on the foundation of existing bilateral and multilateral initiatives, we will enhance cooperation to meet both our increased energy needs and associated challenges, including those related to air pollution, energy security, and greenhouse gas intensities.

To this end, we will work together, in accordance with our respective national circumstances, to create a new partnership to develop, deploy and transfer cleaner, more efficient technologies and to meet national pollution reduction, energy security and climate change concerns, consistent with the principles of the U.N. Framework Convention on Climate Change (UNFCCC).

The partnership will collaborate to promote and create an enabling environment for the development, diffusion, deployment and transfer of existing and emerging cost-effective, cleaner technologies and practices, through concrete and substantial cooperation so as to achieve practical results. Areas for collaboration may include, but not be limited to: energy efficiency, clean coal, integrated gasification combined cycle, liquefied natural gas, carbon capture and storage, combined heat and power, methane capture and use, civilian nuclear power, geothermal, rural/village energy systems, advanced transportation, building and home construction and operation, bio-energy, agriculture and forestry, hydropower, wind power, solar power, and other renewables.

The partnership will also cooperate on the development, diffusion, deployment and transfer of longer-term transformational energy technologies that will promote economic growth while enabling significant reductions in greenhouse gas intensities. Areas for mid-to-long-term collaboration may include, but not be limited to: hydrogen, nano-technologies, advanced biotechnologies, next-generation nuclear fission, and fusion energy.

The partnership will share experiences in developing and implementing our national sustainable development and energy strategies, and explore opportunities to reduce the greenhouse gas intensities of our economies.

We will develop a non-binding compact in which the elements of this shared vision, as well as the ways and means to implement it, will be further defined. In particular, we will consider establishing a framework for the partnership, including institutional and financial arrangements and ways to include other interested and like-minded countries.

The partnership will also help the partners build human and institutional capacity to strengthen cooperative efforts, and will seek opportunities to engage the private sector. We will review the partnership on a regular basis to ensure its effectiveness.

The partnership will be consistent with and contribute to our efforts under the UNFCCC and will complement, but not replace, the Kyoto Protocol.

सत्यमेव जयते

CHAPTER 20

Memorandum of Understanding between the Ministry of Defence of the Republic of India and the Ministry of National Defence of the People's Republic of China for Exchanges and Cooperation in the Field of Defence

Beijing, 28 May 2006

Pursuant to the Declaration on Principles for Relations and Comprehensive Cooperation between India and China signed in June 2003 and the Joint Statement signed in April 2005 by the Prime Minster of the Republic of India and the Premier of the State Council of the People's Republic of China, the Ministry of Defence of the Republic of India and the Ministry of National Defence of the People's Republic of China (hereinafter referred to as "the two sides") are committed, in accordance with the relevant purposes and principles of the Charter of the United Nations, to developing the strategic and cooperative partnership for peace and prosperity between India and China. Such a partnership is based on the principles of the Five Principles of Peaceful Co-existence, mutual respect and sensitivity for each other's concerns and aspirations and equality.

The two sides note the utility of confidence building measures between them, including their armed forces.

The two sides reiterate that strengthening effective contacts in the field of defence is of vital importance to enhancing mutual trust and understanding between their two armed forces, ensuring a peaceful environment in which they can pursue their respective national development objectives, and maintaining peace and stability in the region and the world at large. In order to broaden and deepen defence exchanges between the two countries, the two sides have, through friendly consultations, reached the following understanding:

Article 1

1. Maintain frequent exchanges between the leaders and high-level functionaries of the Defence Ministries and the armed forces of India and China. An annual programme of exchange of visits will be worked out through consultations for timely implementations;

2. Convene an Annual Defence Dialogue at a mutually agreed level, to be hosted alternately by the two sides. The dialogue will review progress in defence exchanges and make suggestions for future exchanges. It will also exchange views on international, security and strategic issues;

3. Endeavour to hold joint military exercises and/or training programmes in the fields of search and rescue, anti-piracy, counter-terrorism and other areas of mutual interest. Each side will invite senior military officers of the other side to witness designated military exercises;

4. Establish a mechanism of study tours for each other's senior and middle level military officers and relevant civilian officials, in order to facilitate better understanding of foreign, defence and national development policies of the host side, and participation in seminars and discussions on themes to be agreed upon. Specific arrangements will be decided through consultations;

5. Establish a mechanism for military officers to study in the military academies of the other side to be identified by the host side. Carry out exchanges between counterpart military academies. The number of officers and academies involved in the above-mentioned exchanges can be increased if necessary; and

6. Have exchanges in other mutually agreed fields to be decided through consultations.

Article 2

For the high level delegations as undertaken under clause (a) of Article 1 and other delegations designated by the two sides, on the basis of balance and reciprocity, the host will bear the local expenses for boarding, lodging and transportation. Other delegations will be self-financed. The delegations may comprise both military and civilian officials. The host will facilitate the visits and assist with visa and other travel arrangements, as necessary.

Article 3

This Memorandum of Understanding shall come into effect on signature by the two sides. It shall remain in force for five years unless terminated in advance by either side giving written notice for termination at least three months in advance. At the end of the five-year period, the Memorandum of Understanding shall be automatically extended by another five-years, unless either side gives written notice for its non-extension at least three months before the expiry date.

Done at Beijing on May 29, 2006 in two originals, each in the Hindi, Chinese and English languages, all texts being equally authentic. In case of any divergence in interpretation, the English text shall prevail.

(Sd.) Defence Minister of the
Republic of India

(Sd.) Defence Minister of the
People's Republic of China

St. Petersburg G-8 Summit—Position Paper by Declaration by the Heads of State and/or Government of Brazil, China, India, Mexico, South Africa

St. Petersburg, 16 July 2006

Introduction

1. Global challenges today in the areas of energy security, education and infectious diseases can only be adequately dealt with through intensified international coordination and cooperation. In this regard we reiterate our proposal, made last year in Gleneagles, for a new paradigm for international cooperation, focused on the achievement of concrete and properly assessed results, taking fully into account the perspective and needs of developing countries. The increased participation of developing countries in the decision-making processes of the United Nations system and other international organizations, is essential to ensure more balanced and legitimate results.

2. In addition to the three topics to be examined at the Summit (energy security, education and infectious diseases), we also wish to call attention to the importance of mobilising financial resources for development, through innovative mechanisms supplementing the commitments made at the United Nations International Conference on Financing for Development. We reaffirm the importance of concluding negotiations on the Doha Development Agenda in 2006, as an important outcome in enabling developing countries to benefit more fully from international trade.

3. In addressing the issues brought to the attention of the G-8, we emphasize the need to follow-up on the work programme on

Africa launched at Gleneagles. As we focus on the issues before the Summit, we agree on the need to look carefully at the special needs of Africa.

4. We recognize that Africa is going through a period of renewed hope, based on its leaders' vision of promoting further regional integration with the goal of ensuring the socio-economic development of the continent. The resolution of violent conflicts which for decades have thwarted African potential is crucial. We stress the need to address the root causes of instability which are closely linked to poverty, social inequality and exclusion.

5. The international community should continue to co-operate with the African countries in their quest for peace, development and social justice. A true partnership must be established bearing in mind the views and needs of African countries and people. South-South co-operation is of particular value in that regard.

Energy Security

6. Energy security constitutes a vital and strategic issue for producing and consuming countries alike. Affordable and reliable energy resources are basic requirements for sound economic and social development as well as world peace and stability. The international community must endeavor to put in place fair and equitable conditions for the long-term sustainability and predictability of energy supplies, at reasonable, competitive prices. Energy security can be enhanced by exploiting locally available resources in a sustainable manner. Development of all feasible hydro-power potential in an optimal manner needs to be accelerated.

7. We express concern at the negative impact of soaring energy prices on our development efforts in recent years. We favour the establishment of an international energy order that is fair, equitable, secure and stable, to the benefit of the entire international community. We support an inclusive dialogue on energy, capable of creating a political environment conducive to the peaceful settlement of disputes through consultation. This dialogue should involve exporters and consumers and the International Energy Forum. In this regard we welcome

the initiative taken to hold two Round Tables in New Delhi, in January and November last year, which brought together principal Asian consumers with important regional producers.

8. Global and regional integration is a fundamental dimension of the debate on energy security. We stress the importance of more compatible and balanced regulatory frameworks both at the regional and global levels. Expanding regional cooperation can facilitate faster development of energy resources by sharing best practices and promoting regional trade in energy.

9. We emphasize the significance of technological cooperation in energy research and development to augment and diversify the energy supply by developing more efficient, affordable and cost effective energy technologies, including fossil fuel technologies and renewable energy technologies aiming at energy production and consumption, and thereby leading to greater efficiency. We call for improved access to these technologies and pledge to work with developed and developing countries in sharing knowledge and expertise for development of such technologies. In this context we also emphasize the need to develop new forms of cooperation in nuclear energy.

10. Diversification is a central element in any definition of energy security. We encourage the development and use of alternative sources of energy to enhance sustainability. New forms of energy that are clean, safe and economically efficient should be fully explored. In this regard, ethanol, biodiesel and other bio-fuels—can play a greater role in the diversification of the global energy mix, as well as in reducing emissions of greenhouse gases from anthropogenic sources.

11. Energy security is not an end in itself. We must look beyond energy security towards broader development objectives in order to ensure successful synergies among energy security, development and the environment. As our economies develop, our energy consumption will inevitably grow, which in turn will require individual and collective efforts to ensure economic and environmental sustainability.

Education

12. We call upon the international community and G-8 members, as well as UNESCO and all International agencies to strengthen cooperation towards the achievement of the Millennium Development Goals and the Dakar Goals. In this context we welcome and support the development of UNESCO Global Action Plan to achieve core "Education for All" goals and recognise the importance of the Monterrey Declaration of the E-9 countries.

13. We recognize the need for the education system to instill respect for diversity in terms of race, culture and religion. Governments have a primary role to play in ensuring a conducive environment and improving cooperation in this regard.

14. We encourage the sharing of good practices, both between countries of the North and the South and among developing countries, for accelerating progress towards EFA. The use of Information and Communication Technologies has proved essential towards improvement of educational systems. We urge developed countries to share their expertise and transfer technologies and resources, thereby enabling developing countries to employ more advanced technologies.

15. We welcome the development of mechanisms such as debt cancellation, debt reconstruction and debt swaps. International initiatives such as the Fast Track Initiative and the International Funding Facility have wide political support and have demonstrated their utility. However, donor countries need to step up their assistance with a view to consolidating long term and predictable financial support.

Infectious Diseases

16. Infectious and chronic diseases are a common enemy of mankind. We stress the urgency of dealing with infectious diseases by addressing them as a strategic issue, affecting both economic growth and social stability worldwide. Through a global partnership, we must strive to make a decisive contribution to international efforts to prevent and treat infectious diseases.

17. While communicable diseases pose a particular challenge in developing countries, the increasing importance of chronic

diseases needs to be recognized. Further attention is required to monitor and contain human influenza and other vaccine preventable diseases.

18. Infectious diseases such as HIV/AIDS, tuberculosis, malaria, and avian influenza, pose daunting challenges that must be tackled through more efficient cooperation and greater financial resources as mentioned in the Millennium Development Goals. No nation is invulnerable and no disease can be effectively controlled without international cooperation. A comprehensive response is necessary to end the unacceptable scale of mortality, which is particularly high in developing countries.

19. We reiterate the need to reduce major trade barriers to facilitate access to new affordable quality vaccines, medicines, diagnostics and technology aimed at preventing and controlling infectious diseases. The flexibilities contained in the WTO Agreement on Trade-Related Aspects of Intellectual Property Rights and recognised by the Doha Ministerial Declaration on TRIPS and Public Health should be fully used to protect public health.

20. An effective global response requires a global monitoring system that can help to prevent, identify and control the spread of infectious diseases. We encourage G-8 countries to help setting up a platform for sharing and exchanging information and best practices on the prevention and control of infectious diseases. We urge the Leaders of the G8 to collaborate with developing countries in improving capacity as regards health services, and access to treatment and research, with special focus on Africa.

21. We welcome the Political Declaration adopted by the 2006 High Level Meeting on HIV/AIDS "Uniting the World Against AIDS". We reaffirm our commitment towards the goal of universal access to comprehensive prevention programmes, treatment, care and support for persons affected by HIV/AIDS by 2010.

22. We express our support for and urge donor countries to maintain, and if possible increase, funding in a sustained and timely manner to benefit initiatives such as the Global Fund to Fight AIDS, Tuberculosis and Malaria, the Global Fund to combat

Polio and the Global Outbreak Alert and Response Network that are helping to fight, prevent and control other infectious diseases. We welcome the proposal for the establishment of an international drug purchase facility, to be known as UNITAID, which represents an effort to raise additional funds through innovative means. Efforts have to take into consideration that, while fighting infectious diseases, it is important to give special attention to vulnerable groups in order to target the disease through intensive actions, for example: TB with AIDS, TB/AIDS with Injecting Drug Users, TB/AIDS with Poverty.

23. We stress the need for adequate mechanisms through which developing countries, in particular least developing countries, can receive support from international organizations and financing sources in order to: strengthen their epidemiologic surveillance systems; build human resources and provide training; produce vaccines, medicines and inputs necessary to control infectious diseases and guarantee their availability.

Trade and the Doha Agenda for Development

24. We are committed to strengthening the multilateral trading system and view with great concern trends towards raising protectionism in developing countries. The World Trade Organization is the sole forum for global trade rule-making and liberalization. The majority of WTO members are developing countries and their interests must be at the heart of the current round of trade negotiations. The Doha Round is the best chance we have to open world markets, level the playing field, share wealth and create jobs. This is a Development Round and it must create new opportunities for the developing world.

25. Poverty alleviation and development promotion are not only ethical and economic imperatives, they are also essential for a stable world economy. All nations, especially the poorest ones, must benefit from the opportunities created by international trade. A significant substantial reduction of agricultural subsidies and improved market access for agricultural and other products will increase the competitiveness and improve living standards of developing countries.

26. Subsidies, high tariffs, tariff peaks and tariff escalation in developed countries and other trade barriers in developed countries generate distortions in the world agricultural market that affect the lives livelihood and survival needs of millions of people around the world, particularly in poor countries heavily dependent on agriculture. The elimination of such practices must not be deferred indefinitely. The international community is increasingly aware of the fact that agricultural subsidies in developed countries are not only immoral but often illegal. By keeping these privileges for themselves, rich countries are exporting more poverty to already poor countries. In addition to the elimination of export subsidies, it is necessary urgent for developed members to undertake serious effective commitments in both domestic support and market access to unblock the round. In the negotiations, the issue of recently acceded developing members should be addressed properly and effectively.

27. Deadlines have been set and repeatedly missed. Some offers on the table have fallen short of the level of ambition and of the principle of proportionality found in the Doha mandate. A consensus can be reached only if development is made the kernel of the negotiating Round and the principle of special and differential treatment incorporated integrally in all aspects.

28. Believing that concessions made by developing countries will magically unblock negotiations is an illusion. In order for the Round to live up to its development goals, developed countries must assume their responsibility in moving the process forward. The key to the end of distortions lies in the hands of those who distort. The world's poor must stand as the main beneficiaries of a fair, balanced and comprehensive outcome. Our vision of a final deal is one where rich countries will make larger concessions, developing countries will also contribute with important efforts and the least developed will not be expected to make concessions. In addition, developed members should implement duty free and quota free treatment to least developed members as early as possible. A number of pressing issues need to be addressed in the coming weeks. Time is running out. The engagement of world leaders is urgently required to break the deadlock. New impetus must be given to the negotiations. A fresh impetus needs

to be given to the negotiations that are underway in all areas. All parties must show a readiness to look beyond their narrow interests. Parties must work together to ensure that international trade will be based on open, equitable and non-discriminatory rules. We urge leaders attending the summit to strive for a high level of ambition, with equitable results, and rise to the challenge of ensuring a speedy and successful conclusion of the Doha Round in 2006. We urge leaders attending the Summit to strive for a high level of ambition, with fair and equitable results of the Doha Round in 2006, which meet the development imperatives of the developing countries.

Mobilisation of Financial Resources

29. The Millennium Summit represents the culmination of a historical process seeking to locate the fight against poverty as a key priority in the international agenda. Building upon the spirit of the Millennium Declaration, the International Conference on Financing for Development, held in Monterrey in 2002, brought focus to the timely implementation of the Millennium Development Goals (MDGs) which is of paramount importance to achieve stability, security and world peace.

30. As a result of the commitments undertaken by the international community in the Monterrey Consensus, progress has been registered in moving towards the achievement of the Millennium Development Goals, particularly in matters such as: i) debt elimination for a relevant number of highly indebted poor countries; ii) increase of ODA flows; and iii) a higher and better coordination among economic multilateral institutions in order to achieve the MDGs.

31. Additional efforts are necessary if we are to comply with the MDGs within the deadlines originally agreed upon in 2000. The Action against Hunger and Poverty initiative, launched by the Heads of State and Government of Brazil, Chile and France and supported by a significant number of countries, identified and agreed to develop possible innovative mechanisms to finance development. With the aim of advancing further, the Paris Conference on Innovative Financing for Development, held last March, examined different options for new and innovative

financing mechanisms. These mechanisms should be geared to mobilise public, private, domestic and external sources in order to increase and supplement the ones identified in the Monterrey Consensus.

32. The timely and successful fulfilment of the MDGs constitutes the starting point for the definition of long-term development strategies capable of resulting in the permanent elimination of hunger and poverty. Reaching the goal of 0.7% of GNP for ODA is a real and urgent need.

33. Further steps towards international agreements on financing for development, should take into account criteria different from those related exclusively to total GDP, given that in the developing countries which do not belong to the HIPC initiative, poverty and hunger often continue to afflict large segments of the population. At the same time, it is understood that special efforts must be directed towards the least developed countries.

34. The need to intensify efforts to raise additional financial resources for development is relevant to the debate on the issues placed before the G-8 Saint Petersburg Summit. In order to win the fight against hunger and poverty, infectious diseases and inadequate education, we must assume our shared responsibility in the search for mechanisms capable of channelling the necessary resources to fulfil common development objectives.

CHAPTER 22

Statement by the G-8, the Leaders of Brazil, China, India, Mexico, South Africa, Chairman of the Council of the Heads of State of the CIS, Chairman of the African Union, and the Heads of the International Organizations, St. Petersburg

St. Petersburg, 17 July 2006

"We are outraged by the barbaric terrorist acts, carried out on 11 July 2006 in Mumbai and other parts of India. We stand in solidarity with the Government and the people of India and express our deepest condolences to the victims and their families.

"We are determined to continue the fight against terrorism by all legitimate means. We express our readiness to undertake all necessary measures to bring to justice perpetrators, organizers, sponsors if these and other terrorist acts, and those who incited the perpetrators to commit them. We shall do it in accordance with our obligations under international law, in particular international human rights law, refugee law and humanitarian law.

"We are united with India in our resolve to intensify efforts to fight terrorism which constitutes a threat to each of our country, as well as to international peace and security."

CHAPTER 23

Joint Declaration by the Republic of India and the People's Republic of China

New Delhi, 21 November 2006

1. H.E. Mr. Hu Jintao, President of the People's Republic of China, is currently paying a State visit to the Republic of India from 20 to 23 November 2006 at the invitation of H.E. Dr. A.P.J. Abdul Kalam, President of the Republic of India.

2. President Hu Jintao held talks with Prime Minister Dr. Manmohan Singh, earlier today. He will call on President Dr. A.P.J. Abdul Kalam later in the day. Vice President Shri Bhairon Singh Shekhawat, Speaker, Lok Sabha Shri Somnath Chatterjee, and Leader of the Opposition in Lok Sabha Shri L.K. Advani will pay courtesy calls on President Hu Jintao. Smt. Sonia Gandhi, Chairperson, United Progressive Alliance, will meet him. Earlier today, Minister of External Affairs Shri Pranab Mukherjee called on the visiting Chinese President. President Hu Jintao will deliver a policy address at the Vigyan Bhawan and attend the India-China Friendship Year commemorative function. He will also visit Agra and address a business summit in Mumbai, among other engagements.

3. The leaders of the two countries have noted with satisfaction the all-round progress made over recent years in India-China relations and their regional and multilateral cooperation. They reiterate the shared vision and fundamental principles for the future development of India-China relations, as embodied in the Declaration on Principles for Relations and Comprehensive Cooperation of 23 June 2003 and the Joint Statement of 11 April 2005 signed between the Prime Ministers of the two countries.

4. Both sides agree that the relationship between India and China, the two biggest developing countries in the world, is of global and strategic significance. Both countries are seeking to avail themselves of historic opportunities for development. Each side welcomes and takes a positive view of the development of the other, and considers the development of either side as a positive contribution to peace, stability and prosperity of Asia and the world. Both sides hold the view that there exist bright prospects for their common development, that they are not rivals or competitors but are partners for mutual benefit. They agree that there is enough space for them to grow together, achieve a higher scale of development, and play their respective roles in the region and beyond, while remaining sensitive to each other's concerns and aspirations. Strategic partnership between the two countries with a similar world-view is consistent with their roles as two major developing countries. With the growing participation and role of the two countries in all key issues in today's globalising world, their partnership is vital for international efforts to deal with global challenges and threats. As two major countries in the emerging multi-polar global order, the simultaneous development of India and China will have a positive influence on the future international system.

5. In order to promote the sustainable socio-economic development of India and China, to fully realise the substantial potential for their cooperation in a wide range of areas, to upgrade India-China relations to a qualitatively new level, and to further substantiate and reinforce their Strategic and Cooperative Partnership, the leaders of the two countries have committed themselves to pursuing the following "ten-pronged strategy":

I. Ensuring Comprehensive Development of Bilateral Relations:

6. Both sides are committed to making the positive development and diversification of India-China relations in recent years an irreversible trend.

7. The two sides agree to hold regular Summit-level meetings, in each other's country and in multilateral forums. They agree that high-level exchanges between Governments, Parliaments

and political parties play an important role in expanding overall bilateral cooperation.

8. In order to sustain, facilitate and promote greater engagement between the two countries, an additional Consulate General shall be opened in each other's country. The Indian side shall open a new Consulate General in Guangzhou, while the Chinese side shall open a new Consulate General in Kolkata. In this context, the mutually satisfactory resolution of the long-pending issue of the property of the Consulate General of India in Shanghai is a positive development.

II. Strengthening Institutional Linkages and Dialogue Mechanisms:

9. The two sides shall strengthen institutional linkages between their Governments in different areas and levels with a view to foster synergy and cooperation and promote greater understanding of each other's policies and positions on important national, regional and international issues. The concerned ministries and organisations of the two countries shall intensify exchanges under the existing dialogue mechanisms and revitalise those that have not been regularly used. The signing of the Protocol of Cooperation between the Ministry of External Affairs of India and the Ministry of Foreign Affairs of China during the visit is an important step in this direction.

III. Consolidating Commercial and Economic Exchanges:

10. Both sides believe that comprehensive economic and commercial engagement between India and China is a core component of their Strategic and Cooperative Partnership. They will endeavour to raise the volume of their bilateral trade to US$ 40 billion by 2010. They shall make joint efforts to diversify their trade basket, remove existing impediments, and optimally utilise the present and potential complementarities in their economies, in order to sustain and further strengthen bilateral commercial and economic cooperation. Towards this end, both sides will attach utmost priority to an early implementation of the decisions taken in March 2006 by the Ministerial-level Joint Economic Group, including the recommendations of the Joint Study Group, through mechanisms already created for this

purpose. The Joint Task Force set up to study the feasibility and benefits of an India-China Regional Trading Arrangement shall complete its work by October 2007.

11. The conclusion of the Bilateral Investment Promotion and Protection Agreement during the visit is a welcome development that will provide the institutional and legal basis to encourage and promote greater investment flows between the two countries.

12. The Chinese side has invited India to participate in the World Exposition Shanghai 2010. The Indian side expressed its appreciation and stated that it will actively support and participate in the event.

IV. Expanding All-Round Mutually Beneficial Cooperation:

13. The two sides agree to further strengthen positive trends in the all-round development of relations and fully realize the substantial potential of cooperation, including in trade, industry, finance, agriculture, water resources, energy, environment, transportation, infrastructure, information technology, health, education, media, culture, tourism, youth affairs and other fields.

14. Both sides agree to fully implement the provisions of the Memorandum on Cooperation in the field of Oil and Natural Gas signed in January 2006 and encourage collaboration between their enterprises, including through joint exploration and development of hydrocarbon resources in third countries.

15. Given the complementarities that India and China enjoy in the area of information and communication technology, the two sides agreed to strengthen mutually beneficial cooperation in this sector, through closer policy dialogue and enhanced collaboration among their enterprises, including in third countries.

16. The two sides shall fully implement the Memorandum of Understanding on Agricultural Cooperation, step up the exchange of experience in the field of agriculture and rural development, including food security, and hold discussions and consultations on the standards for agricultural goods at an early date in order to facilitate trade in such goods.

17. The two sides will set up an expert-level mechanism to discuss interaction and cooperation on the provision of flood season hydrological data, emergency management and other issues regarding trans-border rivers as agreed between them. The on-going provision of hydrological data for the Brahmaputra/Yarlung Zangbo and the Sutlej/Langqen Zangbo Rivers by the Chinese side to the Indian side has proved valuable in flood forecasting and mitigation. The two sides agree to continue bilateral discussions to finalise at an early date similar arrangements for the Parlung Zangbo and Lohit/Zayu Qu Rivers.

18. Both sides shall intensify their consultations, bilaterally and in multilateral fora, on sustainable development, bio-diversity, climate change and other related environmental issues of common concern. The cooperation in wildlife conservation, particularly in tiger conservation, shall be stepped up.

V. Instilling Mutual Trust and Confidence through Defence Cooperation:

19. The exchange of visits in the field of defence has resulted in building of mutual trust and enhancement of mutual understanding between the defence establishments of the two countries. Both sides shall fully implement the provisions of the Memorandum of Understanding for Exchanges and Cooperation in the field of Defence signed on 29 May 2006, which provides a sound foundation and institutional framework for further development of defence cooperation.

VI. Seeking Early Settlement of Outstanding Issues:

20. Both sides are committed to resolving outstanding differences, including on the boundary question, through peaceful means and in a fair, reasonable, mutually acceptable and proactive manner, while ensuring that such differences are not allowed to affect the positive development of bilateral relations.

21. The Special Representatives of India and China on the boundary question have taken steps and shall continue to strive to arrive at a boundary settlement on the basis of the Agreement on Political Parameters and Guiding Principles for the Settlement

of India-China Boundary Question signed on 11 April 2005. An early settlement of the boundary question will advance the basic interests of the two countries and shall, therefore, be pursued as a strategic objective. The Special Representatives shall complete at an early date the task of finalising an appropriate framework for a final package settlement covering all sectors of the India-China boundary. Pending the resolution of the boundary question, both sides shall maintain peace and tranquillity in the border areas in accordance with the agreements of 1993, 1996 and 2005.

22. Along with the talks between the Special Representatives, the Joint Working Group on the India-China Boundary Question shall expedite their work, including on the clarification and confirmation of the line of actual control and the implementation of confidence building measures. It was agreed to complete the process of exchanging maps indicating their respective perceptions of the entire alignment of the LAC on the basis of already agreed parameters as soon as possible.

VII. Promoting Trans-border Connectivity and Cooperation:

23. Both sides shall promote greater trans-border cooperation at mutually agreed sites in India-China border areas with the objective of transforming their border from being a dividing line into a bridge that unites them in cooperative pursuits. In this context, border trade between India and China, including the recent resumption of border trade through the Nathula La Pass, is of significant importance. The two sides shall strengthen border trade through the existing locations, while continuing to explore the possibility of opening additional trading routes in India-China border areas.

24. The two sides welcome the organisation of a car rally, recommended by the BCIM Forum, between Kolkata and Kunming via Bangladesh and Myanmar.

25. The Chinese side shall provide greater facilitation to Indian pilgrims for the Kailash Mansarovar Yatra. Both sides shall explore the possibility of opening an additional route for the Yatra.

VIII. Boosting Cooperation in Science and Technology:

26. Bearing in mind the priority attached by India and China to scientific and technological development and innovation as a cornerstone of their efforts towards sustainable socio-economic development, the two sides shall establish an India-China Partnership in Science and Technology. The two sides welcome the establishment of the Ministerial-level Committee on Science and Technology Cooperation as a positive step in guiding, coordinating and facilitating cooperative activities. They agree to launch joint projects in the areas of (i) earthquake engineering, (ii) climate change and weather forecasting, (iii) nano-technology with focus on advanced materials, and (iv) biotechnology and medicines with focus on bio-nano. The cooperation framework shall include entrepreneurs on both sides, besides the two Governments and their respective institutions.

27. Considering that for both India and China, expansion of civilian nuclear energy programme is an essential and important component of their national energy plans to ensure energy security, the two sides agree to promote cooperation in the field of nuclear energy, consistent with their respective international commitments. As two countries with advanced scientific capabilities, they stress the importance of further deepening cooperation bilaterally as well as through multilateral projects such as ITER, and enhance exchanges in the related academic fields.

28. As countries, which have made advances in space technologies, both sides reiterate their commitment to the use of outer space for peaceful purposes. They agree to strengthen their cooperation in the use of space-based technologies for peaceful and developmental applications, including through satellite remote sensing, satellite communications, satellite meteorology and satellite launch services. Cooperation in practical applications of space technology, such as those related to disaster management and distance education, shall also be actively explored. Towards this end, both sides shall fully implement the provisions of the Memoranda of Understanding on the peaceful use of outer space signed between India and China in December 1991 and January 2002.

IX. Revitalising Cultural Ties and Nurturing People-to-People Exchanges:

29. The centuries-old cultural contacts between the two peoples provide a strong foundation for enduring friendship between India and China. The initiatives to rediscover these historical linkages and revitalise them in the present day context, including through an early completion of the Xuanzang Memorial in Nalanda and the Indian-style Buddhist Shrine in Luoyang, will further strengthen these bonds. The two sides agree to strengthen cooperation in the area of spiritual and civilizational heritage, discuss collaboration in the digitisation of Buddhist manuscripts available in China as well as the redevelopment of Nalanda as a major centre of learning with the establishment of an international university on the basis of regional cooperation. In order to promote greater awareness of each other's culture, the two sides shall organise a "Festival of India" in China and a "Festival of China" in India, with a joint logo. Detailed modalities in this regard will be decided by the concerned authorities through mutual consultations.

30. In order to promote greater academic exchanges between India and China, the two sides agree to work towards the establishment of an "India-China Exchange Foundation". Detailed modalities of the Foundation will be worked out through mutual consultations.

31. India-China relations in the field of education will be further strengthened through a new Educational Exchange Programme concluded during the visit.

32. The two sides also agree to launch a five-year programme for mutual exchange of youth delegations. In this context, the Chinese side invites five hundred youth from India over the next five years.

33. With a view to vigorously promoting tourism between India and China, the two sides shall organise the "India-China Year of Friendship Through Tourism" in 2007 with a joint logo and take other initiatives, such as opening of the office of the China National Tourism Administration in India and an

Indian Tourism Office in China, improved air connectivity, and continued liberalisation of the visa regime.

34. The two sides welcome cooperation linkages between the Indian States and the Chinese provinces in order to promote greater people-to-people exchanges.

X. Expanding Cooperation on Regional and International Stage:

35. The two sides shall hold regular exchange of views on the emerging security environment in the Asia-Pacific and in the world, and undertake proactive consultations on issues of immediate and emerging concern, so as to coordinate their positions and to make positive contribution towards peaceful resolution of such issues. They shall also have regular consultations on issues pertaining to regional peace, security and stability, such as regional maritime security, proliferation of weapons of mass destruction and related materials and their means of delivery, pandemics, natural disasters, illegal trafficking in arms, narcotics and people, and environmental degradation.

36. The two sides positively assess the trilateral dialogue mechanism among India, China and Russia and agree that exchanges and cooperation under it should be further substantiated.

37. Recognising that terrorism constitutes a crime against humanity that cannot be justified on any ground and condemning it in all forms and manifestations, the two sides agree to revitalise and broaden the India-China Dialogue Mechanism on Counter-Terrorism. They shall strengthen their efforts, bilaterally as also in the international fora, to fight against terrorism, separatism and extremism, and the linkages between terrorism and organized crime and illicit arms and drugs trafficking.

38. Recognising the central role of the United Nations in promoting international peace, security and development, both sides reiterate their determination to strengthen the UN system. The reform of the UN should be comprehensive, ensure balanced representation of developing and developed countries in the UN Security Council, and add to the efficiency and efficacy of the UN and its Security Council. The two sides shall conduct

consultations on the question of UN reform, including the reform of the UN Security Council. The Indian side reiterates its aspirations for permanent membership of the UN Security Council. China attaches great importance to the status of India in international affairs. It understands and supports India's aspirations to play a greater role in the United Nations.

39. Energy security constitutes a vital and strategic issue for producing and consuming countries alike. It is consistent with the common interest of the two sides to establish an international energy order, which is fair, equitable, secure and stable, and to the benefit of the entire international community. Both sides shall also make joint efforts, bilaterally as well as in multilateral fora, to diversify the global energy mix and to increase the share in it of renewable energy sources. Global energy systems should take into account and meet the energy needs of both countries, as part and parcel of a stable, predictable, secure and clean energy future. In this context, international civilian nuclear cooperation should be advanced through innovative and forward-looking approaches, while safeguarding the effectiveness of international non-proliferation principles.

40. Both countries are committed to non-proliferation objectives and agree to expand their dialogue on the related issues, in bilateral and international fora.

41. As two large developing countries with relatively successful developmental experiences, India and China share unique responsibilities to protect and promote the interests of the developing world in the emerging international order and to help them benefit from the positive forces of globalisation. In this context, the two sides shall hold a two-part international seminar in Beijing and New Delhi, co-hosted by their Ministries of Finance, to share their developmental experience with other developing countries and the international community at large.

42. The two sides agree to strengthen their cooperation in the World Trade Organisation. They support the establishment of an open, fair, equitable, transparent and rule-based multilateral trading system, early resumption of Doha negotiations, and are determined to safeguard the legitimate rights and interests of

the developing countries. As founder Members of the G-20 and the G-33, they are determined to strengthen their cooperation and to coordinate with other members of the WTO, especially the developing countries, in order to secure an early resumption of the negotiations on the Doha Work Programme, placing the development dimension at its heart.

43. Recognising that regional integration is an important feature of the emerging international economic order, the two sides agree to expand their coordination within regional organisations and explore a new architecture for closer regional cooperation in Asia. They positively view each other's participation in Asian inter-regional, regional and sub-regional cooperation process, including in the progress towards the East Asian Community. In this context, the two sides agree to cooperate closely in the East Asia Summit. The Indian side welcomes China's attainment of observer status in the South Asian Association for Regional Cooperation. The Chinese side welcomes India's membership of the Asia-Europe Meeting. The two sides agree to expand their cooperation on issues on common interest under the Shanghai Cooperation Organisation.

44. The Indian side recalls that India was among the first countries to recognize that there is one China and that its one China policy has remained unaltered. The Indian side states that it would continue to abide by its one China policy. The Chinese side expresses its appreciation for the Indian position.

45. The Indian side reiterates that it has recognized the Tibet Autonomous Region as part of the territory of the People's Republic of China, and that it does not allow Tibetans to engage in anti-China political activities in India. The Chinese side expresses its appreciation for the Indian position.

46. The following agreements were signed during the visit:

I. Protocol on the Establishment of Consulates-General at Guangzhou and Kolkata;

II. Protocol on Cooperation between the Ministry of External Affairs of India and the Ministry of Foreign Affairs of China;

III. Agreement on the Issue of Property of the Consulate General of India in Shanghai;

IV. Agreement on Bilateral Investment Protection and Promotion;

V. Memorandum of Understanding on Inspection of Export Cargo (Iron Ore);

VI. Protocol on Phytosanitary Requirements for Exporting Rice from India to China;

VII. Memorandum of Understanding between Forward Markets Commission of India and China Securities Regulatory Commission regarding Commodity Futures Regulatory Cooperation;

VIII. Memorandum of Understanding on Cooperation between the Indian Institute of Public Administration and the Central Party School of the Communist Party of China;

IX. Agreement on Forestry Cooperation;

X. Memorandum of Understanding between the Indian Council of Agricultural Research and the Chinese Academy of Agricultural Sciences;

XI. Exchange Programme on Cooperation in the Field of Education;

XII. Memorandum of Understanding on Cooperation in the Conservation of Cultural Heritage; and

XIII. Agreement on Preventing Theft, Clandestine Excavation and Illicit Import and Export of Cultural Property.

47. The two sides believe that the highly successful visit of President Hu Jintao to India marks the high point of the India-China Friendship Year in 2006, promotes mutual understanding and trust, helps in substantiating the Strategic and Cooperative Partnership between the two countries and leads to a qualitative and quantum improvement in bilateral relations. They also agree that this Joint Statement provides a valuable blueprint for enduring development and diversification of the relations between India and China and sustained enrichment of their strategic partnership.

48. President Hu Jintao extended invitations to President Dr. A.P.J Abdul Kalam and Prime Minister Dr. Manmohan Singh to visit China. The invitations were accepted with appreciation. The timing of the visits will be decided through diplomatic channels.

CHAPTER 24

Joint Communiqué on the Results of the Trilateral Meeting of the Foreign Ministers of India, Russia and China

New Delhi, 14 February 2007

A trilateral meeting of the Foreign Ministers of the Republic of India, the Russian Federation, and the People's Republic of China was held in New Delhi on February 14, 2007.

The Ministers noted that the mechanism of trilateral meetings is a manifestation of enhanced mutual understanding and trust among the three countries and positively assessed the outcome of their meetings. They agreed that the Summit level trilateral meeting held in St. Petersburg on July 17, 2006 on the sidelines of the G-8 Summit demonstrated the willingness of the three sides to carry forward consultations on issues of shared interest, at the highest political level, with the aim of promoting the development objectives of the three countries as well as peace, security and stability in the region and the world. They reaffirmed that trilateral cooperation was not directed against the interests of any other country and was, on the contrary, intended to promote international harmony and understanding and find common ground amidst divergent interests. They also emphasized the strong commitment of India, Russia and China to multilateral diplomacy.

The Ministers discussed the political, security and economic aspects of the current global situation, besides exchanging views on how international relations are being presently conducted. They noted that globalization opens up opportunities for a more even distribution of development resources and influence in the world thus creating a foundation for a more stable and balanced international system. They also emphasized the need to preserve the cultural and civilizational diversity of the contemporary world and to promote the existing initiatives for dialogue among civilizations and religions. They expressed their conviction that democratization of international relations is the key to building an increasingly multi-polar world order that would be based on principles of equality of nations—big or small, respect for sovereignty and territorial integrity of countries, international law and mutual respect. The Ministers acknowledged that the UN is an appropriate instrument for promoting and attaining such a world order. The Sides stressed the importance of reforms at the UN, including the UN Security Council, in order to deal with the myriad challenges of today's world more effectively. They shared the view that member states should aim to make the UN more transparent, efficient and reflective of contemporary realities. The Sides agreed to take steps in this direction. In this context, the Foreign Ministers of Russia and China reiterated that their countries attach great importance to the status of India in international affairs, and understand and support India's aspirations to play a greater role in the United Nations.

The Ministers noted that international terrorism continued to pose a grave threat to all nations and expressed concern about the new and evolving forms of the menace. They agreed that under central and coordinating role of the UN and within the framework of its Global Counter—Terrorism Strategy collective action must be strengthened further by taking into account the mutating character of terrorism and its networks. They agreed that an early entry into force of International Convention for the Suppression of Acts of Nuclear Terrorism and the earliest possible adoption in the UN of the India-sponsored draft Comprehensive Convention on International Terrorism would lead to further consolidation of the international legal basis for combating terrorism. The Sides underlined the substantial potential of their counter-terrorism cooperation in regional organizations. They agreed that there can be no justification for any act of terrorism, irrespective of motivations, wherever and by whosoever committed. They stressed that selective approaches in counter-terrorism cannot yield sustainable results and it should be combated in a consistent, sustained and comprehensive manner without any double standards. The Sides also agreed to coordinate action against all factors that feed international terrorism, including its financing, illegal drug trafficking and trans-national organized crime.

The Ministers agreed that India, Russia and China, as countries with growing international influence, can make substantive positive contribution to global peace, security and stability. In this context, the Ministers exchanged views on various regional and international issues of concern. They agreed that cooperation rather than confrontation should govern approaches to regional and global affairs. While welcoming India's joining the Shanghai Cooperation Organization (SCO) as an observer country, the Foreign Ministers of Russia and China stated that they would actively facilitate early realization of mutually beneficial contribution of India to the SCO.

The Ministers paid specific attention to the high potential of trilateral cooperation and synergy in the economic field. The Ministers reiterated the considerable potential for mutually beneficial economic interaction among the three countries in areas such as energy, transport infrastructure, health, high technologies, including IT and biotechnology. Recognizing the important role of the business and industrial circles of the three consistently growing and large economies, the Ministers agreed to advice their respective apex business bodies to organize a trilateral business forum taking into account the capabilities and potential of the three countries. The Ministers agreed to monitor this process with a view to facilitating the agreed business meeting which would take place during 2007.

The Ministers expressed satisfaction at the results of the trilateral meeting in New Delhi and agreed to hold their next meeting in China.

CHAPTER 25

Joint Statement by the German G8 Presidency and the Heads of State and/or Government of Brazil, China, India, Mexico and South Africa on the Occasion of the G8 Summit in Heiligendamm, Germany

Berlin, 8 June 2007

Today's purposeful discussions between the G8 and Brazil, China, India, Mexico and South Africa mark an important step towards an equal and enduring partnership for building the framework conditions of a globalized and competitive world economy. In a globalizing world, we have to look beyond national and regional boundaries and work together.

Towards this endeavour, we commit to cooperate in the following fields:

Promoting Cross Border Investment to our Mutual Benefit

We recognize that cross-border direct investment is a major factor shaping the world's economy. Such inflows can make a major positive contribution to economic growth and sustainable development. We share a common interest in promoting investment and to safeguard and further develop a sound global investment environment. To this end, we shall work together to promote more favourable conditions in our countries for investment, both domestic and foreign, with the aim of fostering economic growth and sustainable development. This may also include the encouragement of responsible business conduct.

Promoting Research and Innovation

Strategies to encourage and support research and innovation are key elements for future sustainable development of our economies. In this context, we underline the importance of integrating the promotion and protection of innovation in our national policies and legislation. We encourage a positive exchange of views on international experiences related to the crucial role and economic value of intellectual property rights (IPR) protection and implementation of agreed international IPR protection standards. In this exchange we also need to consider the protection of IPRs in conjunction with common good of human kind for the purposes of protecting the environment and supporting public health. In this regard, we recall the Doha Declaration on the TRIPs Agreement and public health. We affirm our commitment for further cooperation in capacity building, human resource development and public awareness programmes in the field of intellectual property.

Fighting Climate Change

We face serious challenges in tackling climate change and achieving sustainable development globally. We reaffirm our commitment to the United Nations Framework Convention on Climate Change (UNFCCC) and to its objective through both mitigation and adaptation in accordance with our common but differentiated responsibilities and respective capabilities. On this basis and taking into account the scientific knowledge as represented in the recent IPCC reports, we remain committed to contribute our fair share to tackle climate change in order to stabilize green house gas concentrations at a level that would prevent dangerous anthropogenic interference with the climate system. To this end we need a flexible, fair and effective global framework and concerted international action. We underline the crucial role of economic incentives, in particular by carbon markets, for the necessary investments in climate friendly technologies at large scale. The adaptation to climate change will be a major challenge for all countries, in particular for developing countries, and means for adaptation need to be included in a future agreement along with enhanced technology cooperation and financing. We call on all parties to actively and constructively participate in the negotiations on a comprehensive agreement at the UNFCCC Conference in Indonesia in December 2007.

Energy

We recognise the need for closer, more practical and result-oriented regional and international cooperation in the energy sector, especially in ensuring secure and affordable supplies of energy as well as in improving energy efficiency and the access to advanced and affordable energy technologies. We confirm our commitment to promote energy efficiency, through cost-effective solutions, to advance the effective use of fossil fuels, such as the clean coal technology, and to increase the use of cleaner and renewable energy sources, such as biofuels and biomass, as an important step towards secure, stable and competitive energy supplies for achieving sustainable development.

Development, Particularly in Africa

We reiterate our commitment to the Millennium Development Goals (MDGs), the eradication of poverty and sustainable global development. In view of our responsibility regarding the challenges of development we shall strengthen cooperation and coordination between us to achieve these goals.

We commit to embark on a high-level dialogue on specific challenges as proposed by the G8 (Heiligendamm Process) as a follow up to continue our discussion in a more structured manner for a period of two years until the G8 Summit in 2009 where we will review the progress made on the following issues: Promoting cross border investment to our mutual benefit, Promoting Research and Innovation, Development, particularly Africa, and Sharing Knowledge for improving Energy Efficiency.

CHAPTER 26

Joint Communiqué of the Meeting of the Foreign Ministers of the People's Republic of China, the Republic of India and the Russian Federation

Harbin, 24 October 2007

1. The Foreign Ministers of the People's Republic of China, Republic of India and the Russian Federation met in Harbin, China on 24 October 2007.

2. The three Foreign Ministers positively assessed the important role played by the Foreign Ministers' meeting mechanism in enhancing mutual trust and understanding and increasing trilateral exchanges and cooperation. They believe that trilateral cooperation has excellent prospects for development. They reaffirmed that trilateral cooperation is not targeted against any other country or organization and is intended to promote international harmony and mutual understanding and seeks to broaden common ground amidst divergent interests.

3. The three Foreign Ministers exchanged views on the international situation and reaffirmed that they would abide by the principles and purposes of the UN Charter and other accepted principles of international law. They further emphasized that they would continue to promote democratization of international relations and evolution of a more just and rational international order.

4. The three Foreign Ministers believe that the development of China, India and Russia is a major contribution to peace and development of the region and world and is beneficial to the process of global multipolarity. The three countries have chosen their respective development paths in accordance with their

domestic situation and past experience and have contributed to the diversity of world civilization and world development patterns. With their continuous development and growing role in international affairs, China, India and Russia will further contribute to world peace, security, stability and prosperity.

5. The three Foreign Ministers believe that in order to safeguard the diversity of world civilization and increase mutual understanding, further steps to enhance multilateral cooperation in conducting dialogue among civilizations would be useful.

6. The three Foreign Ministers emphasized that globalization has brought about closer interrelation and interdependence among all nations, and that multilateralism and collective action should be promoted in addressing urgent issues and meeting new challenges and threats. Drawing lines on the ground of ideologies and values is inconsistent with the trends of the times and does not help solve various global issues facing the international community.

7. The three Foreign Ministers underlined that the United Nations is the most representative and authoritative international organization. In order to deal with various problems and challenges facing the international community more effectively, it is important to strengthen the role of the United Nations, improve its efficiency and conduct a comprehensive reform of the United Nations. The Foreign Ministers of China and Russia reiterated that their countries attach importance to the status of India in international affairs, and understand and support India's aspirations to play a greater role in the United Nations.

8. The three Foreign Ministers said that the three countries attach great importance to the issue of climate change and reiterated the principles and provisions of the UN Framework Convention on Climate Change and its Kyoto Protocol, including the principle of "Common but Differentiated Responsibilities". They stated their adherence to the Convention and its Kyoto Protocol as the major framework for tackling climate change, and agreed that the three countries will actively participate in the Conference of the Parties to the Convention and the Protocol to be held in Bali, Indonesia in December 2007. The

three Foreign Ministers said that the three sides will enhance technical cooperation in implementing the Convention and its Kyoto Protocol, including adapting to climate change, increasing energy efficiency and develop renewable energy resources.

9. The three Foreign Ministers reiterated their strong condemnation of terrorism in all its forms and manifestations. No act of terrorism can be compartmentalized, and there can be no justification for terrorism on any grounds. It is imperative for the international community to come together to combat terrorism in a long-term, sustained and comprehensive manner. Collection action within the framework of the UN Global Counter Terrorism Strategy and under the central and coordinating role of the United Nations and its Security Council should be strengthened. Double standards should not be adopted. It is imperative to finalize the draft UN Comprehensive Convention on International Terrorism urgently. The three sides agreed to further coordinate their action against all factors that feed international terrorism, including its financing, drug trafficking and trans-national organized crime.

10. The three Foreign Ministers had in-depth discussions on the Asian regional situation. They believe that peace, development and cooperation are the mainstream in the evolution of the Asian situation. Asia is one of the most vibrant regions enjoying the fastest economic growth in today's world. At the same time, Asia is also faced with pressing issues of imbalanced development and non-traditional security threats. The three Foreign Ministers stated that the three countries will enhance cooperation in all areas including coordination within the framework of regional organizations and dialogue mechanisms to the benefit of the people of Asia.

11. The three Foreign Ministers decided that there is the necessity to set up a consultation mechanism at the level of Director-General/Division Head between the three Foreign Ministries to strengthen trilateral coordination and cooperation on regional and international issues and to implement the agreements reached at the three Foreign Ministers' meetings.

12. The three Foreign Ministers discussed the process for launching cooperation in economic and cultural interactions. They felt that pragmatic cooperation in these areas has enormous potential and complementarity.

13. The three Foreign Ministers decided that working-level mechanisms of Division Head/Director-General should be established between Ministries of the three Governments looking after agriculture, disaster management, medicine and health to explore concrete ways and methods of cooperation for the development of agricultural resources, processing of agriculture produce, research and development, capacity-building and application of technology in disaster risk mitigation, exchange of information on the prevention and control of contagious diseases and in traditional medicine, etc.

14. The three Foreign Ministers stated that the three countries will encourage and promote entrepreneurs and regions to enhance contacts and launch cooperation among them and facilitate this process. They expressed appreciation that the trilateral business forum will be held in New Delhi on 15 December 2007.

15. The three Foreign Ministers positively assessed the role of meetings among their scholars in promoting mutual understanding and cooperation among the three sides and expressed support for scholars of the three countries to further expand exchanges and cooperation in all forms. They noted India's offer to host a trilateral seminar on the evolution of geopolitical strategic trends with the participation of officials as well as scholars and agreed to hold it in 2008.

16. The three Foreign Ministers expressed satisfaction at the results of this round of meeting and decided to hold the next meeting in Russia.

CHAPTER 27

सत्यमेव जयते

A Shared Vision for the 21st Century of the Republic of India and the People's Republic of China

Beijing, 14 January 2008

A Shared Vision for the 21st Century of the Republic of India and the People's Republic of China

H.E. Dr. Manmohan Singh, Prime Minister of the Republic of India and H.E. Mr. Wen Jiabao, Premier of the State Council of the People's Republic of China, meeting in Beijing on 14 January 2008, resolve to promote the building of a harmonious world of durable peace and common prosperity through developing the Strategic and Cooperative Partnership for peace and prosperity between the two countries.

India and China (hereinafter referred to as the "two sides") are the two largest developing nations on earth representing more than one-third of humanity. The two sides recognize that both India and China bear a significant historical responsibility to ensure comprehensive, balanced and sustainable economic and social development of the two countries and to promote peace and development in Asia and the world as a whole.

The two sides are convinced that it is time to look to the future in building a relationship of friendship and trust, based on equality, in which each is sensitive to the concerns and aspirations of the other. The two sides reiterate that India—China friendship and common development will have a positive influence on the future of the international system. India-China relations are not targeted at any country, nor will it affect their friendship with other countries.

The two sides believe that in the new century, Panchsheel, the Five principles of peaceful Co-existence, should continue to constitute the basic guiding principles for good relations between all countries and for creating the conditions for realizing peace and progress of humankind. An international system founded on these principles will be fair, rational, equal and mutually beneficial, will promote durable peace and common prosperity create equal opportunities and eliminate poverty and discrimination.

The two sides hold that the right of each country to choose its own path of social, economic and political development in which fundamental human rights and the rule of law are given their due place, should be respected. An international system founded to tolerance and respect for diversity will promote the cause of peace and reduce the use, or threat of use, of force. The two sides favor an open and inclusive international system and believe that drawing lines on the ground of ideologies and values, or on geographical criteria, is not conducive to peaceful and harmonious coexistence.

The two sides believe that the continuous democratization of international relations and multilateralism are an important objective in the new century. The central role of the United Nations in promoting international peace, security and development should be recognized and promoted. The two sides support comprehensive reform of the United Nations, including giving priority to increasing the representation of developing countries in the Security Council. The Indian side reiterates its aspirations for permanent membership of the UN Security Council. The Chinese side attaches great importance to India's position as a major developing country in international affairs. The Chinese side understands and supports India's aspirations to play a greater role in the United Nations, including in the Security Council.

The two sides support and encourage the processes of regional integration that provide mutually beneficial opportunities for growth, as an important feature of the emerging international economic system. The two sides positively view each others' participation in regional processes and agree to strengthen their coordination and consultation within regional cooperation mechanisms including the East Asia Summit, to explore together and with other countries a new architecture for closer regional cooperation in Asia, and to make joint efforts for further regional integration of Asia. The two sides will strengthen their coordination under the framework of Asia-Europe Meeting, and are committed to strengthening and deepening Asia-Europe comprehensive partnership.

The two sides take a positive view on each other's participation in sub-regional multilateral cooperation processes between like-minded countries, including South Asian Association for Regional Cooperation, Bay of Bengal initiative for Multi-Sectoral Technical and Economic Cooperation and Shanghai Cooperation Organization. The two sides hold that this does not affect either country's existing friendly relations or cooperation with other countries.

The two sides welcome the positive facets of economic globalization, and are ready to face and meet its challenges, and will work with other countries towards balanced and mutually beneficial economic globalization. The two sides believe that the establishment of an open, fair, equitable, transparent and rule-based multilateral trading system is the common aspiration of all countries. The two sides favour the early conclusion of the Doha Development Round, placing the issues that affect the poorest of the poor at its core. The two sides are determined to strengthen their coordination with other developing countries in order to secure their shared objectives.

The two sides are convinced that it is in the common interest of the international community to establish an international energy order that is fair equitable, secure and stable, and to the benefit of the entire international community. The two sides are committed to making joint efforts to diversity the global energy mix and enhance the share of clean and renewable energy, so as to meet the energy requirements of all countries.

The two sides welcome the opportunity for their outstanding scientists to work together in the International Thermonuclear Experimental Reactor (ITER) project, which is of great potential significance in meeting the global energy challenge in an environmentally sustainable manner. As two countries with advanced scientific capabilities, the two sides pledge to promote bilateral cooperation in civil nuclear energy, consistent with their respective international commitments, which will contribute to energy and to dealing with risks associated with climate change.

The two sides recognize the challenge that humankind faces from climate change. The two sides the issue of climate change seriously and reiterate their readiness to join the international community in the efforts to address climate change. The two sides also stand ready to enhance technological cooperation between the two countries. The two sides welcome the outcome of the United Nations Framework Convention on Climate Change (UNFCCC) meeting in Bali in December 2007 and agree to work closely during the negotiation process laid out in the Bali Road Map for long term cooperative action under the convention. The two sides emphasize the importance of addressing climate change in accordance with principles and provisions of the UNFCCC and its Kyoto Protocol, in particular the principle of common but differentiated responsibilities.

The two sides appeal to the international community to move forward the processes of multilateral arms control, disarmament and non-proliferation. Outer space is the common heritage of humankind. It is the responsibility of all space faring nations to commit to the peaceful uses of outer space. The two sides express their categorical opposition to the weaponisation and arms race in outer space.

The two sides strongly condemn the scourge of terrorism in all its forms and manifestations, and in all regions of the world. The two sides pledge to work together and with the international community to strengthen the global framework against terrorism in a long-term, sustained and comprehensive manner.

The two sides believe that cultural and religious tolerance and dialogue between civilizations and peoples will contribute to overall peace and stability of our world. The two sides endorse all efforts to promote inter-civilizational and inter-faith dialogues.

The two sides believe that their bilateral relationship in this century will be of significant regional and global influence. The two sides will therefore continue to build their Strategic and Cooperative Partnership in a positive way. As major economies in their region, the two sides believe that the strong growth in their trade and economic relations is mutually beneficial, and welcome the conclusion of a Feasibility Study on a Regional Trading Arrangement (RTA) between the two countries. According to the report of the Feasibility Study, an India—China RTA will be mutually advantageous. Against the backdrop of accelerating regional economic integration in Asia, the two sides agree to explore the possibility of commencing discussions on a mutually beneficial and high-quality RTA that meets the common aspiration of both countries, and will also benefit the region.

The two sides will continuously promote confidence building measures through steadily enhanced contacts in the field of defence. The two sides therefore welcome the commencement of the India-China Defence Dialogue and express their satisfaction at the successful conclusion of the first joint anti-terrorism training between their armed forces in December 2007. The two sides also welcome their efforts to set an example on trans-border rivers by commencing cooperation since 2002. The Indian side highly appreciates the assistance extended by China on the provision of flood season hydrological data which has assisted India in ensuring the safety security of its population in the regions along these rivers. The two sides agree that this has contributed positively to building mutual understanding and trust.

The two sides remain firmly committed to resolving outstanding differences, including on the boundary question, through peaceful negotiations, while ensuring that such differences are not allowed to affect the positive development of bilateral relations. The two sides reiterate their determination to seek a fair, reasonable and mutually acceptable solution to the boundary question and to build a boundary of peace and friendship on the basis of the Agreement on Political Parameters and Guiding Principles for the Settlement of the India-China

Boundary Question concluded in April 2005. The Special Representatives shall complete at an early date the task of arriving at an agreed framework of settlement on the basis of this Agreement.

The Indian side recalls that India was among the first countries to recognize that there is one China and that its one China policy has remained unaltered. The Indian side states that it would continue to abide by its one China policy, and oppose any activity that is against the one China principle. The Chinese side expresses its appreciation for the Indian position.

The two sides recognize the responsibilities and obligation of the two countries to the international community. The two sides are determined to enhance mutual understanding and friendship between the peoples of India and China for the betterment of both countries and to bring about a brighter future for humanity.

(Dr. Manmohan Singh)
Prime Minister of the Republic of India

(Wen Jiabao)
Premier of the State Council of the
People's Republic of China

Joint Communiqué on the Outcome of the Meeting of the Foreign Ministers of the Russian Federation, the People's Republic of China and the Republic of India

Yekaterinburg, 15 May 2008

1. The Eighth Meeting of the Foreign Ministers of the Russian Federation, the People's Republic of China and the Republic of India was held on May 14-15, 2008 in Yekaterinburg, Russia.

2. The Ministers noted with satisfaction the increasing interaction between Russia, China and India, fast growing, multi ethnic countries with rich history and culture. It was underlined that trilateral interaction was contributing to the shaping of a multi polar, stable and harmonious world, to democratization of international relations and a more just and rational international order.

3. The Ministers positively assessed the efforts made by the three Parties to build up the potential of cooperation in accordance with the outcome of the Harbin Meeting on October 24, 2007.

4. The first round of consultations between the Heads of Departments of the Russian, Chinese and Indian Foreign Ministries held in February 2008 in Moscow was highly appreciated. It signals the beginning of regular exchange of views at this level on implementation of understandings reached during the Russia-China-India Foreign Ministers' meetings and preparation for their future meetings. Russia-China-India forum on agricultural cooperation on April 28, 2008 in Beijing is an important step towards promotion of trilateral interaction in this sphere. Substantial work to establish cooperation between

experts of the three countries on health & medicine and disaster mitigation & relief has also been started. It was agreed that the first trilateral meetings on these subjects would be held in 2008.

5. The Ministers highlighted the importance of enhancing contacts between the business communities of Russia, China and India and in this regard commended the outcome of the first trilateral business forum held in New Delhi in December 2007. A meeting of the Chambers of Commerce and Industry of Russia and India and the China Council for the Promotion of International Trade will be held in Moscow in the autumn of 2008. The second trilateral business forum is scheduled to take place in China in 2009.

6. The Ministers appreciated the holding of the trilateral Seminar on Evolution of Geo-Political Strategic Trends in New Delhi in March this year with the participation of officials and experts from Russia, China and India which further encouraged the multifaceted dialogue between the official circles and academic communities of the three countries.

7. The Ministers reiterated their intention to actively deepen dialogue and interaction between the three countries. Special attention was paid to the wide-ranging possibilities of cooperation in the humanitarian field. In this context, Russia, China and India stated that they attach great importance to international cooperation in promoting and protecting human rights and basic freedoms. Bearing in mind that drawing lines on the ground of ideologies and values or on geographical criteria is not conducive to peaceful and harmonious coexistence, the Ministers believe that such cooperation should take due account of specific characteristics of cultural and historical development of each of the countries and respect for traditional values of civilizations. The Ministers emphasized that international humanitarian assistance should focus on disaster relief, reconstruction etc. and refrain from interference in internal affairs.

8. The Ministers discussed in detail the global situation and the major international and regional problems and reaffirmed the commonality in the approaches of the three countries.

9. The Ministers reiterated that today's world order should be based on the rule of international law and the strengthening of multilateralism with the United Nations playing the central role. They reaffirmed the need for a comprehensive reform of the UN with a view to make it more efficient so that it can deal with the current global challenges more effectively. The Ministers of Russia and China reiterated that their countries attach importance to the status of India in international affairs, and understand and support India's aspirations to play a greater role in the United Nations.

10. The Ministers confirmed their countries' commitments made under the UN Framework Convention on Climate Change and the Kyoto Protocol and underlined the need to develop greater interaction in international cooperation to combat global climate change. They declared the intention of the three nations to take all necessary efforts to implement the Bali Plan of Action.

11. The Ministers agreed that elaboration of a common position in the field of counteracting new challenges and threats within the framework of the United Nations is of particular importance. They expressed their confidence that their anti-terrorism cooperation should be actively supported both within the framework of the UN system and regional organizations. They also called upon all member states to comply with relevant international terrorism conventions and related protocols, and the Security Council resolutions on counter-terrorism. While supporting the implementation of the UN Global Counter-Terrorism Strategy the Ministers emphasized that all member states should make concerted efforts towards expeditious finalization of a Comprehensive Convention on International Terrorism at the UN. They reaffirmed their commitment to further strengthening cooperation among their countries to combat terrorism.

12. Reviewing the situation in the Asia-Pacific Region (APR), the Ministers stated that it is defined by the aspiration of the region towards peace and sustainable economic development. Guided by the principles of multilateralism and equal security they stressed the necessity of a regional security system based

on mutual confidence, mutual taking into account the interests of the other sides, equality and cooperation. They expressed themselves in favor of expanding the economic integration in the APR on a mutually beneficial and non-discriminatory basis in accordance with the principles of open regionalism.

13. The Ministers reaffirmed their countries' common desire to expand multifaceted cooperation with the Central Asian countries, including in the fields of combating terrorism, separatism, extremism, illegal drug trafficking and trans-boundary crime. The Ministers spoke in favor of identifying various forms of trilateral interaction in order to promote further development of the region. The Ministers of Russia and China welcome India's aspirations for playing an enhanced role as an Observer State within the SCO framework.

14. The Ministers praised the achievements of Afghanistan on the way for its reconstruction, but at the same time expressed concern at the continuing deterioration of the security situation there due to continued terrorist attacks and resurgence of the Taliban and Al Qaeda. They stressed the importance of rendering assistance to the Afghan government in fulfilling its tasks in the field of security, in improving the functioning of governmental institutions and social and economic development of the country. They highlighted the need for strict observance of the sanctions regime against Afghan extremist leaders and other persons and entities listed by UN Security Council Committee 1267, tough rebuff to the forces of terrorism and extremism in Afghan territory as also for further increasing the efforts to eradicate the drug threat coming from Afghanistan. The Sides noted the importance of international and regional cooperation in creating a comprehensive system of anti-drug security belts alongside the borders of Afghanistan with the UN playing a central coordinating role and cooperation of the neighboring countries.

15. The Ministers noted the need to continue the efforts to achieve at the earliest a political and diplomatic settlement of the situation around the Iranian nuclear program through negotiations. The purpose of these negotiations is to find a long-term comprehensive solution that provides for the trust of

the international community to be restored in the exclusively peaceful nature of the program to ensure that Iran can exercise its right to the peaceful use of atomic energy and to open up the path to wider international cooperation with Iran.

16. The Ministers call upon all interested parties to continue active efforts to promote the six-party talks on resolving the Korean Peninsula nuclear problem towards peaceful and full denuclearization of the Peninsula in accordance with all relevant agreements achieved earlier in Beijing.

17. The Ministers noted the importance of settling the issue of the status of Kosovo in accordance with norms of international law with the UN playing the leading role and on the basis of an agreement between the parties. The unilateral declaration of independence of Kosovo is contrary to the UN Security Council Resolution 1244, which should remain the legal basis for the settlement of Kosovo issue till new decisions by the UN. The Ministers call upon Belgrade and Pristina to act within the framework of international law in order to search for an appropriate solution to the problem through negotiations.

18. The Russian and Indian Ministers reaffirmed their countries' support to the Beijing Olympic Games and efforts to ensure their successful holding.

19. The Ministers expressed satisfaction with the outcome of the meeting and decided to hold the next trilateral meeting in India.

CHAPTER 29

G-5 Political Declaration

Sapporo, 8 July 2008

We the Leaders of Brazil, China, India, Mexico and South Africa, gathered in Sapporo, Japan, on 8 July 2008, have resolved to issue this Political Declaration:

1. Mankind is at a critical historical crossroad. The potential of globalization and innovation to raise living standards is unprecedented, but so are social and sustainable development challenges around the world.

2. The interrelationships of a global economic slowdown marked by financial uncertainty, the persistence of trade protectionist distortions, soaring food and oil prices, and the threats posed by climate change add complexity to the current scenario.

3. Our increasing interdependence demands an integrated and concerted response to these global challenges. We must ensure development and prosperity on a sustainable path, both within and across nations. That is the historical challenge of our generation. To achieve this fundamental goal, we must act in a coordinated manner to ensure equitable growth with care for the environment, taking appropriate account of cross-border interactions in fulfillment of our shared responsibility.

World Economy

4. The global economy continues to expand, but at a slower rate than in previous years. Most emerging and developing economies have proved resilient so far to adverse circumstances. Nevertheless, the international community as a whole faces important policy challenges to maintaining financial stability and mitigating global economic risks. Headline inflation is of particular concern.

5. We reaffirm our commitment to the establishment of a stable and orderly international financial system, more transparent and legitimate. The voice and representation of developing countries in the decision making of international financial institutions should be significantly improved, especially at the International Monetary Fund and the World Bank.

6. Given current global macroeconomic imbalances, it is essential to enhance policy coordination not only among advanced economies but also with emerging market economies, including by reinforcing existing multilateral mechanisms for coordination. The Financial G-20 is an appropriate forum for this endeavor.

7. The global financial architecture and its surveillance capacities must be also strengthened to contribute to the prevention and resolution of potential financial crises but, more importantly, to support sustainable development. In particular, it is necessary to provide international financial institutions with an adequate array of instruments to preserve global financial stability and smoothen the supply shocks derived from higher food and oil prices, especially in support of least developed and middle income countries.

8. The world economic outlook lends urgency to the establishment of a just, open, reasonable and non-discriminatory international trade system. It is essential to achieve an early conclusion to the Doha Round that fully supports development in accordance with its agreed mandate. Developed countries must dismantle barriers and distortions, especially agriculture subsidies and domestic support that affect the overall efforts of developing countries. This would provide a much needed impetus to global economic growth and would positively contribute to an enabling environment for development.

Food Security

9. The rise in global food prices poses a new challenge to the fight against poverty and hunger. To ensure food security is a shared responsibility that calls for swift and resolute action by all Governments and relevant actors.

10. The world produces enough food, but not enough people have access to it. We call upon the international community to devise better ways and means of producing and distributing food. Multi-billion agricultural trade-distorting support in developed countries have hampered the development of food production capacity in developing countries, critically reducing their possibilities of reaction to the present crisis. We therefore reaffirm the imperative of creating an enabling international environment for agro-produce related trade, establishing a just and reasonable international trade regime for agricultural products and concluding the Doha Round with meaningful commitments to agricultural subsidies reductions. Also, it is necessary to combat speculation and minimize the use of measures that could increase volatility of international food prices.

11. The food security crisis demands a rapid and substantial increase in the allocation of resources to support rural development and combat hunger and poverty. We urge developed countries, in particular, to increase their emergency aid at an early date. Innovative mechanisms of financing and enhanced flows of investment can also play an important role in addition to the required increase in flows of official aid.

12. Technological innovations and international cooperation can significantly increase agricultural productivity and contribute to combating the current food security crisis. Intellectual property rights in the agricultural domain should strike a balance between the greater good of humankind and incentives to innovation. In particular, we encourage collaborative action for better seeds and farm outputs that are sustainable and environmentally sound as well as a comprehensive approach in all fields including finance, trade, aid, environment, intellectual property rights and technology transfer, so as to create a conducive international environment for food security.

13. The current food security crisis has multiple and complex causes whose assessment requires objectiveness. It is essential to address the challenges and opportunities posed by biofuels, in view of the world's food security, energy and sustainable development needs. If developed sustainably, biofuels

can effectively contribute to generating opportunities and achieving food and energy security altogether. To this purpose, it is important that public policies for production of biofuels contribute to sustainable development and the well-being of the most vulnerable people and do not threaten food security.

Climate Change

14. We urge the international community to address the challenge of climate change through long term cooperative action in accordance with the United Nations Framework Convention on Climate Change (UNFCCC) and its Kyoto Protocol, especially the principle of common but differentiated responsibilities and respective capabilities. We take our responsibilities seriously and welcome the Bali Action Plan and the Bali Roadmap and are committed to the completion of negotiations by 2009.

15. Negotiations for a shared vision on long-term cooperative action at the UNFCCC, including a long-term global goal for greenhouse gases (GHG) emissions reductions, must be based on an equitable burden sharing paradigm that ensures equal sustainable development potential for all citizens of the world and that takes into account historical responsibility and respective capabilities as a fair and just approach. It is essential that developed countries take the lead in achieving ambitious and absolute greenhouse gas emissions reductions in accordance with their quantified emission targets under the Kyoto Protocol after 2012, of at least 25 40 per cent range for emissions reductions below 1990 levels by 2020, and, by 2050, by between 80 and 95 per cent below those levels, with comparability of efforts among them.

16. We also urge the international community, particularly developed countries, to promote sustainable consumption patterns and lifestyles responsive to mitigation requirements.

17. For developing countries, adaptation is of cardinal importance, particularly given their vulnerability, limited capacity and inadequate means. We stress the need of scaling up resources for adaptation and strengthening of adaptive potential in developing countries in order to reinforce capabilities to

prevent and confront the increased frequency and scale of natural disasters and the other adverse effects of climate change.

18. We, on our part, are committed to undertaking nationally appropriate mitigation and adaptation actions which also support sustainable development. We would increase the depth and range of these actions supported and enabled by financing, technology and capacity-building with a view to achieving a deviation from business-as-usual. In this regard, in the negotiations under the Bali Road Map, we urge the international community to focus on the core climate change issues rather than inappropriate issues like competitiveness and trade protection measures which are being dealt with in other forums.

19. Affordable access to adaptation and mitigation technologies, achieved through a suite of funding mechanisms, investment structures and policy tools, is a key enabling condition for developing countries to tackle climate change. We call upon the international community to work towards a strengthened scheme for technology innovation, development, transfer and deployment, and a comprehensive review of the intellectual property rights regime for such technologies in order to strike an adequate balance between rewards for innovators and the global public good.

20. Enhanced financial support for developing countries must cover incremental and opportunity costs to meet the challenges of climate change. New and innovative financial mechanisms must mobilize additional resources beyond the flexibility mechanisms of the Kyoto Protocol and other instruments of the carbon market, without diverting national or multilateral and ODA resources from the imperatives of development and poverty alleviation.

21. Developed countries should commit clearly to significant additional financing to support both mitigation and adaptation in developing countries. We recognize the need for further financing options to complement, not substitute, the financial arrangements under the Kyoto Protocol. In this regard, we welcome for further exploration, inter alia, the proposal by China

for setting a climate financing goal for all developed countries, such as 0.5% of GDP (in addition to ODA) for climate action in developing countries, as well as the Mexican initiative for a World Climate Change Fund.

Energy Security

22. Energy security is essential to ensure the steady growth of the global economy. We call upon the international community to strengthen overall cooperation on energy development and utilization, with emphasis on renewable energy and energy efficiency and giving adequate consideration to solar, wind and hydro-electrical power, and bio-fuels such as ethanol and bio-diesel without adversely affecting food security.

23. More efforts should be made to develop clean energy technologies that are affordable, environment-friendly and suitable to the conditions of developing countries, ensuring that these technologies be adequately transferred to developing countries.

24. We must take an integrated approach to international energy cooperation and international development cooperation, ensuring access to energy by developing countries on an equitable and sustainable manner.

Millennium Development Goals and Monterrey Consensus

25. The global community of nations has recognized that achieving the internationally agreed development goals, including those contained in the United Nations Millennium Declaration, demands a new partnership between developed and developing countries.

26. This was stated in the Monterrey Consensus, whereby the international community agreed to work in a coordinated manner to support development by mobilizing domestic resources, attracting international resource flows, developing innovative financial mechanisms, harnessing the benefits of international trade, increasing international financial and technical cooperation, achieving sustainable debt financing and external debt relief, and enhancing the coherence and consistency of the international monetary, financial and trading systems.

27. As we reach with uneven success the mid-point in the process to achieve the Millennium Development Goals, particularly in the least developed countries in Africa and other regions, the international financial community should join efforts to preserve financial stability and resume the path of vigorous and sustainable economic growth as necessary conditions to attaining these goals. We urge developed countries to renew their resolve to support these processes in the global interest, particularly regarding trade openness, the fulfillment of their commitments to allocate at least 0.7% of their GNP to ODA, and the reform to global governance.

28. The international community should ensure that, from their holistic perspective, the upcoming UN Millennium Development Goals High-level event and the Doha Follow-up International Conference on Financing for Development contribute to achieving all-round and balanced progress towards the Millennium Development Goals at the global level. A follow-up mechanism to continue to monitor the implementation of the Monterrey Consensus should be one of the results of the Doha Conference.

South-South Cooperation

29. We reaffirm the role of South-South cooperation in the context of multilateralism, and the need to strengthen it as an important platform for developing countries to jointly respond to development challenges.

30. We reiterate that South-South cooperation enjoys important comparative advantages and complements rather than replaces North-South cooperation. In this context, we call upon Governments, international organizations and all relevant actors, to support South-South cooperation, by fully tapping the synergies of triangular cooperation.

31. While acknowledging progress in South-South cooperation in recent years, we are committed to continue broadening its reach and impact through innovative models of cooperation based on the principles of equality and mutual benefit.

The Role of the G5

32. In fulfilling our shared responsibility as major developing countries, we are determined to continue engaging in all efforts leading to achieve the improved global economic governance and other major global changes required to ensure that globalization and interdependence work for the benefit of all.

33. We thus commit ourselves to a strengthened multilateralism, keeping fully engaged to intensified international cooperation under the leadership of the United Nations. We will continue to strive for a comprehensive reform of the United Nations that includes strengthening the General Assembly, revitalizing ECOSOC, reforming the Secretariat, strengthening the UN gender architecture and, in particular, achieving an early reform of the UN Security Council. We urge the international community to faithfully implement the outcomes of major World Summits, especially the Millennium Development Goals,

34. The Monterrey Consensus and the Johannesburg Plan of Implementation and to continue promoting shared initiatives to rise to the new global challenges and opportunities of our era.

35. As a key strategic objective, we will continue contributing to multilaterally promote an action-oriented global partnership for equitable and sustainable development, including by making positive contributions in such critical areas as global governance, financial stability, climate change as well as food and energy security.

36. With these purposes, based on the principles of equality, mutual respect and cooperation for the common good, we are ready to consolidate bilateral relations, improve our cooperation level and mechanisms, and continue the dialogue and collaboration with the G8 and the international community at large.

CHAPTER 30

Declaration of Leaders Meeting of Major Economies on Energy Security and Climate Change

Toyako, Hokkaido, 9 July 2008

We, the leaders of Australia, Brazil, Canada, China, the European Union, France, Germany, India, Indonesia, Italy, Japan, the Republic of Korea, Mexico, Russia, South Africa, the United Kingdom, and the United States met as the world's major economies in Toyako, Hokkaido, Japan, on 9 July, 2008, and declare as follows:

1. Climate change is one of the great global challenges of our time. Conscious of our leadership role in meeting such challenges, we, the leaders of the world's major economies, both developed and developing, commit to combat climate change in accordance with our common but differentiated responsibilities and respective capabilities and confront the interlinked challenges of sustainable development, including energy and food security, and human health. We have come together to contribute to efforts under the U.N. Framework Convention on Climate Change, the global forum for climate negotiations. Our contribution and cooperation are rooted in the objective, provisions, and principles of the Convention.

2. We welcome decisions taken by the international community in Bali, including to launch a comprehensive process to enable the full, effective, and sustained implementation of the Convention through long-term cooperative action, now, up to, and beyond 2012, in order to reach an agreed outcome in December 2009. Recognizing the scale and urgency of the challenge, we will continue working together to strengthen implementation of the Convention and to ensure that the agreed

outcome maximizes the efforts of all nations and contributes to achieving the ultimate objective in Article 2 of the Convention, which should be achieved within a time frame sufficient to allow ecosystems to adapt naturally to climate change, to ensure that food production is not threatened, and to enable economic development to proceed in a sustainable manner.

3. The Major Economies Meetings constructively contribute to the Bali process in several ways:

I. First, our dialogue at political, policy, and technical levels has built confidence among our nations and deepened mutual understanding of the many challenges confronting the world community as we consider next steps under the Convention and continue to mobilize political will to combat global climate change.

II. Second, without prejudging outcomes or the views of other nations, we believe that the common understandings in this Declaration will help advance the work of the international community so it is possible to reach an agreed outcome by the end of 2009.

III. Third, recognizing the need for urgent action and the Bali Action Plan's directive for enhanced implementation of the Convention between now and 2012, we commit to taking the actions in paragraph 10 without delay.

4. We support a shared vision for long-term cooperative action, including a long-term global goal for emission reductions, that assures growth, prosperity, and other aspects of sustainable development, including major efforts towards sustainable consumption and production, all aimed at achieving a low carbon society. Taking account of the science, we recognize that deep cuts in global emissions will be necessary to achieve the Convention's ultimate objective, and that adaptation will play a correspondingly vital role. We believe that it would be desirable for the Parties to adopt in the negotiations under the Convention a long-term global goal for reducing global emissions, taking into account the principle of equity. We urge that serious consideration be given in particular to ambitious IPCC scenarios. Significant progress toward a long-term global goal

will be made by increasing financing of the broad deployment of existing technologies and best practices that reduce greenhouse gas emissions and build climate resilience. However, our ability ultimately to achieve a long-term global goal will also depend on affordable, new, more advanced, and innovative technologies, infrastructure, and practices that transform the way we live, produce and use energy, and manage land.

5. Taking into account assessments of science, technology, and economics, we recognize the essential importance of enhanced greenhouse gas mitigation that is ambitious, realistic, and achievable. We will do more. We will continue to improve our policies and our performance while meeting other priority objectives in keeping with the principle of common but differentiated responsibilities and respective capabilities. Achieving our long-term global goal requires respective mid-term goals, commitments and actions, to be reflected in the agreed outcome of the Bali Action Plan, taking into account differences in social and economic conditions, energy mix, demographics, and infrastructure among other factors, and the above IPCC scenarios. In this regard, the developed major economies will implement, consistent with international obligations, economy-wide mid-term goals and take corresponding actions in order to achieve absolute emission reductions and, where applicable, first stop the growth of emissions as soon as possible, reflecting comparable efforts among them. At the same time, the developing major economies will pursue, in the context of sustainable development, nationally appropriate mitigation actions, supported and enabled by technology, financing and capacity-building, with a view to achieving a deviation from business as usual emissions.

6. We recognize that actions to reduce emissions, including from deforestation and forest degradation, and to increase removals by sinks in the land use, land use change, and forestry sector, including cooperation on tackling forest fires, can make a contribution to stabilizing greenhouse gases in the atmosphere. These actions also reduce climate change impacts and can have significant co-benefits by maintaining multiple economic goods and ecological services. Our nations will continue to cooperate

on capacity-building and demonstration activities; on innovative solutions, including financing, to reduce emissions and increase removals by sinks; and on methodological issues. We also stress the need to improve forest-related governance and cooperative actions at all levels.

7. We recognize that adaptation is vital to addressing the effects of inevitable climate change and that the adverse impacts of climate change are likely to affect developing countries disproportionately. We will work together in accordance with our Convention commitments to strengthen the ability of developing countries, particularly the most vulnerable ones, to adapt to climate change. This includes the development and dissemination of tools and methodologies to improve vulnerability and adaptation assessments, the integration of climate change adaptation into overall development strategies, increased implementation of adaptation strategies, increased emphasis on adaptation technologies, strengthening resilience and reducing vulnerability, and consideration of means to stimulate investment and increased availability of financial and technical assistance.

8. We affirm the critical role of technology and the need for technological breakthroughs in meeting the interlinked global challenges of energy security and climate change. In the near term, broader deployment of many existing technologies will be vital for both mitigation and adaptation. In particular, energy conservation, energy efficiency, disaster reduction, and water and natural resource management technologies are important. We will promote the uptake and use of such technologies including renewables, cleaner and low-carbon technologies, and, for those of us interested, nuclear power. Technology cooperation with and transfer to developing countries are also vital in this effort, as is promoting capacity building. For the longer term, research, development, demonstration, deployment, and transfer of innovative technologies will be crucial, and we acknowledge the need to enhance our investment and collaboration in these areas. Mindful of the important role of a range of alternative energy technologies, we recognize, in particular, the need for research, development, and large-scale demonstration of and

cooperation on carbon capture and storage. We also note the value of technology roadmaps as tools to promote continuous investment and cooperation in clean energy research, development, demonstration, and deployment.

9. We recognize that tackling climate change will require greater mobilization of financial resources, both domestically and internationally. There is an urgent need to scale up financial flows, particularly financial support to developing countries; to create positive incentives for actions; to finance the incremental costs of cleaner and low-carbon technologies; to make more efficient use of funds directed toward climate change; to realize the full potential of appropriate market mechanisms that can provide pricing signals and economic incentives to the private sector; to promote public sector investment; to create enabling environments that promote private investment that is commercially viable; to develop innovative approaches; and to lower costs by creating appropriate incentives for and reducing and eliminating obstacles to technology transfer relevant to both mitigation and adaptation.

10. To enable the full, effective, and sustained implementation of the Convention between now and 2012, we will:

Work together on mitigation-related technology cooperation strategies in specific economic sectors, promote the exchange of mitigation information and analysis on sectoral efficiency, the identification of national technology needs and voluntary, action-oriented international cooperation, and consider the role of cooperative sectoral approaches and sector-specific actions, consistent with the Convention;

Direct our trade officials responsible for WTO issues to advance with a sense of urgency their discussions on issues relevant to promoting our cooperation on climate change;

Accelerate enhanced action on technology development, transfer, financing, and capacity building to support mitigation and adaptation efforts;

Support implementation of the Nairobi Work Programme on impacts, vulnerability, and adaptation to climate change;

Improve significantly energy efficiency, a low-cost way to reduce greenhouse gas emissions and enhance energy security;

Continue to promote actions under the Montreal Protocol on Substances That Deplete the Ozone Layer for the benefit of the global climate system; and

Intensify our efforts without delay within existing fora to improve effective greenhouse gas measurement.

11. Our nations will continue to work constructively together to promote the success of the Copenhagen climate change conference in 2009.

CHAPTER 31

Joint Statement of the BRIC Countries' Leaders

Yekaterinburg, 16 June 2009

We, the leaders of the Federative Republic of Brazil, the Russian Federation, the Republic of India and the People's Republic of China, have discussed the current situation in global economy and other pressing issues of global development, and also prospects for further strengthening collaboration within the BRIC, at our meeting in Ekaterinburg on 16 June, 2009.

We have arrived at the following conclusions:

1. We stress the central role played by the G20 Summits in dealing with the financial crisis. They have fostered cooperation, policy coordination and political dialogue regarding international economic and financial matters.

2. We call upon all states and relevant international bodies to act vigorously to implement the decisions adopted at the G20 Summit in London on 2 April, 2009. We shall cooperate closely among ourselves and with other partners to ensure further progress of collective action at the next G20 Summit to be held in Pittsburgh in September 2009. We look forward to a successful outcome of the United Nations Conference on the World Financial and Economic Crisis and its Impact on Development to be held in New York on 24-26 June 2009.

3. We are committed to advance the reform of international financial institutions, so as to reflect changes in the world economy. The emerging and developing economies must have greater voice and representation in international financial institutions, and their heads and senior leadership should be appointed through an open, transparent, and merit-based selection process. We also believe that there is a strong need for a

stable, predictable and more diversified international monetary system.

4. We are convinced that a reformed financial and economic architecture should be based, inter alia, on the following principles:

I. democratic and transparent decision-making and implementation process at the international financial organizations;

II. solid legal basis;

III. compatibility of activities of effective national regulatory institutions and international standard-setting bodies;

IV. strengthening of risk management and supervisory practices.

5. We recognize the important role played by international trade and foreign direct investments in the world economic recovery. We call upon all parties to work together to improve the international trade and investment environment. We urge the international community to keep the multilateral trading system stable, curb trade protectionism, and push for comprehensive and balanced results of the WTO's Doha Development Agenda.

6. The poorest countries have been hit hardest by the financial crisis. The international community needs to step up efforts to provide liquidity for these countries. The international community should also strive to minimize the impact of the crisis on development and ensure the achievement of the Millennium Development Goals. Developed countries should fulfill their commitment of 0.7% of Gross National Income for the Official Development Assistance and make further efforts in increasing assistance, debt relief, market access and technology transfer for developing countries.

7. The implementation of the concept of sustainable development, comprising, inter alia, the Rio Declaration, Agenda for the 21st Century and multilateral environmental agreements, should be a major vector in the change of paradigm of economic development.

8. We stand for strengthening coordination and cooperation among states in the energy field, including amongst producers and consumers of energy and transit states, in an effort to decreasing uncertainty and ensuring stability and sustainability. We support diversification of energy resources and supply, including renewable energy, security of energy transit routes and creation of new energy investments and infrastructure.

9. We support international cooperation in the field of energy efficiency. We stand ready for a constructive dialogue on how to deal with climate change based on the principle of common but differentiated responsibility, given the need to combine measures to protect the climate with steps to fulfill our socio-economic development tasks.

10. We reaffirm to enhance cooperation among our countries in socially vital areas and to strengthen the efforts for the provision of international humanitarian assistance and for the reduction of natural disaster risks. We take note of the statement on global food security issued today as a major contribution of the BRIC countries to the multilateral efforts to set up the sustainable conditions for this goal.

11. We reaffirm to advance cooperation among our countries in science and education with the aim, inter alia, to engage in fundamental research and development of advanced technologies.

12. We underline our support for a more democratic and just multi-polar world order based on the rule of international law, equality, mutual respect, cooperation, coordinated action and collective decision-making of all states. We reiterate our support for political and diplomatic efforts to peacefully resolve disputes in international relations.

13. We strongly condemn terrorism in all its forms and manifestations and reiterate that there can be no justification for any act of terrorism anywhere or for whatever reasons. We note that the draft Comprehensive Convention against International Terrorism is currently under the consideration of the UN General Assembly and call for its urgent adoption.

14. We express our strong commitment to multilateral diplomacy with the United Nations playing the central role in dealing with global challenges and threats. In this respect, we reaffirm the need for a comprehensive reform of the UN with a view to making it more efficient so that it can deal with today's global challenges more effectively. We reiterate the importance we attach to the status of India and Brazil in international affairs, and understand and support their aspirations to play a greater role in the United Nations.

15. We have agreed upon steps to promote dialogue and cooperation among our countries in an incremental, proactive, pragmatic, open and transparent way. The dialogue and cooperation of the BRIC countries is conducive not only to serving common interests of emerging market economies and developing countries, but also to building a harmonious world of lasting peace and common prosperity.

16. Russia, India and China welcome the kind invitation of Brazil to host the next BRIC summit in 2010.

CHAPTER 32

BRICS' Joint Statement on Global Food Security

Yekaterinburg, 16 June 2009

The fluctuations of global food prices coupled with the global financial crisis is threatening global food security. As a result, the number of people suffering from hunger and malnutrition grows and the progress towards the achievement of the Millennium Development Goals may be reversed. This challenge should be addressed without delay in a comprehensive manner through resolute action by all Governments and the relevant international agencies.

The developed and developing countries should address the food security issue according to the principle of common but differentiated responsibility. The developed countries should provide financial and technology support for developing countries in the field of food production capacity. The BRIC countries welcome various initiatives in this field by the UN and its special agencies. The BRIC countries renew their commitment to contribute to the efforts to overcome the global food crisis.

Countering effectively the global food crisis is impossible without a clear and full understanding of its causes. Attempts to explain food price hikes by an increase in consumption in developing countries obscure the true causes which have a complex and multifaceted nature. Global Climate Change and natural disasters have direct implications on food security through changes in agro-ecological conditions. Current global economic and financial crisis also has negative impact on food security through shrinking financial resources available to agriculture sector. Restricted market access and trade-distorting subsidies in developed countries have also hampered the development of food production capacity in developing countries over the last thirty years. Further, global market conditions have not created adequate incentives for the expansion of agricultural production in developing and least developed countries that have become main importers of food products.

It is also important to assess the challenges and opportunities posed by the biofuels production and use in view not only of the world's food security, but also of the energy security and sustainable development needs. An international cooperation mechanism needs to be established to review and re-evaluate the long-term implications of the development of biomass energy, and develop relevant policy guidance accordingly. The BRIC countries welcome, therefore, the exchange of experiences on biofuels technologies, norms and regulations, in order to ensure that production and use of biofuels is sustainable, in accordance with the three pillars of sustainable development—social, economic and environmental—and that it takes into account the need to achieve and maintain global food security. Sustainable biofuels can constitute a driving force for social inclusion and income distribution mainly in the impoverished rural areas of developing and least developed countries, where most of the world's famine problems are located.

Tackling effectively the food crisis requires a fully coordinated international response and should include both short-term and long-term measures. The international community needs to work out and consistently implement a comprehensive strategy to resolve this global problem. In this respect, the BRIC countries welcome the outcomes of relevant international fora, including the Food and Agriculture Organization (FAO) High-Level Conference on World Food Security in Rome.

The BRIC countries also welcome the results of the World Grain Forum which was held in Saint Petersburg and call on all interested states and international organizations to take necessary steps to implement the measures agreed upon at the Forum.

Ensuring food security requires a well-functioning world market and trade system for food and agriculture based on the principles of fairness and non-discrimination. In this regard, it is of paramount importance to accelerate the Doha round of talks at the World Trade Organization (WTO) in order to find compromise solutions for radical reductions of multi-billion subsidies in the agricultural sector, which distort terms of trade and prevent developing countries from increasing their agricultural production. We are committed to opposing protectionism, establishing a just and reasonable international trade regime for agricultural products, and giving farmers from developing countries incentives to engage in agricultural production.

The BRIC countries support the adoption of a wide range of mid- to long-term measures in order to provide for a solution to the issue of food security. Such measures may include:

1. rendering additional resources and assistance to the agricultural sector through the channels of respective national budgets and international development institutions, mainly to household agriculture, which is the main source for food production;
2. joint technological innovations and international cooperation to introduce advanced technologies in the agricultural sector of developing countries to significantly increase agricultural productivity. Intellectual property rights in the agricultural domain should strike a balance between the common good of humankind and incentives to innovation;
3. upgrading agricultural infrastructure, including irrigation, transportation, supply, storage and distribution systems and promoting technical assistance, access to credit and crop insurance policies. In this context public-private partnerships could play a significant role;
4. improving the exchange of knowledge and commercialisation of sustainable biofuels;
5. ensuring wider access to food at the national and international level through appropriate policies and well functioning distribution systems especially for the poor and most vulnerable people in developing countries;

6. sharing of best practices of operating successful public distribution programmes; and
7. equipping developing countries with financial and technological means to fully implement adaptation measures to minimize the adverse impacts of climate change on food security.

Agreed by the national authorities in advance of the BRIC Summit and issued in Ekaterinburg, Russia.

CHAPTER 33

Joint Communiqué of the Ninth Meeting of Foreign Ministers of India, Russia & China

Bengaluru, 27 October 2009

1. The Ninth Meeting of the Foreign Ministers of Republic of India, the Russian Federation and the People's Republic of China was held on 27 October 2009 in Bengaluru.

2. The Ministers noted the ongoing trilateral cooperation between India, Russia and China and explored new avenues for deepening and strengthening this interaction on various issues for the benefit of the people of the three countries and peace and stability in the region.

3. Despite the impact of the international financial crisis, the pace of development of the three countries has improved contributing to faster growth among them. Enhanced engagement among them strengthens their influence on the process of democratisation of international relations and development of multi-polar world order reflecting the diversity of world cultures and civilizations.

4. While reviewing the implementation of the Trilateral initiatives, the Ministers noted with satisfaction the holding of the trilateral meeting of experts of India, Russia & China in the area of Disaster Mitigation and Relief held in Samara, Russia on 28 July 2008. The prospective areas of cooperation in this important area were identified as—interaction between research institutes; exchange of experts/specialists; exchange of experience in practical response to major disasters; exchange of information between the National Disaster Management Authorities on major emergencies; training of instructors/specialists; and holding joint conferences and seminars. The

next meeting of this group of experts is due to be held in China in 2009.

5. The Ministers welcomed the holding of the next meeting of the India-Russia-China trilateral expert group on agricultural cooperation, scheduled to be held in November/December 2009 in New Delhi.

6. The Ministers noted that according to the understanding arrived at in the first meeting of trilateral group of experts on Health and Medicine held in India in September 2008, the next meeting of the trilateral group of experts on Health and Medicine would be held in 2010 in Russia.

7. The Ministers reviewed the trilateral interaction among the business communities of the three countries and discussed the 2nd Trilateral Business Conference held on 17-19 September 2009 in Changchun, China. They noted that interaction among business communities was increasing and areas like pharmaceuticals, infrastructure, IT and energy have been the focus areas. The Ministers discussed ways in which the meetings of this forum could be more meaningful to the business communities in the time ahead so that new opportunities may be grasped to expand trade and investment. They looked forward to the next meeting in Russia.

8. The Ministers discussed ways of enhancing interaction in the trilateral format. India, Russia and China, which together stretch over 20% of the total global landmass and represent 39% of the global population, are important members of the international community playing a significant role in world affairs. The Ministers agreed that trilateral dialogue in areas such as global economic governance architecture, climate change, trade policy and development cooperation would contribute greatly to global peace and prosperity and that concerted trilateral action against international terrorism, trans-national crime and drug-trafficking would promote stability and all-round development in today's inter-dependent world.

9. The international situation was reviewed by the Ministers and the major global developments were discussed. The Ministers welcomed the decision made at the Pittsburgh Summit to

designate G20 as the premier forum for international economic cooperation. They stressed that the future global economic governance should feature in balanced representation, equality and result-orientedness, and ensure the voice and representation of emerging market and developing countries. The three countries advocated that future G20 summits should be held in developed countries and emerging market and developing countries by rotation based on the principle of transparency and equity. The Ministers emphasized that one of the ultimate goals of governance structure reform for international financial institutions is equitable distribution of voting power between developed countries and developing ones. The Ministers called for early implementation of the quantified targets on the governance structure reform of the international financial institutions endorsed by the G20 Pittsburgh Summit, speedy shift in IMF quota share of at least 5% to emerging market and developing countries and a significant increase of at least 3% of voting power in the World Bank for developing and transition countries, while avoiding erosion in voting shares of developing countries.

10. The three countries reiterated that they take the issue of climate change very seriously and that they are ready to strengthen international cooperation and make active effort to jointly tackle climate change. The three countries stressed that the UN Climate Change Conference in Copenhagen presents an important opportunity for strengthening international cooperation in addressing climate change in accordance with the principles and provisions of the UNFCCC and the Bali Action Plan, taking into account the principle of common but differentiated responsibilities and respective capabilities. The Ministers reiterated the willingness of the three countries to contribute to the success of the Conference.

11. The Ministers reiterated that there was a need for a comprehensive reform of the United Nations with a view to make it more efficient so that it can deal with the current global challenges more effectively. The Ministers of India, Russia and China reiterated that their countries attach importance to the status of India in international affairs, and understand and

support India's aspirations to play a greater role in the United Nations.

12. The Ministers strongly condemned terrorism in all its forms and manifestations and reiterated that there can be no justification for any act of terrorism anywhere. They underlined that the fight against terrorism needs strong international cooperation, particularly within the framework of the United Nations. The Ministers stressed that all concerned must implement relevant resolutions of the UN General Assembly and the UN Security Council, particularly UNSC Resolution 1267, 1373 and 1540 and international conventions and protocols against terrorism as well as contribute to implementation of the UN Global Counter-Terrorism Strategy. In the context of strengthening international cooperation against terrorism, the Ministers urged all UN member states to urgently conclude and adopt the Comprehensive Convention on International Terrorism.

13. The Ministers agreed that there exists a natural complementarity between India, China and Russia in the energy sector. Russia is a dominant supplier of oil and gas; India and China are energy deficit, but significant suppliers of manufactured products and services. Trilateral relations can be further reinforced by establishing mutually advantageous relations in the energy sector. India, China and Russia welcome the growing trend of discussing energy security issues in multilateral fora. Energy matters are best addressed in a framework that reconciles the long-term interests of both energy-consuming and energy-producing nations. India, Russia and China look to intensifying international cooperation in the energy sector on a new basis to promote openness, transparency and competition in the energy market and reflect in a balanced manner the interest of all parties concerned.

14. The Ministers noted that the Afghan presidential and provincial council elections were held on August 20, 2009, and a second round of the presidential elections is due to be held on November 7, 2009. The Ministers expressed the hope that the election process will be conducted peacefully and with the active participation of the Afghan people. The Ministers emphasised

the necessity of the international community maintaining its commitment to render assistance to the government and people of Afghanistan in ensuring security and development, and restoring peace and stability and building a democratic, pluralistic and prosperous Afghanistan. The Ministers agreed that terrorism must be combated firmly by the international community and expressed concern at the continuing deterioration of the security situation there due to continued terrorist attacks. The Ministers condemned the terrorist attack on the Indian Embassy in Kabul on October 8, 2009. The Ministers highlighted the need to bring the perpetrators of all terrorist attacks to justice and the need for strict observance of the sanctions regime against persons and entities listed by the UNSC Committee 1267.

15. The Ministers stressed the need for sustained international efforts to effectively combat production and trafficking of narcotics in the region. In this regard, they called for close cooperation between the International Security Assistance Force and the coalition forces and the Government of Afghanistan in fighting this threat to regional stability and security.

16. The Ministers welcomed the recent talks between Iran and representatives of the P5+1 and the EU in Geneva and emphasised the need to continue efforts to achieve a political and diplomatic settlement of the Iran nuclear issue. They shared the view that Iran is entitled to the right to use nuclear energy for peaceful purposes and at the same time should fulfill its due international obligations. The Ministers emphasized that all possible efforts should be made to address the Iran nuclear issue by peaceful means through dialogue and negotiation and that the IAEA should play an important role in resolving outstanding issues.

17. The Ministers noted that the Shanghai Cooperation Organization (SCO) is steadily becoming an important factor of emerging architecture of security, economy, culture, people-to-people contacts and cooperation in Asia. They spoke in favour of further enhancement of interaction of the SCO Member-States with Observer-States and dialogue partners and other states and international organizations concerned for the benefit of strengthening security and stability in the region.

18. The Foreign Ministers of China and Russia expressed satisfaction that the Indian delegation to the SCO Summit was led by the Prime Minister for the first time and at Indian participation at appropriate levels in other SCO meetings held in 2009. The External Affairs Minister of India reiterated India's interest in participating in SCO activities particularly economic activities (SCO Business Forum, SCO Energy Club and Inter Banking Consortium), counter-terrorism (Regional Counter Terrorism Structure) and SCO Contact Group on Afghanistan. The Foreign Ministers of China and Russia welcomed India's constructive engagement in SCO activities.

19. The Foreign Ministers of India and China expressed support to Russia's efforts to maintain peace and stability in the Caucasus region.

20. The Foreign Ministers of India and China welcomed the decision that Russia would officially join the mechanism of Asia-Europe Meetings (ASEM) at the 8th ASEM Summit in Brussels.

21. The Ministers reiterated their support for the Six Party talks to achieve the objective of full denuclearization of the Korean peninsula and called upon all parties concerned to work towards bringing about peace and stability in the region.

22. The Ministers expressed satisfaction with the outcome of the meeting and decided to hold the next trilateral meeting in China.

Chapter 34

Joint Communiqué at 10th RIC Ministerial Meeting at Wuhan

Wuhan, 15 November 2010

1. The Foreign Ministers of the People's Republic of China, the Russian Federation and the Republic of India held their 10th meeting in Wuhan, China on 15 November 2010.

2. The Ministers expressed conviction that the trilateral meeting mechanism had deepened coordination and cooperation among the three countries on international and regional issues and helped promote multilateralism and democracy in international relations. The Foreign Ministers reiterated that the cooperation between China, Russia and India does not target any other country.

3. The Ministers expressed satisfaction with the follow-up efforts made by the three parties on the decisions arrived at during the Bangalore meeting on 27 October 2009. The Ministers reviewed the progress of trilateral cooperation in various fields and agreed that the cooperation between think-tanks and businesses and in the fields of agriculture, disaster mitigation and relief, and medical and health services furthered their trilateral relations. They renewed their solid commitment to advancing existing cooperation, further exploring cooperation potential and reinforcing cooperation in, inter alia, energy, high-tech sectors, innovation and modernization, aerospace, people-to-people and cultural exchanges.

4. The Ministers noted that the three countries have suffered loss of life and property due to natural disasters during the current year. The Ministers appreciated the outcome of the China-Russia-India trilateral expert meeting on disaster mitigation and relief held on 12-13 November in New Delhi and

looked forward to the next meeting scheduled for the second half of 2011 in Russia.

5. The Ministers noted the large potential for mutually beneficial cooperation in the field of healthcare and medicine. They looked forward to the report of the next Expert-Level Meeting on Cooperation in the field of Healthcare and Medicine to be convened in Russia in the first half of 2011. They also noted that further interaction would include shaping effective mechanisms for combating infectious diseases and for food safety.

6. The Ministers underlined the importance of exchanging experiences in the agricultural sector, and looked forward to the recommendations of the Trilateral Expert-Level Meeting on Agricultural Cooperation to be held in New Delhi in 2011.

7. The Ministers noted with satisfaction the growth in trade and investment relations among the three countries. They hoped that the business chambers in their meeting in New Delhi on 30 November, preparatory to the 2011 Trilateral Business Forum in Russia, would be able to chart out innovative mechanisms for true, meaningful trilateral business alliances in identified priority sectors.

8. The Ministers commended the trilateral meetings of scholars for their significant contribution in stimulating scholarly discourse on political and strategic issues of policy relevance to the three countries. They welcomed the outcomes of the tenth meeting of scholars from China, Russia and India held in September 2010 in Moscow, and looked forward to the eleventh meeting to be held in 2011 in China.

9. The Ministers welcomed the proposals by Russia on sectoral cooperation in the field of energy and innovation and agreed to hold expert-level consultations in these areas.

10. The Ministers exchanged views on the current international situation and agreed that they share close or similar views on various international and regional issues and their cooperation is solidly grounded. The Ministers shared the perception that the world is undergoing major and swift changes. They expressed their support for a multi-polar, equitable and

democratic world order, based on principles of international law, mutual respect, cooperation, coordinated action and collective decision-making by all states. The Ministers expressed their strong commitment to the use of multilateral instruments for finding common solutions to global and regional problems.

11. The Ministers noted that this year marks the 65th Anniversary of the end of the Second World War and paid tribute to all those who fought against fascism and for freedom. The Ministers reiterated that the three countries would continue to work with all peace-loving countries and peoples to establish a fair international order and prevent war and conflict.

12. The Ministers noted that the global economic recovery remains uneven, fragile, unbalanced. They agreed that major economies shall work together and step up macro-economic policy coordination. They called for global coordinated efforts to promote strong, sustainable and balanced world growth.

13. The Ministers reiterated their support for the G20 as the premier forum for international economic cooperation, and welcomed the decisions of the G20 summit in Seoul including on IMF quota reform. They reiterated that the goal of the reform of international financial institutions was to achieve, step by step, equitable distribution of voting power between developed and developing countries.

14. The Ministers urged all parties to take concrete actions to oppose all forms of protectionism and work for early, comprehensive and balanced outcomes from the Doha Development Agenda, consistent with its mandate, based on the progress already made, including with regard to modalities. The Ministers emphasized that international trade frictions should be handled in the spirit of equality, consultation, mutual benefit and within the framework of WTO. The Ministers of China and India supported Russia's accession to the WTO in 2011.

15. The Ministers called for continued international adherence to the principles of the UN Framework Convention on Climate Change (UNFCCC) and its Kyoto Protocol including that of "common but differentiated responsibilities". The Ministers of Russia and India appreciated China's hosting

of the 12th session of the Ad Hoc Working Group on Long-term Cooperation under the Convention (AWG-LCA) and the 14th session of the Ad Hoc Working Group on Further Commitments for Annex I Parties under the Kyoto Protocol (AWG-KP) in October this year. The Ministers reiterated their commitment to step up their cooperation to enable positive outcomes at the Cancun conference.

16. The Ministers expressed the view that global energy security is of great significance to advancing world economic recovery and development, and such security can be achieved through greater dialogue and cooperation between producing and consuming countries. The international community should work together to ensure stable energy supply, the security of international energy transportation and stable energy prices so that the energy demand of all countries, especially developing ones, are met. Efforts should be made to build an open and transparent energy market system and an advanced energy technology R&D and dissemination system for enhanced technological transfer and financial support to developing countries consistent with existing international non proliferation obligations and relevant national policy. The Ministers agreed to step up cooperation in the field of energy security, taking into account, inter alia, the initiative of President Medvedev to negotiate an international legal instrument in this area.

17. The Ministers reiterated the importance of the UN Millennium Declaration and the implementation of the Millennium Development Goals, welcomed the outcomes of the UN high-level meeting on the MDGs held in September 2010 and urged members of the OECD Development Assistance Committee to honor their commitment of devoting 0.7% of their Gross National Income to official development assistance as early as possible.

18. The Ministers commended the indispensable role played by the United Nations in international affairs. The Ministers reiterated the need for a comprehensive reform of the United Nations to make it more democratic, representative and efficient so that it can deal with today's global challenges more effectively. The Ministers of China and Russia appreciated the role played

by India in international affairs and welcomed India's election to the UN Security Council for the 2011-2012 term, and looked forward to deepening cooperation with India within the Council.

19. The Ministers stressed that proliferation of weapons of mass destruction and their means of delivery as well as its association with international terrorism poses a grave threat to international peace and security and represents a cause for deep concern. The Ministers proceed from the understanding that dialogue over the problems of preventing risks and threats to the global non-proliferation regime must be built on the basis stipulated by the international obligations of states. The prospects for the non-proliferation regime to a large extent depend on ensuring the security of all states, as well as states' ability to establish an effective export control system and to secure sensitive materials.

20. The Ministers reiterated their strong condemnation of terrorism in all its forms and manifestations and stressed that there could be no justification for any act of terrorism anywhere. They emphasized the need for full international cooperation in counter-terrorism efforts, particularly within the framework of the United Nations, to prevent terrorist attacks and to prosecute terrorists and their supporters. In this context, the Ministers urged all UN member states to urgently conclude and adopt the Comprehensive Convention on International Terrorism. The Ministers exhorted the UN Member States to implement relevant resolutions of the UN General Assembly and the UN Security Council, particularly UNSC Resolution 1267, 1373, 1540 and 1624 and international conventions and protocols against terrorism as well as to contribute to implementation of the UN Global Counter-Terrorism Strategy. The Ministers emphasized the importance of joint efforts to counter the use of information and communication technologies for terrorist and criminal purposes. They also underscored the importance of joint efforts in countering the financing of terrorism.

21. The Ministers emphasized the imperative for the international community to maintain its commitment to render assistance to the Government and people of Afghanistan in

ensuring security and development and to make concerted efforts to restore peace and stability in Afghanistan. They expressed concern at the deteriorating security situation and underlined the need for adequate development of the Afghan National Security Forces to enable Afghanistan to defend its sovereignty and independence. The Ministers reaffirmed their long term commitment to a peaceful, stable and prosperous Afghanistan. The Ministers expressed their support to the transition to increasing Afghan responsibility on national security, and to the Afghan Government's Peace and Reintegration Program. The Ministers stressed the importance of cooperation among three countries on the issue of Afghanistan within current mechanisms. The Ministers considered the SCO as an important platform for regional cooperation on this issue. The Ministers underlined the need to step up the coordinated fight of the international community against illegal trafficking of Afghan drugs.

22. The Ministers recognized that Iran is entitled to the right to use nuclear energy for peaceful purposes, and should at the same time restore international confidence to the exclusively peaceful nature of its nuclear activities. The Ministers emphasized that there is no alternative to the intensification of efforts to address the Iranian nuclear issue by peaceful means through dialogue and negotiation.

23. The Ministers reiterated the importance of maintaining peace and stability on the Korean Peninsula and in the region through dialogue, and called on the parties concerned to return to the Six-Party Talks at the earliest date and to fully implement the Joint Statement of 19 September 2005.

24. The Ministers of China and India expressed support to Russia's policy to protect its core interests, and to contribute to regional peace and stability in the Caucasus region.

25. The Ministers stressed the need to develop an open transparent inclusive and balanced security and cooperation architecture in the Asia Pacific region based upon universally agreed principles of international law and giving due consideration to the legitimate interests of all states. The Ministers agreed that experts from three countries should study this issue.

26. The Ministers expressed their determination to work toward strengthening cooperation within BRIC which is acquiring growing importance in the modern world. The Foreign Ministers of Russia and India reiterated their readiness to coordinate with China as it prepares for the third BRIC Summit and other related events in 2011.

27. The Ministers of Foreign Affairs of China and India welcomed Russia to the East Asia Summit process and looked forward to Russia's positive contribution to the emerging economic and security architecture in the region.

28. The Ministers of China and India welcomed Russia's membership in the Asia-Europe Meeting (ASEM).

29. The Foreign Ministers of China and Russia welcomed India's constructive participation in the Shanghai Cooperation Organization as an Observer Country and attached importance to India's intention to play a larger role in the SCO.

30. The Ministers expressed their gratitude to the Government and people of Hubei Province for their hospitality and arrangements for the 10th meeting of the Foreign Ministers.

31. The Ministers tasked the Heads of relevant Departments of the MFAs of China, Russia and India to hold close consultations on issues related to trilateral cooperation.

32. The Ministers decided to hold their next meeting in Russia in 2011.

CHAPTER 35

Agreements Signed during Visit of the Chinese Premier Wen Jiabao

New Delhi, 16 December 2010

Sr. No.	Name of the MOU/ Agreement	Chinese Signatory	Indian Signatory
1.	Programme of Cultural Exchange for the years 2010-2012	H.E.MR. CAI WU Minister of Culture	SHRI S.M. KRISHNA Hon'ble Minister of External Affairs
2.	Memorandum of Understanding on Cooperation in Green Technologies	MR. ZHU ZHIXIN Vice Chairman of the National Development and Reform Commission	SHRI JAIRAM RAMESH Hon'ble Minister of State (Independent Charge) of the Ministry of Environment and Forests
3.	Memorandum of Understanding between the Ministry of External Affairs of the Republic of India and the State Council Information Office of the People's Republic of China on Media Exchanges	H.E. MR. ZHANG YAN Ambassador of China to India	SMT. NIRUPAMA RAO Foreign Secretary
4.	Memorandum of Understanding between the Ministry of Water Resources of the Republic of India and the Ministry of Water Resources of the People's Republic of China on Provision of Hydrological Data on the Sutlej River in Flood Season by China to India	MR. HU ZHENGYUE Assistant Minister of Foreign Affairs	SHRI D.V. SINGH Secretary, Ministry of Water Resources

5.	Memorandum of Understanding between the Reserve Bank of India and the China Banking Regulatory Commission	MR. WANG ZHAOXING Vice Chairman, China Banking Regulatory Commission (CBRC)	SMT SHYAMALA GOPINATH Deputy Governor, Reserve Bank of India
6.	Memorandum of Understanding between Export-Import Bank of India and China Development Bank Corporation	MR. GAO JIAN Vice Governor, China Development Bank Corporation	SHRI T.C.A. RANGANATHAN Chairman & Managing Director, Export-Import Bank of India

CHAPTER 36

Joint Communiqué of the Republic of India and the People's Republic of China

New Delhi, 16 December 2010

1. At the invitation of H.E. Dr. Manmohan Singh, Prime Minister of the Republic of India, H.E. Mr Wen Jiabao, Premier of the State Council of the People's Republic of China, is on a State visit to the Republic of India from 15 to 17 December 2010. Premier Wen Jiabao held talks with Prime Minister Dr. Manmohan Singh and will call on Smt. Pratibha Patil, President of India. Leaders of the two countries had an in-depth exchange of views on bilateral relations and regional and international issues of mutual interest in a sincere and friendly atmosphere and reached/broad consensus.

2. The two sides agreed that as the two largest developing countries in the world, India and China shoulder important and historical responsibilities of ensuring their comprehensive and sustainable economic and social development. They also make a vital contribution to advancing peace and development in Asia and in the world at large. India-China relations go beyond their bilateral scope and have acquired global and strategic significance.

3. The two sides welcome each other's peaceful development and regard it as a mutually reinforcing process. They believe that their growing relationship offers increasing opportunities to advance their cooperation. There is enough space in the world for the development of both India and China and indeed, enough areas for India and China to cooperate.

4. The two sides reviewed with satisfaction the comprehensive and rapid progress of India-China relations in the last ten years, and reaffirmed their commitment to abiding by the basic

principles and consensus concerning the development of India-China relations set out in the Declaration of Principles for Relations and Comprehensive Cooperation between India and China in 2003, the Joint Statement of India and China in 2005, the India-China Joint Declaration of 2006 and A Shared Vision for the 21st Century of India and China of 2008. The two sides decided to enhance strategic communication, advance functional cooperation,/broaden cultural exchanges, and deepen and enrich the India-China Strategic and Cooperative Partnership for Peace and Prosperity on the basis of the Five Principles of Peaceful Co-existence, mutual respect and sensitivity for each other's concerns and aspirations.

5. Reflecting this partnership, the two sides decided to establish the mechanism of regular exchange of visits between Heads of State/Government. They welcomed the opening of the telephone hotline between the Prime Minister of India and Chinese Premier and agreed on regular consultations between the two leaders on issues of importance to both countries. They also agreed to establish the mechanism of annual exchange of visits between the two Foreign Ministers.

6. While expressing satisfaction at the growing quantum of bilateral trade and investment ties, the two sides agreed to further/broad base and balance trade and economic cooperation, and identify new opportunities to realize the vast potential for future growth. Towards this objective, the two sides:

(a) Positively viewed the growing opportunities in the economic relationship and agreed to establish a Strategic Economic Dialogue to enhance macro-economic policy coordination, to promote exchanges and interactions and join hands to address issues and challenges appearing in the economic development and enhance economic cooperation.

(b) Set a new bilateral trade target of USD 100 billion by 2015. The two sides agreed to take measures to promote greater Indian exports to China with a view to reduce India's trade deficit. This includes support for Indian participation in China's national and regional trade fairs, advancing of trade facilitation, enhancing exchange and cooperation of pharmaceutical supervision, stronger relationships between Chinese enterprises and Indian IT industry and speedier completion of phyto-sanitary negotiations on agro products.

(c) Agreed to expand cooperation in infrastructure, environmental protection, information technology, telecommunications, investment and finance on a priority basis to draw on each other's strengths and pursue mutual benefit and win-win results. India welcomed Chinese enterprises to invest and participate in India's infrastructure development such as in roads, railways and in the manufacturing sector. The two sides agreed to encourage greater mutual investment and project contracting cooperation between businesses of the two countries, appropriately handle economic and trade frictions and differences and jointly oppose protectionism in all forms. They constituted an India-China CEO's Forum to deliberate on business issues and make recommendations on expansion of trade and investment cooperation.

(d) Concluded a Memorandum of Understanding between the Reserve Bank of India and China Banking Regulatory Commission to increase banking and financial cooperation. India and China also agreed to grant permission to the banks of the other country to open/ branches and representative offices. Modalities will be worked out by the concerned authorities.

7. Both sides reviewed with satisfaction the celebration activities of the 60th anniversary of the establishment of diplomatic relations between the Republic of India and the People's Republic of China in 2010. The two sides declared 2011 as the "Year of India-China Exchange". The two sides further decided to encourage greater exchanges between the civil society organizations, youth, media, scholars, think-tanks, artists and cultural personalities. The two sides agreed to continue youth exchange activities in the next five years. China will invite 500 Indian youth from various fields to visit China within the year 2011. Memorandum of Understanding

on Media Exchanges as well as the Programme of Cultural Exchanges between the Government of the People's Republic of China and the Government of the Republic of India for the year 2010-2012 were signed. Both sides agreed to discuss compiling an encyclopedia on India-China cultural contacts.

8. Both sides recognized the importance of educational exchanges, including promoting wider knowledge of each other's languages. In this context, the Chinese side welcomed the decision by the Central Board of Secondary Education (CBSE) of India to introduce Chinese as a foreign language in the curriculum of schools in India from the next academic session (April 2011). China will offer support for training Chinese language teachers and providing Chinese language training materials. The two sides declared the establishment of the India-China Outstanding College Students Exchange Programme and would work out the modalities of the Programme through consultations. To facilitate and strengthen intercollegiate and student exchanges, the two countries agreed to consider the finalization of an agreement on mutual recognition of degrees and diplomas.

9. The two sides noted the good cooperation between China and India in the field of trans-border rivers. The Indian side appreciated the flood-season hydrological data and the assistance in emergency management provided by the Chinese side. The two sides reiterated that they will promote and enhance cooperation in this field.

10. The two sides reiterated their firm commitment to resolving outstanding differences including the boundary question at an early date through peaceful negotiations. They reiterated that resolution of the boundary question is one of the ten-pronged strategies agreed by leaders of the two countries. The two sides reaffirmed their commitment to the Agreement on Political Parameters and Guiding Principles for Settlement of the Boundary Question agreed in 2005 and the process of negotiations being undertaken by the Special Representatives and resolved to actively seek a fair, reasonable and mutually acceptable solution from the political and strategic perspective. Pending the resolution of the boundary question, the two sides

shall work together to maintain peace and tranquility in the border areas in line with the previous agreements.

11. Both countries called for continued international adherence to the principles of the UN Framework Convention on Climate Change (UNFCCC) and its Kyoto Protocol including that of "common but differentiated responsibilities". Both sides also appreciated the joint efforts of India and China in the international negotiations towards arriving at fair and balanced climate agreements with the aim of further enabling the full, effective and sustained implementation of the UNFCCC and its Kyoto Protocol according to the mandate of Bali Roadmap. Both sides appreciated bilateral cooperation in the area of mitigating and adapting to climate change and agreed to strengthen such cooperation. They welcomed the signing of a Memorandum of Understanding between the two countries on Cooperation in Green Technologies. China appreciated India's hosting the 11th meeting of the Conference of the Parties of the Biodiversity Convention in 2012.

12. Both sides underlined their unequivocal opposition to terrorism in all its forms and manifestations and stressed that there is no justification for any act of terrorism anywhere. They committed themselves to countering terrorism through joint efforts that include disrupting the financing of terrorism. They also recognized the need to implement all relevant UN resolutions, in particular UNSC resolution 1267, 1373, 1540 and 1624.

13. India and China, being each other's neighbour, have a shared interest in the stability, prosperity and security of the wider region. They agreed to intensify their dialogue on various aspects pertaining to this region and work together on realizing their common goals. The two sides believed that as members of the Asian family, stronger neighbourly relations and mutually beneficial cooperation between India and China help foster a peaceful and stable regional environment that promotes equality, mutual trust and mutual respect. India and China expressed their commitment to assisting Afghanistan to become a peaceful, stable, prosperous nation. They emphasized the importance of

a coherent and united international commitment to Afghan-led initiatives.

14. The two sides reaffirmed their support for the multilateral cooperation mechanisms in Asia and their positive view on each other's participation in the cross-regional, regional and sub-regional cooperation processes in Asia. The two sides agreed to/broaden cooperation within the framework of the East Asia Summit, the Asia-Europe Meeting, the Shanghai Cooperation Organization, the Russia-India-China trilateral cooperation mechanism and the South Asian Association of Regional Cooperation (SAARC). Both sides agreed that EAS is making a meaningful contribution to building an open, inclusive and transparent architecture in the Asia-Pacific region. Both sides agreed to work together on projects which strengthen bonds between the peoples of East Asia. In this context, China welcomed India's efforts to revive the Nalanda University. Both sides appreciated the work of the Nalanda Mentor Group and the progress made so far. India welcomed China's contribution of US$ 1 million for the Nalanda University.

15. The two sides expressed their commitment to promoting the multilateral arms control, disarmament and non-proliferation processes. They supported the complete prohibition and thorough destruction of all nuclear weapons, and called on the international community to move forward together to achieve the goal of global nuclear disarmament, The two sides reaffirmed their firm opposition to the weaponization of and an arms race in outer space.

16. The two sides reaffirmed the importance of maritime security, unhindered commerce and freedom of navigation in accordance with relevant universally agreed principles of international law. In this context, they agreed to work together in tackling piracy in the Gulf of Aden.

17. Recognizing common interests and similar concerns on major regional and international issues, the two sides decided to enhance their coordination and cooperation in multilateral forums. China attaches great importance to India's status in international affairs as a large developing country, understands

and supports India's aspiration to play a greater role in the United Nations, including in the Security Council. China welcomed India's election to non-permanent membership of UN Security Council during 2011-2012 and both countries agreed to deepen consultation within the Council. Multilateral issues such as climate change, the Doha Development Round of WTO, energy and food security, international financial and economic reform are a particular focus for closer cooperation. The two sides recognized that as the global economy stabilizes and recovers, China and India would strengthen communication and consultation within the G20 framework, jointly facilitate the improvement of global economic governance and advance economic globalization towards balanced development and shared benefits. They agreed to enhance cooperation within the BRICS framework.

18. Premier Wen Jiabao invited Prime Minister Dr. Manmohan Singh to visit China during 2011 and Prime Minister Singh accepted the invitation with pleasure. The dates of the visit will be decided through diplomatic channels.

Chapter 37

Agreed Minutes of the 1st India-China Strategic Economic Dialogue

Beijing, 26 September 2011

The 1st India-China Strategic Economic Dialogue (hereinafter referred to as 'the Dialogue') was held at Beijing, China on September 26, 2011. The Indian side was led by H.E. Mr. Montek Singh Ahluwalia, Deputy Chairman, Planning Commission, Republic of India and the Chinese side was led by H.E. Mr. Zhang Ping, Chairman, National Development and Reform Commission, People's Republic of China (hereinafter referred to as the 'two sides').

Based on the consensus reached by the governments of India and China, the establishment of the Dialogue was announced in the India-China Joint Communiqué issued during the visit to India by H.E. Mr. Wen Jiabao, Premier of the State Council of the People's Republic of China in December 2010.

The two sides had an in-depth and frank exchange of views on the world economic situation, respective domestic macro-economic situations, the goals and implementation of the mid and long-term economic and social development plans of the two countries as well as their respective industrial, fiscal and monetary policies and agreed to enhance pragmatic cooperation in economic sectors. The two sides agreed that the Dialogue was highly productive and successful.

World Economic Situation

The two sides shared views on the current world economic situation, and agreed that since the beginning of the year, the world economy is picking-up, but with weak momentum. The process of recovery is not firmly established and neither is it balanced. Escalated risk with respect to sovereign debts in major developed economies; large fluctuations in international financial and commodity markets; and growing global inflation, which is particularly acute in emerging markets have brought about additional uncertainties to the global economic outlook. In this scenario, India and China must continue to focus their efforts on domestic economic growth, which can provide stability to the world economy.

Respective Domestic Macro-economic Situations

The two sides introduced their respective domestic macro-economic situations, enumerated the challenges encountered in the course of economic development, and expounded on the policies they would adopt in the coming years. They agreed that, though new problems and issues emerged in the domestic economic operations of the two countries and in the international environment, India and China have continued to maintain sound economic development. The two sides also agreed to strengthen communication on macro-economic policies, share development experiences and enhance coordination in addressing economic challenges.

Mid and Long-term Development Plans

The two sides introduced the major goals, strategic tasks and implementation framework outlined in the respective mid and long-term social and economic development plans of the two countries. The two sides agreed that India and China face the common task of advancing reform and promoting the comprehensive, balanced and sustainable development of each country. The formulation and effective implementation of their mid and long-term development plans are of great significance in sustaining rapid and stable economic and social development in the long run. The two sides will learn from each other and conduct mutually beneficial cooperation in formulating and carrying out their respective mid and long-term development plans.

Improving Investment Environment

The two sides agreed to stay committed to deepening bilateral investment cooperation, further opening markets, and improving the investment environment in India and China so as to lay a solid foundation for pragmatic cooperation between the businesses of the two countries on the basis of complementarities, mutual benefit and win-win outcomes.

Energy Efficiency and Conservation, and Environmental Protection

The two sides agreed to strengthen cooperation on energy efficiency and conservation as well as on environmental protection and actively develop cooperation in energy matters including in the renewable energy sector in order to promote sustainable development. Enhanced exchanges in these spheres would be the new engine for greater cooperation between the two sides.

Infrastructure Cooperation

The two sides discussed the current status of infrastructure development in the two countries as well as prospects of cooperation. They agreed to enhance cooperation in these sectors, particularly in the railway sector on the basis of mutual complementarities and benefit.

Water Use Efficiency

The two sides agreed to enhance communication, encourage bilateral cooperation on water conservation and clean water technologies.

The two sides agreed that the 2nd India-China Strategic Economic Dialogue will be convened in India in 2012. They also agreed that prior to the 2nd Dialogue, there would be a working group meeting to implement the consensus and decisions agreed to by the two sides at the 1st Strategic Economic Dialogue.

(Montek Singh Ahluwalia)
Deputy Chairman
Planning Commission of the
Republic of India

(Zhang Ping)
Chairman
National Development and Reform
Commission of the People's
Republic of China